D0699987

GAY AND LESBIAN THEMES IN LATIN AMERICAN WRITING

The Texas Pan American Series

GAY AND LESBIAN THEMES IN LATIN AMERICAN WRITING

David William Foster

The Texas Pan American Series is published with the assistance of a revolving publication fund established by the Pan American Sulphur Company.

First edition, 1991

⊗The paper used in this publication meets the minimum requirements of American National Standard for Information Sciences—Permanence of Paper for Printed Library Materials, ANSI Z39.48-1984.

Library of Congress
Cataloging-in-Publication Data

Foster, David William.
Gay and lesbian themes in Latin American writing / David William Foster
p. cm. — (The Texas Pan American series)
Includes bibliographical references and index.
ISBN 0-292-77646-2 (alk. paper). —
ISBN 0-292-77647-0 (pbk. alk. paper)
1. Latin American literature—History and criticism.
2. Homosexuality in literature. I. Title. II. Series.
PQ7081.F634 1991
860.9'353—dc20 90-20149
CIP

CONTENTS

When Bob talked of someone who had a good build he would sound jealous and make remarks, even about Jim who was better-looking. But Jim, when he looked at Bob's strong white body, did not envy; rather he felt a twinship, a similarity, a warm emotion which he could not name. He had always felt this way about Bob. Of course it would be silly to say anything for there were no words in his head to describe what he meant; it was an emotion not understood; to consummate it they played tennis together and talked about the girls Bob liked and, now, they were to swim together. Jim wondered as he watched Bob, the sun on his red hair, if he could tell him some of the strange things he thought, carry out in life his most personal dreams.

(G. Vidal 39)

—¿Qué estabas haciendo?—
le pregunté, ya solos en el corredor.
—¿Qué querés que hiciera? Es largo de contar.
No entiendo nada.
Si te lo contara, ¿entenderías?
Al menos trataría de hacerlo.[1]

(Villordo 163)

PREFACE

Of all of the acts of critical inquiry I have indulged myself in, this has been the most thoroughly exhausting. To attempt to pursue doggedly a topic that has no ontological status in most realms of literary criticism, and specifically much less so in the case of Latin American culture, which is generally considered to be even more taboo-circumscribed than American society, is to set oneself up for a heavy dose of frustration. The difficulty of identifying appropriate texts, setting parameters for which texts to examine, and establishing the dialogic relationship between them that critical analysis implies, makes the critic wonder whether he had embarked on a reasonable course of research.

Moreover, to talk about homosexuality in Western culture at the present moment is to venture into a minefield of issues, ideologies, and opinions. In an earlier day, it would have been quite adequate to highlight those texts that recognize the "problem" of homosexuality (a term with nineteenth-century origins in German clinical medicine, meant to be descriptively neutral). Yet the phenomenon of homosexuality may no longer be a problem (medical, moral, or otherwise); what has come to be regarded as the "problem" is the definition of homosexuality as a problem—or even the categorization of one complex of sexual behaviors, perceptions, and outlooks as a conceptually unified something called homosexuality.

There can, nevertheless, be little question that it is legitimate to identify certain works that view homosexuality as a problem; it is perhaps less valid to frame in a study those texts that promote (like so much of Manuel Puig's writing) the view that homosexuality is not a problem, but rather that social classifications of it (literary criticism included) are the problem. In this sense, the critical analysis of lesbian and gay writing does more to perpetuate the "problematization" encouraged by homophobia than it does to promote the cause of an allegedly healthful sexual liberation. Yet only because the bulk of the writing examined in this study focuses on the abyss that continues to exist between liberation and actual sociocultural practice is it possible to claim the ideological validity of this investigation. From those texts that advance the "vampire" theory of homosexuality, through those that reinforce the image of a tragic blemish of nature and a tragic victimization by society, to the more recent ethos of assertive naturalization, the texts discussed in the following chapters assume with a variety of interpretive registers that there is something to write about called homosexuality.

As a consequence of the foregoing, I often had the sense, while composing this monograph, of engaging in something "dirty," not because of the topic itself, which surely large segments of our society continue to classify as such, but rather because it sustains the framing of one constellation of sexual activities when, perhaps, what is most called for is the de-emphasis of problematized erotic practices in favor of a far-ranging project involving the reeroticization of culture in all of the multiple dimensions such a process might imply. Nevertheless, criticism should be dirty work, if it is ever to deal with the real issues of human history and the social dynamics that disable the individual's quest for decency and dignity.

D.W.F.

ACKNOWLEDGMENTS

A study such as this which involves many different sociopolitical perspectives must depend on the intellectual and emotional support of other individuals. Naomi Lindstrom and Enrique Medina played crucial roles in assisting me in defining the scope of this research, while Roberto Reis, Luis Peña, Magdalena Maiz, Roberto Previdi Froelich, Norma Mabee, and Denize Araujo provided me with many occasions for productive dialogue. My research assistants, Daniel Altamiranda, Salvador Oropesa, Roselyn Costantino, and Darrell Lockhart, made enormous contributions to the development of the manuscript and guaranteed its technical integrity, while at the same time offering constructive comments on the content.

D.W.F.

GAY AND LESBIAN THEMES IN LATIN AMERICAN WRITING

CHAPTER ONE

INTRODUCTION

Insofar as individuals subscribing to a homosexual identity, overtly or implicitly, exclusively or complementarily, constitute a stable component of any society (the controversy over percentages is clearly both irrelevant and misleading), there ought not be anything unusual about being able to identify an inventory of works that treat gay concerns and experiences, whether as the dominant issue of a text or as part of the context to other major themes. The contemporary Latin American novel finds itself dealing with broad social and personal concerns, and it would be surprising if there were no appearance of lesbian and gay characters and their experiences in the representative titles. What is surprising is the virtual lack of bibliography on the topic, as though marking off a segment of Latin American writing as specifically interested in homosexuality were of insufficient critical interest. With the exception of the brief survey by Kessel Schwartz and the more detailed appraisal by Robert Howes ("The Literature of Outsiders"), critics, if noting the subject at all, have done little more than refer in passing to the presence of homosexual characters and situations.

Even in the case of major works where homosexuality may be argued to constitute a major point of reference, critics have eschewed any sort of detailed exploration of what this may mean as part of a specific narrative semiotics. José Lezama Lima's *Paradiso* (1966) is recognized to examine homosexuality as particularly relevant to an aesthetic view of experience (see Gustavo Pellón for the controversies surrounding homosexuality in this novel). Manuel Mujica Láinez's *Bomarzo* (1962), both as novel and in Alberto Ginastera's operatic version, presents the homosexual as the paradigmatic outsider (D. W. Foster, "The Monstrous"; Villanueva). *La traición de Rita Hayworth* (1967; *Betrayed by Rita Hayworth*) and *El beso de la mujer araña* (1976; *The Kiss of the Spider Woman*) are two of Manuel Puig's novels to correlate homosexuality with the repression of the individual in a society dominated by violent machismo (Muñoz). Silviano Santiago, in *Stella Manhattan* (1985), presents a Brazilian homosexual living in New York who is caught in the cross fire between the guerrillas and the militarists of his country, a hapless victim of the machismo of both sectors (Lopes Júnior). Matters that may be related to homosexuality like androgyny, bisexuality, and transvestism are recurring themes in the fictional works of José Donoso, Severo Sarduy, and João Guimarães Rosa.

While individual critical studies have referred in varying degrees to these questions, we have neither an adequate inventory of pertinent works nor any satisfactory examination of the particular ways in which Latin American writing may relate homosexuality to larger concerns. Certainly, even if it is true, as Frederick L. Whitam and Robin M. Mathy have maintained in their cross-cultural research, that Latin American societies are in general more tolerant of homosexuality than the United States, cultural texts tend to see homosexual characters as the locus of both social alienation and authoritarian repression. This is particularly striking in the Brazilian plays examined by Luis Canales, since the impressive sexual liberty of Brazilian society is virtually a cliché.

Even when critics like Canales and Schwartz concern themselves with works in which homosexuality is the principal concern, their comments suffer from two damaging limitations. In the first place, they have been content merely to enumerate examples of homosexual characters and situations, without much analysis of the specifics of literary structure these examples might imply (as in Luis Gregorich's superficial notes). That is, the possibility of a "homosexual" view of human society is not raised, nor is the question asked whether there are particular problems of literary representation associated with the multiple forms of homosexual identity. In the second place, critics referring to homosexuality have difficulty in freeing themselves from the homophobic attitudes presumably repudiated by the very fact that they are willing to inquire sympathetically into this topic in Latin American literature. To speak of novels and plays in terms of a vocabulary echoing qualifiers like "perversion," "antisocial behavior," and "sexual aberration" contributes little to the recognition of an aspect of human experience that these writings are struggling to represent and, on occasion, even to legitimate. The result is that one has the impression that Latin American writers have accepted various contemporary hypotheses concerning sexuality and the many dimensions of homosexuality as one form the expression of sexuality may take, while their commentators continue to be tied to a patronizing view of the subject as an unfortunately acute form of psychological and social deviance that can only result in tragic or grotesque emplotments (see also Shaw passim).

A recent survey of modern research on sexuality underscores the need to become conscious of historical dynamics rather than to continue to speak of essential categories alleged to exist independently of social structures:

> But I am suggesting that what we define as "sexuality" is an historical construction, which brings together a host of different biological and mental possibilities—gender identity, bodily differences, reproductive capacities, needs, desires and fantasies—which need not be linked together, and in other cultures have not been. All the constituent elements of sexuality have their source either in the body or the mind, and I am not attempting to deny the limits posed by biology or mental processes. But the capacities of the body and the psyche are given meaning only in social relations. (Weeks, *Sexuality* 15; see also Weeks, *Sexuality and Its Discontents*)

If Latin American writing is characterized by an awareness of history and ideology, homosexuality cannot be viewed as simply the psychological complex of specific individuals, but rather must be seen as an intrasubjective matter that has ultimately to do with the controlling social dynamic and how it defines the individual's participation in it. If this is true, the examination of homosexual topics, like other topics that have the advantage of underscoring differences and pointing out controversies with high ideological stakes, can be an integral part of a study of how Latin American fiction deals with questions of social history.

One could argue that, in view of the incomplete attention devoted so far by critics to homosexual writings and their themes in Latin America and the apparently unreconstructed consciousness some of the descriptive vocabulary might imply, there is a first need for a comprehensive *bibliographie raisonée* of pertinent materials. Yet, aside from the amassing of a very respectable list of titles that would serve to underscore the extent of critical inattention, such a survey would not address the more interesting question of how versions of homosexuality are part of the Latin American writer's especially notable analyses of historical consciousness.

The novels examined in this study demonstrate a dominant concern for varieties of male homosexuality, with only five examples of lesbian writing. This selection in no way intends to privilege gay men. Lesbian interests have yet to be as consistently thematized as male homosexual ones have been. David F. Greenberg's groundbreaking analysis of the historical construction of homosexuality makes reference to the overwhelming preponderance of documents referring to gay men, which certainly matches what I have found with respect to Latin American narrative (see, however, Juanita Ramos's important anthology of U.S. Hispanic lesbian writing, which falls outside the purview of this study; Martin Bauml Dubermgn, Martha Vicinus, and George Chauncey, Jr., also lament the imbalance of the essays they bring together with respect to interpretive material available on women and the larger amount available on men). Also, Western society tends to "see" lesbian relationships as markedly different from those of gay men, and historically lesbians have been more successful in blocking or preventing their being seen, as in the phenomenon of the "Boston marriage" of women who are observed to live together without attracting further attention as regards their sexual bonding. Yet there are many notable examples of lesbian writing in Latin America, especially and overwhelmingly in the field of poetry. I have examined elsewhere a prominent example of lesbian fiction by Argentina's Reina Roffé (D. W. Foster, *Alternate* 76–81), and it is probable that increasing interest in specifically feminist issues in Latin America (which may be cast differently than they are in the United States) will prompt more writing on the specifically lesbian experience. Undoubtedly, there are Latin American feminists who may be studied with special attention to lesbian concerns, like Chile's Gabriela Mistral. As another category of insufficiently examined Latin American writing, lesbian writings merit an independent investigation (see the emerging material on Hispanic lesbians in the United States [Chumu, Ramos]). An interesting speculative proposal for explaining the underproduction of lesbian narratives in Latin America would be that, since the very notion of homosexuality derives from patriarchal programs to control the individual body, as the starting point for total social control, part of a feminist rejection of the patriarchy may simply entail ignoring such a "problematization" of erotic expression between women as irrelevant in the face of other concerns.

Although all of the novels selected deal with the "problem" of being homosexual in Latin American society, many are less interested in personal dramas than they are in the continuities between social dynamics and details of personal orientation and behavior that come into conflict with those dynamics. Therefore, I consider a chapter like the one on the sociopolitical matrix central to an understanding of the particular originality of Latin American gay writing. Thus, one can point to novels that deal in specific ways with questions of historical awareness, in the sense that a correlation is made between individual experience and dominant social structures. This conflict goes beyond the simple matter of the individual whose sexuality is at odds with patriarchal, heterosexist society, since one could argue that all gay and lesbian writing revolves around this fundamental question. Rather, in the case of Latin American novels, the details of characters call up specific issues of Latin American societies. This is obvious in the case of the conflict between, for example, the homosexual male and Judeo-Christian, romantic concepts of love, the institution of matrimony, and forms of social repression and even vengeance. In the case of Oscar Hermes Villordo's novel *La otra mejilla* (The Other Cheek), as an extension of the correlation between sociopolitical and sexual repression in Puig's *El beso de la mujer araña*, the murder of one of the gay characters is a political act. Such novels imply a reading less in terms of the personal biography of their protagonists and more as examples or facets of social history.

The type of homosexual novel examined in this study, from the point of view of literary semiotics, deals with explicit issues of representation and narration. It has become a commonplace to maintain that societies create sign systems that, since they are ideological gestures, exclude certain forms of individual and social experience or account for them in incomplete and prejudicial ways. Homosexuality would appear to be one such area of experience, and the enormous expansion of an ideologically based semiotics in recent decades has provided cultural critics with ways to examine how such phenomena might be examined within the context of prevailing and dominant sign systems (Beaver; Blau; Chesebro). From the point of view of the literary author, problems related to dealing with taboo and denigrated subjects can lead naturally to a metafictional interest in making the representation and narration of such subjects one foregrounded aspect of a text.

All of the texts examined in this study are, therefore, concerned with the semiotics of homosexuality and its representation, both in the social text in the first instance and in the literary text in the specific case of the novel. This is even true of the "primitive" examples discussed in the first two chapters, where Adolfo Caminha's novel reveals a problematical ambiguity between its sympathy for the main character and its continued subscription to a Naturalistic rhetoric of alarm and where José González Castillo's anarchist-inspired play must appeal to a fossilized ruling-class horror of sexual depredation in order to confirm its social thesis. How to define homosexuality and how to locate it within a definition of sociopolitical conduct, how to describe the parameters of certain forms of personal desire within a social discourse that has inadequate names for them, how to recover distinctive forms of identity that the prevailing sign system neutralizes or obliterates, and, quite simply, how to leave a record of personal experiences that seem to be illegitimate and insubstantial because they lack any confirming function within the textual models available for reporting them are questions that constitute the agenda of this study.

To say that there is no such thing as a unitary homosexual experience and much less a unifying gay sensibility (pace Michael Bronski's excellent history of U.S. gay cultural consciousness) is not the same as to say that the complex varieties of homosexual identity are blocked and denied by a social discourse that cannot account for them in its sign system (the problem of "semiotic accounting" has been exceptionally evident with regard to the language of AIDS [Ross]). If one of the goals of cultural texts is to supplement the social text with what it has not been able to assimilate, it is not surprising that gay novelists like those examined in this study are as much concerned with how to narrativize a homosexual identity and its consequences as they are with the experiences arising from that identity. The result is a group of narratives very much different from what has been published in the United States, where a very rapid transition has been made from oblique or dissembled treatments (Austen) to gay writing within the mainstream of American fiction. To judge from recent anthologies in English translation (Leyland, *Now the Volcano* and *My Deep Dark Pain*), Latin American authors do not yet enjoy a similar public recognition.

No argument is made for the uniqueness of the texts examined, in the sense that gay writing in Latin America must necessarily reveal a metafictional concern with representation and narration. However, it is argued that these texts are especially interesting in that they address themselves both to the prevailing emphasis in Latin American culture on the structures of sociohistoric consciousness and to the special problems of textualizing—first individually and then collectively—a homosexual identity within the parameters of that consciousness.

A word concerning the organization of this study. The individual chapters, after the consideration of two founding texts of writing about homosexuality in Latin America, focus on various modalities for entertaining homosexuality in moral, social, and political terms. Such a clustering of the texts may be justified in rather conventional terms of literary inquiry as corresponding to an interpretation of the various ways in which a general topic is diversely thematized in individual texts. Moreover, this organization is historical in a very general way, at least as far as the understanding of homosexuality in Western societies in the last century is concerned: the explicit identification of a homosexual "nature" is pursued by attempts to understand the personal dynamics of that nature, to be followed at this point in the late twentieth century by attempts to defend and to legitimate homosexuality and even to insert it into a utopian vision of social harmonics.

What is less conventional is the fragmentation of strict historical chronology in the grouping of the texts in the individual chapters. Since this is not a historical inquiry into the development of a particular theme in Latin American writing, I sometimes juxtapose texts which may be separated by several decades but which may be linked by similar strategies of viewing, of semiotizing, homosexuality. The critic's need to discuss individual texts, rather than submerging them in a Foucaultian manner into an underdifferentiated social text, will make this practice of juxtaposition, within the framework of the more conventional order of the chapters in relation to each other, more vivid than I mean it to be for the purpose of analyzing specific textual strategies.

One concluding comment: my purpose is to assess a body of writing that deals, sympathetically or otherwise, with lesbian and gay identities, without wondering whether the writers "are" themselves homosexual—i.e., subscribe to a homosexual self-identity in constructivist sociological terms. While it is reasonable to assume that the writers (at least the sympathetic ones) endorse the identity being assessed (an attribution that legitimately extends to the critic as well), it becomes necessary to set aside ingenuous beliefs that "It takes one to know one" and similar autobiographic fallacies. Both feminist and ethnic writing recognize the need to incorporate the examination of negative images in an overriding "benevolent" treatment for purposes of emphasis and contrast, and there is every reason to believe that research on gay issues should also engage in this form of eloquent juxtaposition, especially when it is revelatory of ideological slippages on the part of both those who defend a gay identity and those who decry it. Had I chosen to write *only* about works that endorse gay sex or *only* about those that condemn it, or that *only* see homosexuality as a social formation or that *only* see it as hormonal destiny, then this study would have more of a unified sociological perspective. Unfortunately, culture itself does not have a unified perspective, and the scholar who chooses to follow along with enormously contradictory ideological postulations will, either lamentably or fortuitously, generate an interpretive discourse that is "flawed" by the lack of a rigorously unifying perspective. Perhaps were there a larger body of gay writing in Latin America, such that I could have dealt only with apologiae or only with hysterical denunciations, the result would have been more unified. But more at issue seems to be a criterion of scholarly exposition attentive to the maddeningly contradictory viewpoints of the texts themselves.

CHAPTER TWO

ADOLFO CAMINHA'S *BOM-CRIOULO*: A FOUNDING TEXT OF BRAZILIAN GAY LITERATURE

> o negro esquecia todos os seus companheiros, tudo que o cercava para só pensar [. . .] no futuro dessa amizade inexplicável.[1] (Caminha 51)

It is customary to recognize the early literature of the Republic in Brazil for the brilliant fiction of Joaquim Maria Machado de Assis, truly the first great nineteenth-century Latin American writer. As befitted Machado's identification with the end of the Second Empire and the emerging national bourgeoisie of the Republic, his novels dealt virtually exclusively with genteel society and the various ideologies within which its members defined themselves. In this and other senses, Machado's novels are founding texts of the literature of the Republic, texts that provide a necessary point of reference for understanding the society of the period and the ways in which culture interpreted it.

Among other founding literary texts of the period, *Bom-Crioulo* (1895) by Adolfo Caminha (1867–1897) is almost a startling discovery (cf. Robert Howes's introduction to the Gay Sunshine Press translation into English and Luis Zapata's introduction to the Spanish translation). Although Brazilian literary history takes note of this and the two other novels Caminha published before his untimely death from tuberculosis, *Bom-Crioulo* has yet to receive adequate critical examination. Many aspects of this novel, nevertheless, argue for its study. In addition to dealing with the details of the shipboard life of sailors during the period and the corresponding popular sectors of society with which they come into contact on land, Caminha's novel also examines the relationship between a black man and a white boy at a time when Brazil was just making the transition from slavery to emancipation (slavery was officially abolished by the monarchy in 1888, less than one year before the creation of the Republic).

However, the most striking quality of *Bom-Crioulo* is that not only is it the first explicit gay novel in Brazilian (and Latin American) literature (Leyland, *Now the Volcano* 82), but that it may be alleged to be one of the first such works in modern Western literature. This is especially true if we define gay literature as writing about questions related to male homosexual identity, whether viewed as inherent character or chosen behavior. Such writing may either be explicit or, more often before recent years, veiled; in the latter case it may be marked with clues taken to be explicit by the cognoscenti. Finally, writing about these issues may (typically) examine the tragedy of being homosexual or it may explore the persecution and hypocrisies befalling the "unfortunate." From the point of view of this definition of gay literature, a group of writings not explicitly (or covertly) gay but marked by a presumed "gay sensibility" is not admitted.

Although recent criticism has been able to read homoerotic themes into other works of nineteenth-century literature (e.g., Leslie Fiedler's famous interpretations) and contemporary attention to gay issues allows one to see how Oscar Wilde's *The Picture of Dorian Gray* (1890) or Herman Melville's *Billy Budd* (written ca. 1886–1891; first published 1924) are almost unquestionably novels based on homoeroticism, not only does Caminha's novel eschew oblique allusions to the matters at hand to deal forthrightly with the emotional and physical aspects of Bom-Crioulo and Aleixo's sexual relationship, but it appears that the novel circulated openly in Brazil, despite the threat of court proceedings against the author. Thus, whatever one may wish to say about elements of sexual repression in Brazilian society, at a time when the Latin American novel as a whole could only deal with heterosexual love with veiled metaphors, *Bom-Crioulo* had established a reference point for Brazil's much-touted twentieth-century sexual openness. The 1969 Olivé edition of the novel reproduces on the flap of the front cover the following anonymous commentary from the period: "Está bem visto que o *Bom-Crioulo* não é obra para se dar de prêmio nas escolas. Escrever para educandas é uma coisa, e escrever para espíritos emancipados é outra coisa"[2] ([*Bom-Crioulo* (review)]). The use of the term *emancipados* is significant in this quote, for it is obvious that the novel is one of both racial and sexual emancipation. Moreover, the very fact that it has circulated freely (whatever the reservations of subsequent literary historiography have been in giving it no more than passing reference or in distorting its significance) cannot be overlooked as significant during a period of Latin American culture customarily noted for its repressiveness. While Spanish-American *Modernism* and Brazilian *Parnassianism* and *Symbolism* may reveal poetic texts here and there deeply marked by European Decadentism, *Bom-Crioulo* as an example of the relatively mass-circulation narrative associated with the rise of a prudish bourgeoisie is indeed historically remarkable.

Echoing a feature often associated with gay fiction, Caminha's novel is essentially utopian in nature, at least in its initial postulation. First as shipboard lovers and then in the refuge of a dingy room in a hostel-cum-house of assignation run by a worldly-wise Portuguese woman in Rio, Bom-Crioulo and Aleixo are involved in flight from a society at large that would, given the public morals of the day, both condemn and persecute them. Thus, Bom-Crioulo, the runaway slave who is the aggressive partner in the relationship, undertakes to create spaces of refuge for himself and his white adolescent lover, Aleixo. Such a space may be a separate sleeping space on board ship or the safe hideaway in the establishment of the knowing D. Carolina—known as Carola Bunda—or it may be simply some place away from the crowd where the two men may be together, as when Bom-Crioulo takes Aleixo aside during a storm at sea.

In all of these cases, the narrator recognizes for the men a disjunctive gesture vis-à-vis the larger heterosexual society: in view of the nature of their relationship, they may only pursue it from within a secret refuge. Of course, this is obvious in terms of real-life experience in the case of practices that are condemned by custom and/or law. What is of special importance about this circumstance in the case of Caminha's novel is the creation of a narrative based on the evolution of the protagonist's movement away from the persecutions of white society not for reasons of race but because of a sexual identity that sets him off from the community, whether that of the other seamen or people in general. The following reflection follows upon Bom-Crioulo's initiation of sexual relations with Aleixo:

> Ao pensar nisso, Bom-Crioulo sentia uma febre extraordinária de erotismo, um delírio invencível de gôzo pederasta . . . Agora compreendia nitidamente que soé no homem, no próprio homem, êle podia encontrar aquilo que debalde procurara nas mulheres.
>
> Nunca se apercebera de semelhante anomalia, nunca em sua vida tivera a lembrança de perscrutar suas tendências em matéria de sexualidade. As mulheres o desarmavam para os combates do amor, é certo, mas também não concebia, por forma alguma, êsse comércio grosseiro entre indivíduos do mesmo sexo; entretanto, quem diria!, o fato passava-se agora

> consigo próprio, sem premeditação, inesperadamente. E o mais interessante é que "aquilo" ameaçava ir longe, para mal de seus pecados . . . Não havia jeito, senão ter paciência, uma vez que a "natureza" impunha-lhe êsse castigo.[3] (62–63)

Leaving aside some phraseology that may appear to exemplify the language of moral condemnation, to which I will return below, it is significant to note both the reference to women as part of the establishment of the separation from the world of others that Bom-Crioulo has now experienced and the allusion to *natureza*, albeit within quotation marks, to suggest a legitimation of Bom-Crioulo's new-found identity.

For what is most impressive about Caminha's novel is the acceptance of the fact of Bom-Crioulo and Aleixo's homosexual relationship as something that is quite natural. Certainly, this "naturalness" cannot be confused with the guiding ideology of one strand of the gay-rights liberation movement, whereby homoerotic love is not only not "unnatural" (in the sense alleged by Natural Theology and its homologies), but is considered a morally neutral biological attraction that must, therefore, be considered natural by virtue of the simple fact that it is found in nature. Rather, Caminha's novel, viewed against the backdrop of late nineteenth-century European Naturalism (Alcoforado), discovers in Bom-Crioulo's sexuality yet another example of biologically driven human nature ignored by the genteel literature against which Naturalism sought to range itself. If tragic consequences devolve from Bom-Crioulo's sexuality, they may be viewed as part of the plot structure dictated by the mechanistic view of biological destiny underlying the Naturalist's conception of the inevitability of human conduct. The result of this process of "naturalization" is that, where the basis of the moralistic repudiation of homosexuality has been based on a belief, and its concomitant rhetoric, that homosexuality is a "sin against nature," Caminha's novel appeals immediately to a modern reader because of its almost nonchalant tone in reporting this homosexual love affair and the choice of hero via whom to legitimize it biologically.

Caminha chose for the protagonist of his homosexual novel not only a black in a society that had only just recently begun the process of establishing racial equality, but one endowed as well with the positive masculine physique cherished by Western society. One frequently sees the complaint that even the most sympathetic treatments of homosexuality in literature incline toward characters who are neurotic, hyperemotional, and effeminate in behavior, as though homosexual acts were pursued by individuals with observable, stereotyped personal characteristics. In conformance with the now widely held conviction that the notion of a specifically homosexual individual is a reactionary ideological concept and that there are no homosexuals, only homosexual acts committed by widely different human beings, there has been an attempt to portray individuals who pursue a homosexual identity or life style as either "normal" in terms of conventional social traits (the American Joseph Hansen in *Job's Year* [1983] and his Brandstetter detective novels) or as embodying prized heroic dimensions (Manuel Puig in *El beso de la mujer araña*, 1976). (By inversion, a writer like Gore Vidal insists on the debasement of aggressive homophobic heterosexuals as an alternate form of ideological compensation.)

Thus, Bom-Crioulo is introduced as a magnificent specimen of masculinity, admired and respected by his shipmates and praised by his superiors for his goodwill and alert seamanship. As a consequence of his benevolent nature, he is given the nickname by which he is known. Yet Bom-Crioulo, for whom the rigors of military life are trivial by comparison to the lot as a slave he had previously endured, undergoes a loss of innocence in the face of the inevitable injustices aboard ship. The novel opens with the administration of floggings to three men for brawling. Two of them receive 20 lashes apiece in an incident that stemmed from masturbation by one of them and voyeurism by the other (Caminha was nothing if he was not candid about how men isolated from women satisfy their creatural needs: "cada qual tem a sua mania . . ."[4] [15]). The third man is Bom-Crioulo, who is sentenced to 150 lashes as the result of beating up a superior whom he felt had made improper advances to Aleixo. Although Bom-Crioulo has yet to bed Aleixo, the awakening of his desire for the boy is tied to a monstrous flogging, not for the homosexual acts he has yet to engage in, but because of his standing as a feared and respected black man who has dared to attack a superior. Caminha records the protagonist's satisfaction with himself at having conducted himself as a man:

> O motivo, porém, de sua prisão agora, no alto-mar, a bordo da corveta, era outro, muito outro: Bom-Crioulo esmurrava despiedadamente um segunda-classe, porque êste ousara, "sem o seu consentimento," maltratar o grumete Aleixo, um belo marinheirito de olhos azuis, muito querido por todos e de quem diziam-se "cousas."
>
> Metido em ferros no porão, Bom-Crioulo não deu palavra. Admiràvelmente manso, quando se achava em seu estado normal, longe de qualquer influência alcooélica, submeteu-se à vontade superior, esperando resig-

> nado o castigo:—Reconhecia que fizera mal, que devia ser punido, que era tão bom quanto os outros, mas, que diabo! estava satisfeito: mostrara ainda uma vez que era homem . . . Depois estimava o grumete e tinha certeza de o conquistar inteiramente, como se conquista uma mulher formosa, uma terra virgem, um país de ouro . . . Estava satisfeitíssimo![5] (22–23)

It is unquestionable that Caminha invests his protagonist with a primitive nobility of spirit that would not have been considered condescending at the time. Moreover, as a prefiguration of the conventionally masculine hero who pursues homosexual interests, Bom-Crioulo betrays none of the outward signs of the neurotic and effeminate "queer" that writers like Oscar Wilde tended to exemplify (if often as a defiant parody of homophobic stereotypes) and that both antagonistic and sympathetic portrayals of homosexuality have routinely echoed.

Moreover, Caminha contrasts Bom-Crioulo's straightforward pursuit of his own needs and the innocence of his defense of Aleixo with the hypocrisy of officers who apply discipline unmercifully while pursuing their own needs in secret (43, 63 inter alia). Indeed, part of Caminha's portrayal of the hypocrisy of the system of military discipline involves recognizing the sexuality inherent in the sadism of the individual who wields the rod of military discipline (15, 23–24). In terms of the process of investing fictional characters with contrasting values, a process characteristic of the high Realism of the period, Bom-Crioulo's innocent masculinity is ranged against the hypocrisy of the individuals, the officers and their agent, who mete out to him an excessive punishment for an act that establishes his involvement with Aleixo. That he is a black man only increases the severity of the punishment he receives, while positing for the universe of the novel a noble savage of heroic dimensions.

If Bom-Crioulo is postulated as a naturally decent man despite his white masters, his masculine sexuality is counterbalanced by the white adolescent whom he pursues. Aleixo is the character in the novel who reveals the stereotypic androgyne or effeminate features routinely associated with the images of Greek boy-love. Since Aleixo comes on board in the south of Brazil, Caminha may even portray him with the blond and blue-eyed features of this stereotype:

> E vinha-lhe à imaginação o pequeno com os seus olhinhos azuis, com o seu cabelo alourado, com as suas formas rechonchudas, com o seu todo provocador.
>
> Nas horas de folga, no serviço, chovesse ou caísse fogo em brasa do céu, ninguém lhe tirava da imaginação o petiz: era uma perseguição de

todos os instantes, uma idéia fixa e tenaz, um relaxamento da vontade irresistivelmente dominada pelo desejo de unir-se ao marujo como se êle fôra do outro sexo, de possuí-lo, de tê-lo junto a si, de amá-lo, de gozá-lo.[6] (41)

In these two sets of oppositions—the noble black Bom-Crioulo versus the hypocritical white officers and the masculine black Bom-Crioulo versus the effeminate white Aleixo—Caminha's narrative cannot avoid an undeniable measure of semantic schematicism. Such schematicism is typical of the late nineteenth-century novel, and writers like Machado are particularly prized for their ability to attenuate it via the subtlety of their narrative texture and the nuances of the details with which characters and events are postulated. By contrast, Caminha, who was not yet thirty when he published *Bom-Crioulo*, is much more primitive in his craft as a novelist. As a result, the lines of opposition in his novel are particularly evident, with none of the complex ambiguities of a Machado. Therefore, there is little mistaking the outlines of what the characters of his novel represent, particularly as regards the two sets of oppositions I have identified.

Bom-Crioulo's pursuit and conquest of Aleixo, highlighted by the physical sacrifice in the form of the flogging he receives for defending the boy, occupies the first half of the novel (chapters 1–5). We see the establishment of a sexual idyll between the two men, first within the relatively protected confines of their shipboard life and then in the refuge of the room in the Rua da Misericórdia where the former slave leisurely fulfills his erotic needs. As part of the affirmation of his influence over the innocent white boy, Bom-Crioulo becomes a demanding master, thereby both echoing contemporary narratives concerning master-slave relationships and inverting radically the pattern of white master and black slave. Caminha is unflinching in narrating the details of sexual enslavement of Aleixo by the older man, and one cannot help but wonder if his portrayal held a doubly morbid fascination for readers who might have been contemplating for the first time both the possibilities of homoerotic passion and a scandalous inversion of the roles of slavery:

Em terra, no quarto da Misericórdia, nem se falava!—ouro sôbre azul. Ficavam em ceroulas, êle e o negro, espojavam-se à vontade na velha cama de lona, muito fresca pelo calor, a garrafa de aguardente ali perto, sozinhos, numa independência absoluta, rindo e conversando à larga, sem que ninguém os fôsse perturbar—volta na chave por via das dúvidas . . .

Uma cousa desgostava o grumete: os caprichos libertinos do outro. Porque Bom-Crioulo não se contentava em possuí-lo a qualquer hora do

> dia ou da noite, queria muito mais, obrigava-o a excessos, fazia dêle um escravo, uma "mulher à-toa" propondo quanta extravagância lhe vinha à imaginação. [. . .]
>
> E o pequeno, submisso e covarde, foi desabotoando a camisa de flanela, depois as calças, em pé, colocando a roupa sôbre a cama, peça por peça.
>
> Estava satisfeita a vontade de Bom-Crioulo.[7] (78–79)

However, this idyll cannot last. Whether because homosexual affairs are inherently unstable or because all relationships based on passion must in time yield to the other events of life, Bom-Crioulo is restationed, and his affair with Aleixo is threatened by the separation of being assigned to different ships with different routines and days off. Throughout the rest of the novel, Caminha traces the tragic dénouement of this perturbation of the sexual idyll attained by the two in their humble, rented Garden of Eden.

Underscoring the breach that develops between Aleixo and Bom-Crioulo, the narrative splits into two threads. On the one hand is Bom-Crioulo's fear that something has gone wrong between him and Aleixo because of the new assignment, his revolt against authority, the terrible flogging he receives for disorderliness, his subsequent hospitalization, his renewed pursuit of Aleixo and his jealous murder of the boy for having become D. Carolina's lover during his "master's" absence. Paralleling the portrait of Bom-Crioulo's agony of loss are the details of Aleixo's second seduction, this time by the men's worldly wise and randy landlady, who sees a special challenge in seducing such a lovely young man and in wooing him away from a male lover in the bargain.

Undertaking a sort of irreflective vindication of heterosexuality, D. Carolina, a white, Portuguese woman who feels that she is denied Aleixo's physical charms by a male lover who is, after all, only a black (132, 151), has little trouble in vindicating her self-attributed rights over the seductive youth. As a consequence, Aleixo becomes little more than a point of reference for a contest of sexual rights between the black slave/male lover and the white Portuguese/female prostitute. While the narrator's omniscient voice implies that Carola Bunda has not completely worked out in her rather primitive mind all of the social consequences of her actions, for the reader it must be obvious that Aleixo is much more than simply a pawn in a contest of erotic wills.

As a black man who has exchanged the slavery of the plantation for the oppressive discipline of the military, Bom-Crioulo bases his initial relationship with Aleixo on the assertion of his mastery over the white boy whom he initiates (as he, in fact, initiates himself) in the details of homoerotic love, a course of behavior that isolates him as much from society as a whole as does his race (hence, the importance of the refuge of the room in the Rua da Misericórdia). Although she explicitly turns against Bom-Crioulo as a black man and as, in her words, a pederast, D. Carolina is not really conscious of having undertaken a form of social revindication against Bom-Crioulo. Nevertheless, what in effect does take place is a form of rehumiliation of the black man, such that in the course of the second half of the novel he is reduced once again to his status as a slave without dignity, respect, or rights. Renounced by Aleixo, whom he kills in a rage of jealousy, and scorned by the white woman whom he had earlier saved from assault, Bom-Crioulo reassumes a condition of total subjection within a society in which there is no place at all for him.

One crucial issue in the novel has not been mentioned so far: Aleixo's right to choose his own sexual partner. But this is never really an issue during the silent contest between Bom-Crioulo and D. Carolina, and, while Aleixo was originally seduced by the former's attentions, he succumbs with equal willingness to D. Carolina's no less aggressive advances. Certainly, Aleixo comes to repudiate Bom-Crioulo's sexual interest in him, but the narrator is insistent in showing his thoughts to be echoes of D. Carolina's erotic persuasiveness. From one point of view, Aleixo may be said to come around, finally, to assuming his "proper" and "natural" sexual role, renouncing the perversion thrust upon him by Bom-Crioulo. While readers may wish to accept and perhaps even endorse this change in his identity, it is important to point out that Caminha's narrator is hardly interested in probing the details of Aleixo's decision, rather, his focus throughout this crucial segment of the novel is on D. Carolina's struggle against Bom-Crioulo, and it is a struggle drawn in the stark terms of an inventory of primary semantic oppositions that quite effectively exclude Aleixo and his own sexual preferences as merely the pretext for the sexual contest between first his "master" and then his "mistress."

Bom-Crioulo's assertion of sexual independence is, to be sure, not a conscious political act, but rather fundamentally the fulfillment of his personal needs as a human being, the biologically neutral naturalness, if not the social legitimacy, of which the narrator clearly acknowledges. But this gesture of independence and the exercise of a sexual mastery over Aleixo cannot last, and Bom-Crioulo's degradation is the reaffirmation of a prevailing if unjust social order. After his unexpected transfer to another ship, a transfer against which he has no recourse, Bom-Crioulo is later flogged unmercifully (by a commander who is notorious for his own homosexuality; see 121–123) for disorderly conduct stemming from his despair at the thought of losing Aleixo in the confusion of his new schedule. The reasons for which he is flogged are significant: "Desobediência, embriaguez e pederastia são crimes de primeira ordem"[8] (123).

This flogging and his confinement as a prisoner in a hospital in order to recover from the lacerations of the rod are the beginning of his degradation as the sailor whose nickname was originally the recognition of his docile and cooperative nature. In a parallel fashion, while Bom-Crioulo is undergoing this public physical humiliation, he has been rejected by Aleixo in favor of a scheming harlot:

> Aleixo dependurou a jaqueta de flanela azul e deixou-se ficar em camisa de meia, ouvindo cantar a água, enquanto D. Carolina ia enxaguando a roupa.
>
> Falaram em Bom-Crioulo e riram à custa do negro, baixinho, à socapa.
>
> —Boa criatura! sentenciou a portuguêsa com um quê de ironia.
>
> —Para o fogo! acrescentou Aleixo.[9] (127–128)

> Grandessíssimo pederasta! Nunca supusera [D. Carolina] que uma paixão de homem a homem fôsse tão duradoura, tão persistente! E logo um negro. Senhor Bom-Jesus, logo um crioulo imoral e repugnante daquele![10] (151–152)

Bom-Crioulo versus Bom-Jesus—this is the disjunction that emerges in the mind of the woman who unwittingly emerges in the novel as the black slave's principal social antagonist. Her reported interior monologue echoes the standard Christian, moral basis for repudiation of Bom-Crioulo's sexual life, adding to it the racial dimension that is fundamental to Caminha's novel. In the final analysis, whatever opportunity may have existed at the time for Bom-Crioulo to seek some measure of physical and sexual liberation—his escape from the plantation, his enrollment in the relatively secure life of the navy, and his successful attempt to establish a relationship with Aleixo—these assertions of independence must not be permanent, and Bom-Crioulo is ultimately humiliated and degraded both by officialdom in the form of his commander and by society at large in the form of D. Carolina. His final death is simply the reconfirmation of his destruction as, to use the phrase from American culture, an uppity nigger, and a queer to boot. Once again throughout this exposition, it must be noted, Aleixo's person—and, finally, his violent death—are not dwelt upon as of separate consequence. Rather, Aleixo never ceases to be a function of the inevitable course of events imposed upon Bom-Crioulo, in quite Naturalistic ways, by his character and his circumstances.

Caminha's omniscient narrator—Caminha himself, of course, in a less rigorous critical distinction—speaks throughout with great sympathy for Bom-Crioulo, with little in the way of condescension toward the noble but ignorant and primitive black. While he does underscore the instinctual nature of Bom-Crioulo's behavior, making it clear that the man's pursuit of Aleixo is a "natural" rather than a conscious political act, to the extent that such a distinction can be made, the narrator concurs unquestionably with the legitimacy of the slave's needs, which are highlighted by the basic nobility of his actions. But in the case of all three of his central characters, the narrator adopts an omniscient tone not just because this is the basic model for nineteenth-century narrators in the novel, but because it derives from the unreflective nature of Bom-Crioulo, D. Carolina, and Aleixo as humble social types.

Perhaps there is a fundamental conflict inherent in Caminha's view of Bom-Crioulo, between a gesture toward the legitimation of his homosexuality because it is a biologically neutral fact and the view of his passion as dooming him inevitably, between seeing in his final destruction the inescapably fatal destiny of the oppressed (whether black or homosexual or both) and considering that destruction the logical consequence of his morbidly fascinating deviation (Flora Süssekind provides excellent comments on Naturalism and Caminha's novel). On the one hand, the narrator has much to say to vindicate the humanness of Bom-Crioulo, if only in the way in which many novelists of Naturalism were wont to engage our sympathy for humble folk whom they proceeded relentlessly to show destroyed by their biological nature and by society's oppressive structures (Thomas Hardy or Frank Norris, for example).

Since the narrator's voice dominates in the novel, with little in the way of direct dialogue, it is often difficult to distinguish between the narrator's voice proper and the indirect discourse he attributes to his characters. The consequence is that the latters' condemnations of Bom-Crioulo's sexuality, condemnations that are often more selfishly motivated than morally based, are complemented by the narrator's descriptions in a language that by the standards of today's defense of gay rights would be considered prejudicial. Thus, when Bom-Crioulo finally beds Aleixo, the narrator closes the chapter with this coda: "E consumou-se o delito contra a natureza" (58).

However, the confusion, by contemporary standards, between the self-serving repudiation of Bom-Crioulo by Aleixo and D. Carolina and the narrator's own beliefs, cannot permit a characterization of *Bom-Crioulo* as antihomosexual. In the sympathetic presentation of Bom-Crioulo in almost heroic terms, in the detailed exposition of the tragedy of his failure to achieve a measure of independence as a (biological) consequence of his race and sexual preferences, and in the harsh representations of official hypocrisy and personal betrayal by two people whom he has defended, Caminha's novel is an eloquent defense of Bom-Crioulo as a human being not despite, but because of, the specific details of his character. Beyond the simple fact of its importance as a founding text of homosexual writing (and this fact is irrespective of how readers understand the novel's stance toward homosexuality), *Bom-Crioulo*, despite certain ambiguities in the narrator's voice, cannot help but be read as based on the forthright recognition of the variegated nature of sexuality, the rhetoric of which is only reinforced by the important combination at a crucial moment in Brazilian social history of racial and homoerotic motifs (Fry, "Léonie"). If Caminha can only consider Bom-Crioulo's sexuality as pathologically anomalous and therefore as leading inevitably to his destruction, his novel is at least a notably morbid example of the Naturalism of the day. In this sense, *Bom-Crioulo* would be simply echoing in a harsher register the accepted beliefs of the nineteenth-century patriarchal society (Reis).

One of the central premises to be drawn from Fredric Jameson's work on the "political unconscious" is that, despite the apparent strong voice with which nineteenth-century fiction speaks about social and political issues, it is a narrative that may be examined for the gaps, silences, and contradictions that lie beneath its superficial compactness. This position only echoes the fundamental axiom of ideological criticism that what a text does not address, what it leaves hanging or unresolved may be as significant as the neat and often schematic structure it appears to draw. Works written under the aegis of Naturalism may be especially significant in this regard. On the one hand, they propose to deal in a "scientific manner" with the hidden forces of the human experience while at the same time addressing themselves to an audience quite secure, if not openly smug, in its beliefs about the social order. It is for this reason that so many of the important texts from this period were considered scandalous and were the object of denunciation if not threats of prosecution. Caminha's novel, written during a period of major social transition in Brazil cannot be seen as an exception, particularly when one considers the taboo nature of the facet of human behavior he chose to treat. Critics have generally agreed that Caminha views the question of homosexuality under the purview of Naturalism: a type of biological destiny that will predetermine specific forms of behavior (Jameson, *The Political Unconscious*; Dowling).

But if, as I believe is the case, there lies behind the gestures toward these beliefs to be found in the form of certain prejudicial tags of the narrator the possibility of legitimizing Bom-Crioulo's person as a figure of racial and sexual oppression, Caminha's novel opens the possibility for a significant opposition to those beliefs. (While restrained in characterizing the details of Bom-Crioulo's sexuality, Dorothy Scott Loos recognizes the differences between the novel and the more typical Naturalism of other Brazilian novels of the period, including Caminha's own *A normalista* [The Grade-School Teacher] [88].)

Toward this end, the novel is carefully constructed in its ranging of Bom-Crioulo versus a series of oppressive elements, generally in the form of brutal naval discipline (from which he suffers repeatedly) and specifically in the form of the self-allegedly socially/racially/sexually superior D. Carolina, who is the principal agent of his downfall. It must be granted that Caminha's Bom-Crioulo is marked by all of the scars of a deleterious determinism. But the fact that he is a victim of his innate sexual identity and the spectrum of repressive social forces (and only in part because of his homosexuality) does not mean that *Bom-Crioulo* can only be read as a denunciation of homosexuality and the disastrous consequences of those who "choose to pursue" it (such a choice would, of course, vitiate the notion of biological determinism). There are those who have read the novel as principally concerned with a racist denunciation of Bom-Crioulo as a black. The most recent such opinion in this vein is provided by David Brookshaw: "The message . . . is basically that the company of blacks is not salubrious as they have no control over their animal instincts, and having therefore no morality of their own, they can create havoc with the lives of those (the whites) who have" (39). But Brookshaw's reading fails to address itself to the repeated image of Bom-Crioulo as victim, even though his sexuality and violent behavior may result from dangerous "animal instincts."

Rather, Caminha's narrator takes great care to present his protagonist as victim, and his behavior toward the other characters and his violent end are consequences of his status as victim. Caminha's narrator may speak contradictorily about how we should view Bom-Crioulo's homosexuality, whether it is an extension of his features that are praised at the outset of the novel or whether it is "*contra natureza*" (again, a contradiction of biological determinism, since what Nature determines cannot be against Nature). But this does not detract from the importance of *Bom-Crioulo* for the striking way in which, so early in modern Brazilian literature, it dealt with one of the great taboo subjects of Western culture.

CHAPTER THREE

VAMPIRE VERSIONS OF HOMOSEXUALITY: SEDUCTION AND RUIN

I

The creation of a well-defined heterosexual matrix in Western society, as Michel Foucault has argued in detail, necessarily involved the delimitation of realms of unhealthy sexuality. One of the abiding arguments against homosexuality is that in addition to representing a constellation of unnatural (perverse, sinful) forms of sexual behavior, it involves the seduction of the innocent by the already corrupt or perverted. Such a view is concomitant with ideologies of so-called healthy reproductive sexuality, which are usually also antierotic insofar as species perpetuation rather than corporal sensuality is their primary focus: if corporal sensuality is tolerated, it must be in the name of the monogamous heterosexual unit and at the service of effective reproduction. Such ideologies are perennially on the alert against the occasions and agents of corruption (Zelmar Acevedo passim).

In the history of Western sexuality, perversion has often been attributed to a corruption-ridden upper or leisure class. Such an attribution is in addition to a notion of corruption from within what came to be constructed, at times loosely (general social customs and values) and at times rigidly (the force of codified civil and ecclesiastic law), as a healthy, sane, or responsible bourgeoisie by its own disaffected or improperly socialized members. It has been held that, for the members of this class, eroticism, including homoeroticism, is but one more form of unproductive self-indulgence. This attribution is likely to be associated with a figure like Oscar Wilde and the eponymous, semiautobiographical hero of his novel *The Picture of Dorian Gray* (Cohen, "Writing Gone Wilde"). However, its most notorious embodiment may be found in the narreme of the aristocratic Count Dracula ravishing village or peasant youth (whom Romantic legend happens to have heterosexualized [Stevenson; Dworkin]). Reaching farther back in history, the cautionary stance toward the possibilities of corruption by the aristocracy may dwell on those princes of the Church for whom innocent altar and choirboys were just so many *boccati* to be consumed.

Yet, the much-maligned Victorian morality has not been the exclusive province of a sexually stern bourgeoisie, and the notions of healthy anerotic genitalism play an integral role in programs in defense of the working class. Such programs whether associated with bourgeois morality or with Stalinized Marxism, in addition to being generally antierotic as a consequence of viewing unproductive sex as of a whole with antisocial degeneracy, have had no problem in viewing homosexuality as an unspeakable perversion of reproductive sexuality. Fidel Castro's persecution of the extensive homosexual subculture in Cuba is as much an application of this traditional Marxist wisdom as it is a confirmation of the exemplification in that subculture, and in the whole fabric of sexual mores in prerevolutionary Havana, of the bourgeois corruption the revolution was obliged to eradicate in order to ensure a healthy socialist body (Karlinsky; Phillips; see also the discussion of Reinaldo Arenas in Chapter 5).

Within the orbit of ideologies in support of the cause of the working class against exploitation from above, whether by a bourgeoisie or the holdover of a feudal aristocracy, turn-of-the-century anarchism (most especially in its Mediterranean varieties) likewise had to concern itself with the threats to a norm of healthy individual life. One of the many threats to such a norm was homosexuality, inasmuch as it could only be viewed as an exploitation of the weak by the powerful and as the corruption of a natural condition of sexual health. Anarchism was not, however, opposed to "healthy" sexual responses, and it is important to note the defense of female sexual independence in Argentina (Bellucci). In the vast culture of anarchism in Argentina, one of the Latin American countries where anarchic theory and praxis flourished vigorously for approximately forty years between 1890 and 1930 (Viñas; Oved), the enormous inventory of concrete examples of the abuse of the individual by corrupt societies and their government has many issues on which to focus its anger other than the threat of homosexuality. But *Los invertidos: Obra realista en tres actos* (The Inverts: A Realistic Play in Three Acts) by the anarchist dramatist José González Castillo (1885–1937) is a notable exception of a cultural text dealing explicitly with the subject (for information on González Castillo's dramas, see Foppa 347–349; Berenguer Carisomo 352, 388–389; Ordaz; Jones 157–158).

Los invertidos was first performed in 1914 and was published as an undated pamphlet in the series "La farsa: Obras teatrales seleccionadas," probably in the same year. The "Carro de Tespis" collection of Argentores, Sociedad Argentina de Escritores (the Argentine equivalent of Equity of which González Castillo was an organizing member) brought out a reedition in 1957. However, to the best of my knowledge, the play remains unstudied. Willis Knapp Jones does mention it in his inventory of the dramatist's thesis plays, but it has otherwise been forgotten, perhaps in part because it represents a sort of thesis drama that, except for the plays of Florencio Sánchez, whose last works were contemporaneous with *Los invertidos*, does not attract much critical interest.

It must be noted from the outset that *Los invertidos* is not alone in dealing with homosexuality in the period. Winston Leyland, in his introduction to *My Deep Dark Pain Is Love*, examines a few, but significant, examples of narratives by writers of the following generation whose personal identities could be aligned intellectually with a still-prevalent climate of sympathy with anarchism in Argentina. Roberto Arlt is surely the most outstanding of these writers, and Leyland discusses a homosexual incident included in his novel *El juguete rabioso* (1926), an incident whose narrativization echoes the aforementioned anarchistic views. Should the inventory of these examples be increased by the sort of diligent archaeological investigation ordinarily necessary to correct a cultural imbalance, one is confident that they would reveal a single voice with respect to homosexuality: it represents the corruption of the innocent by the blackguards of perversion, among whom may be found common men who were themselves previously corrupted.

Moreover, in accord with the narrative schema being described, should the sexual wretch be a member of the downtrodden masses, his desires can only confirm how he has been corrupted by the men who have abused him. While it is customary, in the defense of the inherent nobility of the "natural man" made by both anarchism and socialism, to argue that homosexuality is not to be found among the working class, that it is the result of a degenerate bourgeoisie or a rotten aristocracy, Social Realism proper and its pre-1930s populist and anarchist forerunners (including the sort of writing called muckraking at the time in the United States) might contain characters corrupted by their oppressors in addition to the usually sentimentalized image of the standard-bearers of revolt. Since bourgeois Naturalism dwelt on the bad seed of the humble, the new revolutionary literature was at pains to nurture the spark of inherent nobility in the conflict between the classes. Yet, it could not avoid the simple sociological fact that, because of oppression and exploitation, the members of the working class were broken and corrupted in ways that went far beyond sexual miscreancy.

Los invertidos concerns the secret homosexual life led by Dr. Flórez, a prominent lawyer. As the play opens, his son is copying out the final draft of a report his father has been asked to prepare concerning a man accused of killing his male lover in a fit of jealousy. As Julián copies the report, he reads it aloud, thereby reminding the audience of some of the prevailing concepts of the day concerning homosexual activity. We may call these concepts the vampire theory of homosexuality, in honor of the Dracula narreme. Individuals cursed with the love of other men come out at night to lure unsuspecting victims to their gaudy lairs, where their ravishment initiates them into their perverse form of sexuality. This world is thoroughly corrupt, and raging jealousies and insane desires lead to the sort of violence evidenced in the case at hand. These vampires are the result of a combination of poor genetic stock, an improper moral formation, and a chosen way of life that presents them with the opportunities for corruption and perversion.

Needless to say, the glimpse of this world is disconcerting for Julián, who is, we are given to understand, a fine specimen of a privileged and careful upper middle-class upbringing. His home, including the public image his father projects, is a model of rectitude and moral fortitude, and his mother is a pillar of respectability. Throughout the play, details of Dr. Flórez's comfortable home reinforce the bastion of security that must be built and maintained to protect against the sort of degeneracy this servant of the established order is routinely called on by the police to interpret for them.

One man has free access to the Flórez haven of moral security. Pérez is a close associate of Dr. Flórez, and, during a time when men of the latter's class may have had their professional establishment on the premises of their home but enjoyed an expansive private life in the all-male company of exclusive clubs, Pérez comes and goes in the Flórez home, stopping by to accompany Dr. Flórez to one of their clubs, returning with him from a night of gentlemanly occupation, or simply coming by during his own busy day to pay his respects. Indeed, it is on just such an occasion that Pérez makes amatory advances on Dr. Flórez's wife, Clara. More on this dramatic detail below.

There is, however, a club to which Dr. Flórez and Pérez belong that Clara knows nothing about. This is a circle of sexual perverts of which the two men are the leaders. They meet in Pérez's townhouse, where the two scions of public respectability are accompanied by a band of stereotyped fairies. Dr. Flórez and Pérez enjoy a male-male relationship based on homosexual desire, and these young men enhance the separate reality of the forbidden social milieu Pérez has installed in his apartments. The bourgeois elegance and respectability of the Flórez home that is the scenographic anchor of the play contrast with the highlighted foppery of what is in essence Pérez's homosexual brothel. González Castillo's stage directions are designed to ensure that the decor is as exaggeratedly Wildean as possible.

Clara loses no time in sensing that something is not quite right about the apartment to which Pérez has led her, but he assures her that it is nothing more than his private world which he is offering to her.

> Es mi casa, Clara . . . Mi garçoniere, como dicen los franceses . . . Aquí no entra nadie más que yo, y todo eso que te parece tan femenino no es más que el refinamiento con que me gusta vivir, haciéndome la ilusión de que, solo y triste, hay en esta casa de soltero, un espíritu femenino, delicado y culto, como el tuyo, que todo lo ordena, lo dispone y lo rige . . .[1] (33)

While Pérez is doing his best to calm the discomfort Clara feels but cannot define, he is suddenly interrupted by some of the young men who are accustomed to having access to his home. Although Pérez has ordered his valet not to allow him to be disturbed, the boys barge in on Pérez and Clara. Clara's uneasiness suddenly clicks into sharp focus, and, as she realizes who these men are and what their relationship to Pérez is, she flees in indignation, any sense of guilt she may have had for the transgression she was about to commit with Pérez replaced by repulsion for the nature of the man who sought to seduce her:

> ¡Basta! . . . No necesita explicaciones . . . ¡Es usted un canalla! [. . .] ¿Por quién me ha tomado usted? ¡Degenerado! . . . He oído todo . . . he visto todo . . . ¡Puerco! [. . .] ¡Déjeme pasar le he dicho! . . . ¡Asqueroso! . . . (*Le pega una bofetada y sale precipitadamente por foro, casi sollozando* [. . .]).[2] (39)

Clara's insults mark both the restoration of her moral respectability and the confirmation of Pérez's perverse nature: In addition to his homosexual activities, he would also dare to corrupt a fine family woman like Clara. That he is initially successful does not serve to underscore Clara's moral frailty as a human being or her bourgeois hypocrisy. Rather, within the rhetoric of a thesis play like *Los invertidos*, it functions to frame Pérez's character with unimpeachable clarity.

However, fate has another blow in store for Clara. Clara intercepts a letter sent by Pérez to her husband. The two have had a serious lovers' quarrel, and the letter contains statements that leave no doubts in Clara's mind that her husband is a prominent habitué of Pérez's club. She begins to wonder about their lifelong friendship that antedates her marriage to Dr. Flórez, and she makes inquiries both of her maid, who is an old Flórez family retainer, and of Pérez's manservant. Both confirm her worst fears. When Flórez returns, he is in the company of Pérez:

> FLÓREZ.—¿Qué haces? . . .
> PÉREZ.—Volverte a la realidad de tu propia miseria, de nuestra propia miseria, que está en la sombra . . . Hacerte olvidar de ti mismo, de esa hombría que quieres aparentar y que no es más que el producto de la luz . . . Quiero impedir que te veas . . . que nos veamos . . .
> FLÓREZ.—No . . . vete . . . vete . . .
> PÉREZ.—No, he dicho; no me voy . . . Quiero verte dócil, como lo has sido siempre, sumiso, femenino, que es tu verdadero estado . . . así . . . que te olvides de que eres hombre y de que sea tu propia infamia, tu dicha en la sombra como es tu verdugo a la luz (*lo acaricia*). Así . . . así . . . como lo eras cuando niño . . . y como lo serás toda tu vida ya, irredenta, inconvertible. (*Se inclina sobre él hasta rozar su cuello con los labios. Junto a la puerta, en la semi-obscuridad, ha aparecido la figura de Clara. Viste un peinador blanco. Ansiosamente parece inclinarse a oír. A medida que el diálogo parece ir culminando, ella con el brazo extendido, abre suavemente el cajón del escritorio y saca el revólver.*) No eres tú . . . Vuelve a ser el de siempre . . . (*Se oye un beso, largo y lento. Clara, con ademán rápido ilumina la habitación. Los dos, con asombro quieren incorporarse.*)[3] (57)

Clara, with the words "¡Miserables! . . . ¡Asquerosos! . . ."[4] (57) fires the gun and wounds Pérez. She then offers the gun to her husband, indicating that he should do the honorable thing for the good of his children. Julián appears just in time to hear the gun go off a second time and to receive the sobbing body of his mother in his arms, as the curtain falls.

Certainly, the pivotal character in *Los invertidos* is Clara. She discovers a world of sexual behavior she never even knew existed. Ignorant of her husband's occasional research for the police—she is disturbed when Julián mentions to her the document he has been copying for his father—she is first stunned and then outraged to discover Pérez's world, and her horror is compounded when she comprehends her husband's involvement in it. Moreover, Clara is called upon to be a witness to that world, first by what she sees and overhears in Pérez's garçonnière and then, in the dramatic high point of the play, when she plays voyeur to the final meeting between the two lovers and sees Pérez affirm his "masculine" dominance over the "feminine" Dr. Flórez with an emphatic kiss. By spying on this meeting, Clara discovers the complete truth of her husband's debasement within a perverse underworld that contradicts all his public figure stands for. The gesture of her turning on the switch floods them with the light of discovery and becomes a metonymic assertion of her wrathful indignation, legitimate within the rhetoric of the play, in the face of the shadowy vampire world of their sexual habits. Pérez's kiss on Dr. Flórez's neck in the semidarkness of the latter's study is a sign of Pérez's lifelong, vampirish dominance of the passive Dr. Flórez. Clara's righteous anger prevails to cast out the shadows of their perversion:

> FLÓREZ.—¡Clara! ¡Qué has hecho! ¡Mujer!
> CLARA.—(*Con gesto grave y enérgico, como una orden.*) ¡Calla! . . . ¡Has sido tú! ¡Has sido tú! . . . Toma . . . (*Le da el arma.*) ¡Ahora . . . ahora te queda lo que tú llamas la última evolución . . . tu buena evolución![5] (57)

Clara's role as a witness and her experience of discovery function, there can be little question, as a dramatic interior duplication of the audience, which is asked to accept the existence of people like Pérez and company in society, preying on the young and the weak. It is asked to contemplate without flinching the details of his nocturnal underworld and to scrutinize some significant details of its etiology. It is required to withstand, along with Clara, the horror of the kiss that Pérez implants on Dr. Flórez's neck. And it is asked to react with outrage along with Clara as an appropriate response to the reality it has discovered and witnessed along with her. In this way, the audience can accept the validity of her firing on Pérez, her demand that her husband take his own life, and the sense of emotional destruction that floods her as the curtain falls.

As a thesis play, *Los invertidos* charts its line of exposition very lucidly: the ordered daytime world of Dr. Flórez versus the turbulent nighttime realm of Pérez; the young, healthy masculinity of Julián versus the queerness of the fairies who are denizens of Pérez's garçonnière. Clara functions as a pivotal reference point between these two worlds because of the indiscretion of her incursion into Pérez's world, a lapse that she atones for first by fleeing from the corrupt Pérez and then by bringing moral justice to her own household as the implacable avenger of the threats to it. As a dramatist, González Castillo is implacable in his treatment of Clara, as he exposes her to the danger of being the lover of the same man of whom her husband has been a lover since childhood (thereby confirming the absolute corruption of the vampire Pérez), obliges her to contemplate the brutal truth about her husband's secret life, and guides her as she does what must be done to defend the proper moral order. If the play in early twentieth-century Argentina may be assumed to have been directed at an essentially upper-middle-class audience, Clara is a reasonable stand-in for the audience's introduction to a threat to any society's moral fiber.

Where *Los invertidos*, however, speaks to González Castillo's commitment to an Anarchist point of view is in the handling of the two characters in the work, aside from the brief appearance of Pérez's "boys," who are marginal to the social class the play focuses on: the Flórez's maid and Pérez's valet. Both of these characters are rather bemused by the ignorance about the ways of the world of the main characters, and both tell how they have had considerable contact with "men of that sort" outside in the unprotected milieu of their own social class. Petrona, the maid, overhears Julián read aloud the text he is transcribing for his father:

> PETRONA.—¡Ah! . . . Una manflora . . . ¡bah! . . . He conocido tantos . . . ¿Y cómo dice que le llaman a los manfloras?
> JULIÁN.—Hermafroditas . . . Invertidos . . .
> PETRONA.—Mafrodita . . . ¡Bah! . . . Los médicos y los procuradores siempre le han de inventar nombres raros a las cosas más sencillas . . . En mis tiempos se les llamaba mariquita, no más, o maricón, que es más claro . . . Pá qué tantos términos . . . ¡Yo he conocido más de cien . . . !
> JULIÁN.—¿Usted? . . . ¿En dónde? . . .
> PETRONA.—¿En dónde ha e'ser, pues? . . . ¡En el mundo! . . . ¿Usted qué se cree? Hay más de esos mafroditas que lo que parece. ¿Qué se figura? . . .[6] (10)

Petrona then proceeds to toss out some information that casts the first light on the relationship between Pérez and Dr. Flórez, who have been friends since childhood and whose behavior has always seemed more than a little strange to this servant hardened to both the harsh realities of life and the curious ways of the people she works for. This information, which Julián dismisses by telling Petrona to mind her own business (12), foreshadows Clara's subsequent full discoveries.

To find out the facts for herself, Clara sends for Benito, Pérez's manservant, whom she bribes to tell her what really goes on in his employer's club. Previous to this interview, she has had Petrona repeat for her in greater detail what the latter had told Julián. But from Benito she learns all about Pérez's life and the shadowy world in which he moves. Benito makes it clear that his job is to obey orders and that a man must do what is necessary in order to live. He speaks of his distaste for what he sees and confirms the depravity of his employer and those who frequent the club, including Dr. Flórez:

> BENITO.—Y . . . mujeres falsificadas, ¿no sabe? . . . Varones de ambos "sexos," como dicen . . .
> CLARA.—Pero . . . de modo que . . . ¡No! eso no es posible . . . ¡Usted miente!
> BENITO.—Señora . . . permítame. Yo no miento nada . . .
> CLARA.—Pero . . . ¡dígame! Mi marido . . . ¿Qué hace mi marido ahí? . . . ¿Qué hace? . . .
> BENITO.—Y, señora . . . Son cosas de la vida . . . ¡Qué va a sorprenderse uno! Cada hombre tiene un vicio, tiene.[7] (51–52)

Like Benito, *Los invertidos* is not lying. And like Clara, the audience must accept the bitter truth about the existence and activities of the vampires who pervert the morally healthy. Petrona and Benito may accept with the resignation of the disenfranchised, who must survive in a world they cannot control, the presence of *manfloras* who, particularly in Benito's case, are part of the exploitation to which they are subject in a corrupt world. It is interesting to note that, as part of the confirmation of the extent to which the society they know is pervasively corrupt, both Petrona and Benito acknowledge the extensive existence of men like Pérez and Dr. Flórez, as against the bourgeois wishful thinking, prevalent even today, that homosexuality involves only a miniscule number beyond the pale of decent society.

González Castillo assigns the task of addressing this blight on the social fabric not to the working-class characters who admit to considerable familiarity with it, but to an agent of the very class to which the sexual vampires themselves belong. One might speculate as to the ideological advantage of affirming this correlation between Clara and the likely audience of the play, who themselves are responsible for the moral quality of Argentine society. Concomitantly, the dramatist may have shied away from putting social remedies in the hands of characters who are marginal to the social class that binds the world of the play and the sort of audience it would have had in 1914, almost two decades before Social Realist works sustainedly addressed themselves to working-class audiences (cf., however, Castagnino 133–134 on González Castillo's anarchistic themes). But whatever the explanation for this structural detail of the play may be, it remains clear that the homosexual ringleaders of the play belong to a privileged class from whose protected position they engage in their immoral behavior and corrupt others along with them, including men of Benito's station in life like the boys who interrupt Pérez's and Clara's tryst in his apartment.

As a work of drama, *Los invertidos* places the emphasis on homosexuality as action, as a behavior. Within the context of the debate over whether homosexuality is an inherent condition like other genetically determined traits or whether it is an assumed conduct that can be taken up and set aside according to the varying circumstances of the individual's life (that is, the debate between whether or not "homosexual" can ever be an existential noun or whether it can only be an inanimate adjective to describe acts), Dr. Flórez's professional report refers both to bad genes and to the conditioning effect of environment and education, which is essentially a variety of the Naturalist's deterministic hypothesis about the human condition. The task, then, becomes one of protecting society from the destructive influence of this lamentable condition. Where Julián, in a discussion of the subject with his mother, underscores the pathos of a condition that, nevertheless, provokes nausea in him (25), *Los invertidos* looks toward the legitimate eradication of the vampires by the hand of the morally righteous like Clara.

From the point of view of drama as an arena of actions, it is not the pathetic *condition* of Pérez and company but their perverse *behavior* that holds sway in the development of the play. It is this behavior that Clara witnesses, both directly in her visit to the garçonnière, her reading of the letter from Pérez to her husband, and her spying on their conversation as lifelong lovers and indirectly through the information she extracts from Petrona and Benito, that legitimizes her actions that draw the play to a close.

Los invertidos is a grim piece of theater for the image of a corrupt privileged class it depicts and the solution it proposes, as well as for the counterpoint between that image and subsequent versions of homosexuality, particularly the 1982 dramatic version of Manuel Puig's novel *El beso de la mujer araña* (1976), to mention an Argentine reference (Muñoz). But while the only thing original that González Castillo's play has to say about homosexuality is the legitimation of Clara's Medea-like corrective violence in the name of a sociomoral integrity, its emphasis on the action-based depiction of homosexuality removes the subject from the realm of the cursory references in Argentine literature to the condition of some hapless individuals and provides it with its first forthrightly theatrical representation.

2

—¡Calla, Mónica!—increpó el sacerdote.
—¿Por qué, cuando otros hablarían por mí y, tarde que temprano, llegaría a saber lo que únicamente usted ignora todavía?[8] (D'Halmar 145)

Completed in 1920 and first published in 1924, *La pasión y muerte del cura Deusto* (The Passion and Death of Father Deusto) by the Chilean Augusto D'Halmar (1880–1950) does for Spanish-language Latin American literature what Adolfo Caminha's *Bom-Crioulo* had done thirty years earlier for Brazilian literature: speak unequivocably about homoerotic passion (Stephen Wayne Foster claims that at least ten of D'Halmar's books deal with homosexuality and pederasty; see also R. L. Acevedo). If all of the displaced metaphorical trappings of homoeroticism are present in Rafael Arévalo Martínez's story "El hombre que parecía un caballo" ("The Man Who Looked like a Horse") except for direct lexical signifiers (see Chapter 4), D'Halmar's novel provides a sort of explicitness that contrasts notably with the intriguing evasiveness of Arévalo Martínez's text.

Iñigo Deusto is a dour Basque priest who arrives in Seville as a young man, accompanied by Mónica, a longtime family retainer, to take up residence as the parish priest of San Juan de la Palma. One of the choir urchins, an illegitimate gypsy boy named Pedro Miguel, begins to hang around the priest and quickly ends up his protégé. In time he becomes the parish sacristan, flourishes as a magnificent soloist with the choir, and, as he matures physically, attracts the attention of a fast set that includes a bullfighter, a flamenco singer, a dissolute poet laureate (who is specifically described as a Dorian Gray), and a cynical Jewish painter. The latter win his affections away from Deusto, who is never really able to cope with his feelings for the boy or to offer him anything other than a chaste devotion couched in the holy terms of the spiritual. However, true to the call of his Andalusian blood, Pedro Miguel is unable to renounce the awakening urgings of his flesh, and he becomes a brilliant plaything for the denizens of Sevillian café society. Yet Pedro Miguel continues to nurture a deep bond of love with Deusto and, remorseful over his abandonment of the priest, he attempts suicide. This theatrical gesture brings the two men back together, but only briefly. Pedro Miguel appeals to the priest to recognize the depth of passion that exists between them and to accept it in all of its earthly implications. Deusto, however, cannot forgive the boy his treasonous betrayal (he reproaches him silently for having lain with a woman, although he apparently dares not wonder about his relationship with Oscar Wilde's Sevillian counterpart), and Pedro Miguel feels himself driven from the house. Deusto catches up with him at the train station, where Pedro Miguel plans to run away to seek his fortune in Madrid. Unable to accept Pedro Miguel's pleas for Deusto to leave with him, the priest rushes off and is crushed by the very train Pedro Miguel departs on.

The "love that dare not speak its name" certainly does in D'Halmar's novel, if only to confirm its destructive force. From the outset, it is hardly any secret to the people around Deusto that his relationship with Pedro Miguel has assumed the classic Greek pattern of older mentor and boy lover. Throughout the novel, the unspoken bond of passion between Deusto and Pedro Miguel is acknowledged openly by reprobates who, almost as though playing an elaborate erotic game, eventually entice Pedro Miguel away. It is not surprising that these world-weary demimondains are quick to read the signs of homoerotic passion. Yet they are not alone, for Mónica, with the legendary wisdom of ancient family retainers, is, like the servants in *Los invertidos*, far from reticent with her mutterings, and the self-important sacristan whom Pedro Miguel displaces strikes a direct departing blow: "¡cuidado!, pues quien con chiquillos se acuesta, aviado amanece"[9] (69). Even Deusto's superior, the Cardinal Archbishop of Seville, grasps the nature of the relationship between the two men. After staring intently at Pedro Miguel, whom Deusto has insisted that he meet as the seraphic voice of his choir, the ecclesiastic prince expresses his sympathy: "—'Mi pobre Deusto'—dijo tomándole ambas manos en un movimiento inesperado—. Todo mi favor y mis bendiciones [. . .]"[10] (155–156).

What is singular about D'Halmar's novel is the extent to which those around Deusto acknowledge and virtually accept his emotional involvement with Pedro Miguel. Even someone like the displaced sacristan is more interested in hurting Deusto for having fired him than he is in appealing to conventional heterosexual morality. What is more, the *beatas*[11] who resent Pedro Miguel's intrusion into their jealously guarded domain are unwilling to persecute the priest for his passion. Indeed, when their representative realizes that Deusto is not even aware of how he has compromised himself emotionally, she showers him with compassion (86–89). It is only the priest himself who is unable to accept the nature of his passion for Pedro Miguel.

Although in one sense the trajectory of the novel is Pedro Miguel's attainment of maturity and the consequences of his need to heed the carnal call of his gypsy origins, *Pasión* is more specifically the tragedy of

Deusto's own inabililty to understand that call and how it impinges on the complex relationship he has established with the boy. When he can no longer avoid acknowledging that what he feels for Pedro Miguel is physical love and when it can no longer be explained away with the Baroque language of his religion, Deusto commits suicide rather than assume his homosexual desire. It is at this point, when Pedro Miguel speaks to him in a language that brooks no ambiguities, no duplicitousness, a language beyond the ken of Deusto's codes of religious spirituality, that the priest can no longer hide behind expressions of incomprehension. Deusto confesses repeatedly to not understanding what people mean by their comments regarding Pedro Miguel and the place he has made for himself in the parish house, and incomprehension is his essential reaction to any sign of life around him that he senses to be a challenge to the spiritualized security of his severe Basque Catholicism:

> —¿Qué dice usted de esto, Sem Rubí?
> Hubo un silencio; el muchacho, alzando los hombros, había vuelto a enfrascarse en su tarea; el pintor y Mónica, sin que Deusto se percatara, habían cambiado una mirada por encima de su cabeza.
> —Pues nada—dijo Sem Rubí—. Ya debe esperarse usted ésta y otras muchas cosas.
> —No entiendo—dijo el vasco, usando su palabra favorita—. Debe ser la ociosidad la que mete en la cabeza de esas mujeres [chismosas] ideas tan desprovistas de sentido.[12] (89)

In the face of the rumors about his relationship with Pedro Miguel, only the priest is unable or unwilling to comprehend what is being said. Deusto engages, albeit as an unconsciously stubborn gesture, in a denial of language, and his complaints of not understanding involve the defective decoding of what is being said to him in "plain Spanish." Since what he is called upon to decode is a field of reference about sexuality that he is compelled to deny either because of radical ignorance about the varieties of human passion or because of the "interference" of a code of spirituality that cannot accommodate physical love, homosexual or otherwise, Deusto remains resistant to the (self-)knowledge that is thrust in vain upon him until Pedro Miguel's baldly worded confrontation. As a result, D'Halmar's narrative, in keeping with the tradition of the melodramatic representation of the ramifications of profound psychological blows, must see Deusto impelled blindly toward suicide as the only release possible from truth that Pedro Miguel speaks:

> Con un ardiente reflejo en los ojos, una vibración en la voz, un estremecimiento en todo su ser, Pedro Miguel volvió a apoderarse de su dies-

> tra, y ajustándole al dedo su anillo, tal como en su sueño, se inclinó hasta rozar su oreja.
>
> —Dime—afirmó más bien que interrogó—, ¿has sabido nunca cómo yo te quiero?
>
> Deusto le puso las dos manos en el pecho para rechazarle.
>
> —Ahora lo sé, y, por piedad, no lo digas. ¡También he visto claro en mí![13] (221–222)

Pasión constructs the essential narrative conflict and dénouement of Duesto's story around the cultural disjunction between the Basque country and Seville, where Mónica and the priest feel constantly threatened by a sinful ebullience of life they cannot control and which Deusto confesses repeatedly not even to understand. For D'Halmar, Seville represents a sexual materialism, including homoeroticism, that imposes itself on Deusto through the person of Pedro Miguel, who, in turn, cannot accept the priest's refusal to yield himself up to life. A rigidly defined Basque Catholicism versus a luxuriant hedonism constitute the fundamental cultural primes of D'Halmar's novel, providing the backdrop for the exploration of the eloquence of Pedro Miguel's sexual desire (abetted by the understanding acquiescence of virtually everyone around him), as opposed to the sustained pattern of incomprehension and denial on the part of Deusto.

Where the articulation of a language of homosexuality, or at least a semantic realm for its representation within the society symbolized by Seville in *Pasión*, takes place is in this disjunction between Deusto's perverse silence and the often almost nonchalant eloquence of the society around him. Embedded in a complex religious discourse of antimaterialistic spirituality where the elements of a faith are often presented as displaced erotic fetishes for the human passion Deusto systematically denies and sublimates, the priest's "incomprehension" in the full array of its representation in the novel is an ironic conceit concerning the repudiation of the one defining quality of his human nature. The result of the will toward the nonunderstanding of the language of life incarnate in a seductive Seville can only be emotional self-ruin and, in keeping with the inexorable melodrama of D'Halmar's novel, suicide. It is a suicide, beyond the despair over what is felt by Deusto to be an irresolvable conflict, in the face of a semantics of love the priest must not allow to be uttered. Once it is spoken, as it finally is in unequivocal terms by Pedro Miguel, the priest is impelled toward self-destruction (itself an unpardonable sin within the framework of his Catholicism) in order to restore the silence behind the mask of a seamless incomprehension. (One might mention here that sucide is the "solution" to homosexuality in the Cuban Alfonso Hernández Catá's 1928 *El ángel de la Sodoma* (The Angel of Sodom), which the Spanish physician and cultural historian Gregorio Marañón claims in his introduction to be the first Spanish-language novel to deal with the theme.)

3

En jirones (In Shreds, 1985) by Luis Zapata (born in 1951) is by far the most sexually explicit gay novel published so far in Mexico, perhaps in Latin America. Zapata is an excellent example of the extension of the antiestablishment and countercultural principles of *onda* writing to include the unabashed treatment of homosexual identity, an aspect of human experience that it is safe to say was hardly broached in Mexican literature prior to the present generation of writers. Zapata's *Las aventuras, desventuras y sueños de Adonis García, el vampiro de la colonia Roma* (1979; translated as Adonis García: A Picaresque Novel) is the autobiography of an urban *gazapo* (kid) who openly assumes his sexual identity (Jaén; Blanco, *la paja* 171–173), and the 1981 Gay Sunshine Press translation makes it, to the best of my knowledge, the first specifically gay Latin American novel to appear in English.

Like *El vampiro, En jirones* is a first-person narrative. Sebastián describes in painful detail his destructive relationship with A., a man who cruises for anonymous sex, with which he balances precariously the obligation he feels to fulfill a heterosexual role in Mexican upper-middle-class society. However, with Sebastián, A. struggles against a more permanent male-male relationship and the honest acknowledgment of his own sexual needs. Ultimately unable to accept the latter, A. marries, only to return to Sebastián, with whom in the final pages of the novel he engages in a violent relationship, alternately flinging himself into Sebastián's arms and abusing him verbally and physically for making him the wretched monster he has become.

From one point of view, Zapata's novel hardly champions a positive image for gay sexuality, and one might even be tempted to read it as a homophobically grim example, in the spirit of *Los vampiros*, of what happens to men who "choose" to live this way in blatant defiance of society's good sense: Sebastián, who is a successful researcher, abandons himself to an obsession with A., who appears to be irremediably trapped between his homosexual needs and his drive to maintain the appearance of heterosexuality (concerning the pressures of hypocritical convention on the homosexual in Mexico, see Blanco, *Función* 188–189).

Yet, it may be argued that Zapata never intended his fiction to be a plea for the sympathetic understanding of the tensions of a homosexual identity, and, very much in the tradition of John Rechy (whose Mexican ancestry must surely enhance his recognition in Latin America [Reinhardt]), Zapata's principal concern has been to portray unflinchingly the wrenching conflicts of human relationships. If gay relationships are in fact only variations on the essentially intense and conflictive features of human sexuality that bourgeois society seeks to diminish and to mask, it is no more improper for a writer like Zapata to portray the disastrous quality of Sebastián and A.'s love affair than it is for Ernesto Sábato to portray Martín and Alejandra's equally destructive romance in *Sobre héroes y tumbas* (1961; *On Heroes and Tombs*). What makes Zapata's portrayal stand out, even amidst the most forthright writing in Latin America today, is the detailing of the erotic couplings of Sebastián and A. The description of these couplings, lest the reader wish to repudiate them as an example of the sort of gratuitous sensationalism easily attributed by the censorious to gay writing, is however an integral part of the narrator's chronicle of the frustrations of an emotional and physical union between him and his lover.

As narrative text, *En jirones* establishes correlations between the frustrations of being involved in erotic love and those of writing about it. Framed as a *cuaderno* (notebook) that the narrator dedicates to the elusive object of his desire, the text is a double helix of references to the radical impossibility of establishing a satisfactory relationship and despite laborious descriptions of its details in any of the many guises of writing, the radical impossibility of getting the main points right. Thus, the text proposes a symmetrical relationship between the frustrated semiotics of love and the short-circuited semiotics of writing. As a consequence, throughout the novel there is a semantic overlap or interpenetration between terms that refer to the "story" (that is, the events, the *énoncé*) of Sebastián's relationship with A. and the "story" (its chronicling, the *énonciation*) he proposes to write about it:

> Mi historia (la historia de mi relación con A., la única que importa) ya no está jalonada por sucesos grandilocuentes, operísticos. Ha quedado atrás el tiempo de las manifestaciones de exaltación, del sufrimiento por la falta de correspondencia. Vivo instalado cómodamente entre los plie-

> gues de la petite histoire. La nota roja ha desaparecido del periódico de mi vida; los encabezados, como en principios de sexenio, son boyantes, prometedores; las erratas son mínimas: de repente alguna pequeña discusión con A., cierta incomodidad que se disuelve, como hielo frappé, al contacto de su piel, siempre tibia y húmeda.[14] (Zapata 111–112)

> Si esta historia no tiene clímax (¿o los clímax son los momentos de desesperación?, ¿o las cogidas chingonas?), ¿sólo puede tener desenlace?—¿únicamente la muerte de A., o la mía sería un verdadero desenlace? ¿O ni eso: la historia continuaría, continuará?[15] (265; see also 58, 98, 160, 182, 241)

For Zapata's narrator, writing is not merely the recording of the tortuous—and, ultimately, destructive—love affair with A. It is primarily an act of defining, of seeking language adequate to record the intense emotions that are tearing him apart in the three principal stages of the affair: (1) the initial contact and a coming to terms with respective sexual roles; (2) A.'s abandonment of Sebastián in order to marry because he cannot come to accept a self-perception as a homosexual; and (3) the physically violent reuniting of A. and Sebastián and the projection of their abusive relationship into a very uncertain future. During each of these three moments, Sebastián's text records his desperate attempts to express to A., the ostensible addressee of his *cuaderno*, but also to himself, his own definition of their affair.

For example, Sebastián records three different versions of A.'s visit to him to announce that he has decided to resolve his personal conflict by marrying. At this point in his text, Sebastián's grappling with the problems of expression concerns the formulation of insults strong enough to communicate to A. his anger at being dumped in favor of a sweet, virgin bride, in conformance with prevailing romantic conventions. First he acts out the problem of expressing adequately his anger before A. during their encounter and then he struggles during the act of writing with how to find the proper language to transcribe his anger:

> Quisiera inventar nuevos insultos, nuevas maneras para lograr envilecerte, desprestigiarte . . . no puedo seguir repitiéndote que eres un hijo de la chingada, aunque no seas más que eso . . . quisiera poder inventar insultos más cabrones . . . herirte a de veras; de pensamiento, palabra y obra.[16] (178–179)

The controlling adynaton of this passage, *quisiera*, implies the narrator's inability to succeed in this task of expression, just as he has not succeeded in communicating well enough with A. to save their relationship. Since the *cuaderno* is addressed to A., the equivalence between face-to-face communication and the written text is a double proof of futility, since on neither textual level is Sebastián able to experience any satisfaction that he is expressing himself adequately. While it is true that at the end of the text Sebastián and A. are once again seeing each other, their union has become violent and destructive, and mechanical sex has replaced all of Sebastián's dream of a relationship satisfying in either emotional or physical terms. Thus, he is only able to record over and over again "Viene A. Cogemos"[17] (272–274). All of the narrator's enormous efforts to interpret the complexities of his feelings and A.'s conflicts lead to nothing more than a sort of verbal catatonia as the linguistic sign of the ultimate failure of both the personal contact and its narrative representation.

Where the symmetry between personal experience and its representation via the *cuaderno* is modified is in the recurring implication that the latter may be viewed as a form of supplement in a very Derridian sense of the term: language can never be replaced by transcendent meaning, only supplemented by more language in a continuing, but ultimately frustrated, attempt at transcendent meaning. In one way, it is a supplement in Sebastián's life as regards the way in which he earns his living, which is as a researcher at an unnamed Instituto, apparently somewhere in the Guadalajara area. At the Instituto, he is engaged in preparing the final report of an unspecified *proyecto* (project), upon whose completion he intends to return to Mexico City. His affair with A. comes toward the end of this assignment, and his work on the *cuaderno* overlaps the final draft of the *proyecto*. He sets aside the latter, his point of reference in a scheme of social and professional relationships larger than his affair with A., in order to devote himself monomaniacally to A. and to the *cuaderno* dedicated to him.

But in another sense, the narration is a supplement vis-à-vis lived experience, because it is meant to be both a record and an interpretation of it:

> La necesidad de escribir en este cuaderno se había apagado por completo. Ahora lo hago como placebo para engañar a la impaciencia: sustituyo la presencia de A. con las palabras que intentan cercarlo, dibujarlo apenas, aunque no sea susceptible de descripción: sólo quedan algunos rasgos de su conducta; sólo surge en algunas anécdotas, casi invisibles, como el rastro de semen en el pecho al día siguiente.[18] (107–108)

The set of correlations implied by this fragment are symmetrical: the narrative is an effort to supplement life in the same way that the act of writing supplements the sexual act; therefore, words and semen are analogous terms on different textual levels. Throughout his text, Sebastián struggles with the problems of adequate expression, both in the form of the words he needs to cover what he is going through and the narrative schemata to match the personal drama he and A. enact, or that he enacts during A.'s absence. Within this context, the problematics of the word as displacement, substitution, or supplement are raised, and Sebastián wonders about his need to record his love affair as much as he worries about how to transcribe it:

> Y no, carajo, ¿por qué tengo que pensar en tantas pendejadas? ¿No debería simplemente sentirme satisfecho, contento? ¿Por qué todos mis pinches actos deben tener un corolario de palabras, tan inútiles como gastadas? Uno debería situarse en lo inmediato, en lo palpable; decir únicamente, cuando mucho: A. estuvo presente en mí hoy; cogimos. O ni siquiera eso: desconfiar de lo que es susceptible de verbalizar. Sólo lo que no puede ser escrito, formulado en palabras, es válido; por lo menos en lo que toca al deseo y a su satisfacción. Lo demás son chaquetas.[19] (47)

Perhaps, thus, writing is fetishism, in the Freudian sense, and what Sebastián must learn is that there is nothing *inmediato, palpable* and that his words, as inadequate as they may be, are all that remains of the A. he sought to "have and hold." Concomitantly, when A. returns as a raging monster who makes it quite clear that his goal is to make of Sebastián nothing more than his sex slave, Sebastián's narrative degenerates into a babble that is the pitiful sludge of the lofty notions of affection and communion that he describes as having motivated his attempts to forge a relationship with A. in the beginning: "La impresión de que todo esto ya lo he dicho antes (¿antes, cuándo?, ¿hace mucho tiempo?), *con las mismas palabras*"[20] (255).

The obsessiveness with which Sebastián attempts to achieve a level of narrative adequacy may be seen in his recourse to other texts to provide added dimensions to his own story: texts of popular culture in the form of songs and movie plots, the journalistic note describing with vacuous high-class rhetoric the rituals of A's marriage, and any number of dream and fantasy sequences that are part of the hallucinatory states induced by Sebastián's hysteria and the drugs he takes to calm it. *En jirones* becomes a nightmarish narrative as the result of Sebastián's feverish determination to record all of the destructive consequences of his affair with A. However, the sexual communion the two men are able to establish during one fleeting phase of their affair is destroyed by A.'s ties with a moral code that hampers his giving himself to Sebastián, drives him into a meaningless marriage of social conformity, and, finally, transforms him into an avenging rapist. Hardly a homophobic soap opera, Zapata's novel chronicles the psychological difficulties of homoerotic love and the complexities of narrative as both a representation of those difficulties and a supplement to an ideal of love fragmented and made monstrous by social obstacles internalized by the individual. The result can only be a personal dissolution, here metered primarily by the expressive dead end in which *En jirones* concludes.

CHAPTER FOUR

THE DECONSTRUCTION OF PERSONAL IDENTITY

I

The interpretation of literary texts—i.e., the attempt to decode the meaning of a text by displacing its discourse by another that claims to explicate it—seems to obey two strong cultural traditions in the West, one of long standing and the other of more recent support. The belief that texts constitute allegories that require decipherment is one of the oldest views of literary texts in our culture. Whether because of the inherent defectiveness of language or the artful deceptions of feigning poets, texts would appear to demand that we not take them at face value and that we prefer in the place of their specific discourse another, presumedly transparent but perhaps no less problematic text that we call a "critical interpretation."

We may often wonder why interpretation is necessary, why texts cannot mean what they say and say what they mean, but we have nevertheless constructed an entire intellectual establishment around the need to encrust texts with other texts, and the latter in turn with yet others in a spiraling yet ultimately vain enterprise of getting at the "true meaning" of a text. This undertaking holds such sway over our reading of texts that we are often alarmed when texts do, in fact, seem to mean what they say, and our need to supplement them with a critical interpretation suffers acute frustration in the face of the lack of anything more to say beyond what the text appears to be expressing so lucidly. Interpretation as a cultural project has accrued to it a complex set of protocols meant to circumscribe or limit or legislate what the nature of interpretation is, how interpretations are to be gauged against one another and against the text itself (often in that order), and how we are to understand the cumulative effect of the encrustation of primary texts by successive secondary critical discourses (all of these issues are nicely reviewed by Terry Eagleton's analysis of the ideologies of contemporary literary criticism). That it has now become customary to question the distinction between primary and secondary texts, to doubt whether criticism is legitimate or even possible, and to postulate the metacritical nature of primary texts and the "poetic" character of criticism does not obviate the pervasive sway interpretation holds as a cultural goal in our society in general and the ingenious ways in which interpretation proceeds apace even when cloaked in the raiment of a counterinterpretational theoretical stance.

Abetting the interpretive urge with the eloquence of a newfound theoretical posture, reader response theory holds that texts are only outlines for meaning. Thus, their perceived or attributed meaning is the consequence of the processes of decoding (whether freewheeling or conventionally constrained) practiced by real readers, who come equipped with different and varying principles and strategies of decipherment. Although in an extreme sense, this approach to reading texts could imply that texts mean anything we want them to mean, at least those readers who describe their act of reading in the form of critical discourse are constrained to relate their understanding of meaning to an exposition of the structural details of the text that they can show to have triggered or conditioned it. From this point of view, a text is a problematical encodement of meaning, a position to be maintained with regard to all texts but most especially to the complex varieties of writing that we vaguely call literature, including those texts that may not customarily be recognized as literary but that, for a multiplicity of reasons, we wish to assimilate to the privileged category of literature. The encodement is completed or supplemented (depending on one's view of a hierarchy of text/criticism) by the act of reading, which also ought reasonably to involve a reflection of the problematical nature of that encodement (this is what Jameson's "Metacommentary" is referring to); criticism is, therefore, only a particularly specialized, institutionalized form of reading.

It is not necessary to return to the largely discredited view that texts contain an immanent and unitary meaning that it is the responsibility of the critic to discover in order to accept the premise that we can only read texts by postulating a global structure that allows us to segment the flow of discourse and to map patterns with the goal of establishing a principled meaning to an otherwise jumbled succession of inkblots. The guiding question, of course, becomes how we undertake that process of assignment and toward what ideologized end of criticism. The semiotic process of (re)constructing the underlying conditions of meaning and then assigning meaning itself (and it is always a process of "assigning" rather than merely "un/recovering" meaning) is a type of interpretation, albeit one explicitly tied to another category of cultural texts that we call literary-critical theory. Such a process of interpretation stands apart from the ideology of reading texts merely as independent meanings problematically given discursive substance through allegorical signification.

Interpretation comes to be questioned when it strays beyond the set boundaries of the shifting but nevertheless normative protocols of institutionalized acts of reading. We then may say that the interpretation, whether the identification of a unitary meaning or of a pattern of possible meanings viewed as suggested by the signifying processes attributed to the text, is farfetched or arbitrary. One subcategory of questionable interpretations involves readings that transgress on the ideological limits that a specific culture has erected for containing the meaning of texts. That is to say, to the extent that all cultures, as they crystallize as complex ideological projects, repress inconvenient meanings that threaten the integrity and balance of specific ideological projects, any text, whether "primary" or "secondary," that challenges dominant cultural priorities is suspect as outrageous. Primary texts may be banned or censored; secondary texts may be ridiculed and, if that does not work, then banned or censored. One consequence of the cultural facts of life is that we often prefer not to pursue the interpretation of a text whose meanings may seem to threaten our ideological commitments, even if the cost is to be left to assess such a text as hopelessly vague or ambiguous.

Such is the case with the famous short story "El hombre que parecía un caballo" ("The Man Who Looked like a Horse," 1914) by the Guatemalan writer Rafael Arévalo Martínez (1884–1975). Although there has been a critical undercurrent that has assigned to Aretal, the enigmatic "horse man" of the title, a homosexual identity, primarily because of the association of Aretal with the Colombian poet Porfirio Barba Jacob, widely suspected to have had a homosexual identity (Salgado 102–105; Moody 359), the majority of analyses of the story have preferred to stress its ambiguous or elusive symbology. Thus, there has never been a reading of the text as dealing, no matter how indirectly, with homosexuality, despite all the passing references one might find in the secondary bibliography on Arévalo Martínez (S. W. Foster, however, includes the text in his survey of homosexuality in Central American fiction).

Rather, it has been deemed enough to suggest that Aretal is a literary pseudonym of Barba Jacob, with whom the author enjoyed a personal relationship, and that, if the suspicion that Barba Jacob was a homosexual is valid, the mysteriously alienating and yet magnetic quality of the horse man in the story must, perforce, be a veiled allusion to hideous homoeroticism. Arévalo Martínez's assertion that he did not have Barba Jacob in mind when writing the story and avowals to the effect that Barba Jacob and especially the author himself were not homosexuals have been taken by other critics to be sufficient evidence that homosexuality is not the secret element in the subtle chemistry of human relations described by the story, as though the substance of the story depended on a confirmation of these real-life details.

Critics are in agreement that the story chronicles the first-person narrator's involvement with one Aretal, a man who looks like a horse. Aretal exercises over the narrator a strange fascination that is described with the elliptic and highly metaphorized language of Modernism, Symbolism's very successful Latin American derivate:

> Después de un ritual de preparación cuidadosamente observado, caballero iniciado de un antiquísimo culto, y cuando ya nuestras almas se habían vuelto cóncavas, sacó el cartapacio de sus versos con la misma mesura unciosa con que se acerca el sacerdote al ara. Estaba tan grave que imponía respeto. Una risa hubiera sido acuchillada en el instante de nacer.
>
> Sacó su primer collar de topacios, o mejor dicho, su primera serie de collares de topacios, traslúcidos y brillantes. Sus manos se alzaron con tanta cadencia que el ritmo se extendió a tres mundos. Por el poder del ritmo, nuestra estancia se conmovió toda en el segundo piso, como un globo prisionero, hasta desasirse de sus lazos terrenos y llevarnos en un silencioso viaje aéreo. Pero a mí no me conmovieron sus versos, porque eran versos inorgánicos. Eran el alma traslúcida y radiante de los minerales; eran el alma simétrica y dura de los minerales.[1] (Arévalo Martínez 10–11)

After describing the presentation of a half-dozen additional "necklaces," the narrator concludes:

> Y entonces, en imprevista explosión de dignidad ofendida, creyéndose engañado, el Oficiante me quitó su collar de carbunclos, con movimiento tan lleno de violencia, pero tan justo, que me quedé más perplejo que dolorido. Si hubiera sido el Oficiante de las Rosas, no hubiera procedido así.
>
> Y entonces, como a la rotura de un conjuro, por aquel acto de violencia, se deshizo el encanto del ritmo; y la blanca navecilla en que voláramos por el azul de cielo, se encontró sólidamente aferrada al primer piso de una casa.[2] (11)

Subsequent to this euphoria of initial friendship, the narrator speaks of his consternation at discovering that Aretal is not as completely spiritual as he had thought and that his personality varies drastically in accord with the person with whom he is interacting at a given moment; such a discovery, to be sure, is only meaningful within a culture that privileges spiritual nobility over whatever are presumed to be its antonyms:

> Así de pronto, en el ángel transparente del señor de Aretal, empezó a formarse una casi inconsistente nubecilla obscura. Era la sombra proyectada por el caballo que se acercaba.
>
> ¿Quién podría expresar mi dolor cuando en el ángel del señor de Aretal apareció aquella cosa obscura, vaga e inconsistente?[3] (15)

This detail of psychological perception has been underscored by some commentators, who have been interested alternately in the narrator's awakening to the complexities of human relationships and in the discovery of how an amoebic human character shapes itself to the other characters it comes into contact with (Reedy). The narrator grows concerned over how the "señor de los topacios" is in reality un "hombre caballo," "con rostro humano y cuerpo de bestia"[4] (25). The account of this revelation is accompanied by reference to the low company, in the narrator's opinion, that Aretal often keeps and his bestial speech, behavior, and appearance. Furthermore, within a cultural context that continued to pay homage to a myth of ennobling womanhood, Aretal, despite his many aristocratic ways, not only cannot attract women, but inspires an inexplicable uneasiness in them: "—Pero ¿las ama usted como un hombre? No, amigo, no. Usted rompe en esos delicados y divinos seres mil hilos tenues que constituyen toda una vida"[5] (22). Finally, in addition to confessing to never having been loved by a woman, Aretal acknowledges that he has never had a true friend:

> —Yo no he tenido nunca un amigo. Y sangraba todo él al decir esto. Yo le expliqué que ningún hombre le podría dar su amistad, porque él no era un hombre, y la amistad hubiese sido monstruosa. El señor de Aretal no conocía la amistad y era indelicado en sus relaciones con los hombres, como un animal.[6] (22)

As a consequence of the narrator's discovery of the bestial nature of his former idol, at the end of the story he refers to the violence of his break with Aretal:

> Me separé del señor de los topacios, y a los pocos días fué el hecho final de nuestras relaciones. Sintió de pronto el señor de Aretal que mi mano era poco firme, que llegaba a él mezquino y cobarde, y su nobleza de bruto se sublevó. De un brote rápido me lanzó lejos de sí. Sentí sus cascos en mi frente. Luego un veloz galope rítmico y marcial, aventando las arenas del Desierto. Volví los ojos hacia donde estaba la Esfinge en su eterno reposo de misterio, y ya no la ví. ¡La Esfinge era el señor de Aretal que me había revelado su secreto, que era el mismo del Centauro![7] (25)

The Centaur's secret is to be half man and half horse. But what is the secret of this secret? What is the cultural rationale for a myth of a horse man as a radical outcast? (A variant of the horse-man motif is that of the elephant man, the individual whose essential humanity is concealed or even trapped by his monstrously deformed body, as in Bernard Pomerance's 1979 play; other transformations of this motif are surely the hunchback of Notre Dame, Frankenstein's monster, and so on.) A preliminary hypothesis deals less with the need to expand the definition of what society considers to be acceptable as "human" than with a meditation on the construction, on the one hand, of exclusionary definitions and the need, on the other, to challenge them because of their exclusionary dynamics. Within a Romantic aesthetic that defies fossilized cultural codes, the hunchback, the outcast, the alleged monster, and the marginal individual judged to be subhuman are shown to be bearers of a greater humanity than their persecutors, and the ideology of that aesthetic is found to the present day whenever we would seek to vindicate individuals subjected to the ostracism of social codes that glorify Us as defined by the imperative to discriminate against the Other or Outsider. Certainly, the latter dynamic is at work in the denunciation of alternate sexual identities, and the ideologeme of "greater humanity beyond the abnormal" is marshalled in the normalizing vindication of the sexual outlaw (Rechy).

Arévalo Martínez's narrator is, however, hardly interested in vindicating Aretal's perceived difference, his bestial monstrousness, his defective manhood. This makes "El hombre que parecía un caballo" interesting on at least two levels. In the first place, the story is interesting because of the underspecification of Aretal's character such that he becomes so repulsive to the narrator who once saw in him a spiritual idol and such that he is unable to form friendships with men or to engage the love of women. This is the level of the narrator's conscious description of Aretal and of his effect on his own person. On the level of a reading grounded in an ideological deconstruction, the story is of interest because of its implicit assumption of such a narrow range of acceptable human behavior that deviation results in a person judged to be socially unacceptable and, indeed, bestially monstrous (of interest are other Latin American novels dealing with the monstrous as an encoding of homosexuality, like Manuel Mujica Láinez's *Bomarzo* [1962]; cf. D. W. Foster, "The Monstrous").

It hardly seems possible to avoid spotting metaphors of sexual attraction in this story. In addition to the above-quoted passage built around the metaphor of the "necklaces" as the revelations to the narrator by Aretal and the all-enveloping cloud in which this all takes place, the former speaks of sinking into a well of mystery and of burning in a fire of communion with his new friend:

> ¡Oh las cosas que ví en aquel pozo! Ese pozo fue para mí el pozo mismo del misterio. Asomarse a un alma humana, tan abierta como un pozo, que es un ojo de la tierra, es lo mismo que asomarse a Dios.[8] (12)

> Además me encendí. [. . .]
> Yo ardí y el señor de Aretal me vió arder. En una maravillosa armonía, nuestros dos átomos de hidrógeno y de oxígeno habían llegado tan cerca, que prolongándose, emanando porciones de sí, casi llegaron a juntarse en alguna cosa viva.[9] (14)

Because the narrator's language, because Arévalo Martínez's discourse is so highly metaphorized, any insistence on "El hombre que parecía un caballo" as a ciphered account of homosexual passion found and lost may seem farfetched. Whether or not the author had Barba Jacob in mind and whether or not the latter recognized himself the story—to his alleged horror at being literarily dragged out of the closet—is of little use in assessing the value of such discourse. Suffice it to say that, given the social taboos of the period, other than grim Naturalistic accounts of the dregs of society, it is not reasonable to expect any other treatment of the subject, if indeed it can be treated at all outside Naturalistic conventions (it is significant to note that, despite all of the range of marginal phenomena dealt with by Emile Zola, homosexuality is strikingly absent from his novels). Moreover, given the high degree of semantic indeterminacy of the story, it is even more of an open question whether Aretal's relationship with the narrator is as directly physically erotic as it is with his other associates or whether it is strictly physical with the latter but *blanc* with the narrator. If this second possibility were, in fact, the case, the narrator's intense feelings of betrayal and disgust and his discovery of the animal qualities of Aretal as horse man would be all the more explicable.

The absence of an overt sign that would permit the interpretational decoding of the text or the unraveling of the extravagant metaphors it foregrounds means that, unless the critic is willing to advocate a reading that will seem patently outrageous to other readers, a conservative analysis is left, as Arévalo Martínez may well have intended, with a very nebulous answer to the question of what the secret of the secret of the Centaur is.

The cryptic quality of "El hombre que parecía un caballo" may be a reflex of the impossibility of writing about homoeroticism in any register other than the almost rhetorical. But what is indeed unequivocal about the story is the highlighting of a social code that places certain types of characters beyond the pale. If Aretal is repudiated both by women and men, both of whom he would wish to court, it can only be because they each have in place rigid codes of acceptable social behavior that have the effect of erasing his personal identity. Despite the fact that Aretal outwardly fulfills the criteria of a Victorian gentleman, certain of his personal qualities, beginning, it appears, with the mutability of his character according to the company he is with (i.e., his polyvalent sexuality?), make him unsuitable for the solid relationships his society prizes; such relationships in his case would be monstrous, precisely the sort of lexical item customarily employed by the culture of the day to characterize sexual deviance:

> —El hombre es más que eso: el hombre es la solidaridad. Usted ama a sus amigos, pero ¿los ama con amor humano? No; usted ofende en *nosotros* mil cosas impalpables.[10] (24; emphasis added)

The foregoing discussion does not pretend to be a "homosexual reading" of Arévalo Martínez's story. Rather, by examining the particular—almost peculiar—rhetoric of the story within the context of the limits of the interpretation of the nuclear meaning of a literary text, with special reference to circumspection of allusion to homoeroticism in the cultural texts of the period, the goal here has been to suggest that "El hombre que parecía un caballo" echoes the dominant practice of social exclusion, personal repudiation, and identity erasure in the face of alleged sexual deviance. Even if one does not decipher the allusions to hidden mysteries and burning attraction as veiled metaphors for explicit or latent homosexual passion, it is virtually impossible to ignore how the social ideology that informs the text is based on the principle of the legitimate exclusion from human commerce of those individuals, the horse men, whose bestiality is not that they are animals—Aretal only *appears* to be a horse—but of a character that confuses the boundaries of identity. Whether this identity is essentially sexual or whether it is an unspecifiable global quality of character (but to what extent may individual sexual identity be a global key to character rather than merely a circumstantial and isolatable feature?) remains impossible to determine in a text that is an exercise in semantic indeterminacy and a masterpiece of discursive resistance to the imperative to interpret categorically.

2

Micky, Miguel Antonio Casas Planas, the fish-out-of-water figure of Isaac Chocrón's *Pájaro de mar por tierra* (Landlocked Seagull, 1972) is the confused and slightly schizophrenic homosexual who is unable to define adequately for himself his place in the world and the nature of his sexual feelings (see Chocrón's own comments on this novel in Vestrini). Micky is the product of almost the caricature of a sprawling Venezuelan middle-class family whose father is the paradigmatic drunken and cursing macho and whose mother is the long-suffering, perennially pregnant victim of her husband's authoritarian tyranny.

Micky escapes this oppressive family nucleus, whose most terrible aspects are intensified by the quirks of his dozen siblings, and flees to New York, as much a mecca for Latin Americans in search of a new beginning as it has customarily been for dislocated, especially gay, Americans. In New York, Chocrón's Venezuelan foundling undergoes a series of picaresque adventures as a hustler and kept lover and studies English and design art. Wandering the streets of New York and tracing the map of Manhattan (Chocrón 55–56), he learns quickly the basic rules for survival. No longer able to tolerate the jealous demands of the man who keeps him and the emotional extortions of a mutual friend, a psychiatrist of Honduran origin whom he marries in order to remain in the United States, Micky returns to Caracas. As a graphic designer, he continues his trajectory of picaresque wanderings through various settings of moral hypocrisy and corruption, only to fall victim to a destructive relationship that results in his mysterious disappearance.

Throughout *Pájaro de mar por tierra*, there are two intersecting narrative circumstances: Micky's bewildered search for self-identity and the constant attempts of the men and women with whom he comes in contact to exploit his alluring sexuality.

Micky's desperate struggle to come to terms with himself arises from his differentness within a family nucleus that can afford only one conventional definition of human behavior. Although one of his brothers is also a homosexual and lives openly as a kept lover, Micky's complex emotions cannot allow him merely to accept a predefined female role as his brother has done, which would allow him some sort of refuge within a facile reversal of conventional sexual patterns. Although willing to support himself in New York as the hustler paid for services without undertaking any act that would indicate that he is the seeking partner, Micky is unable to formulate any understanding of his own needs and what might be for him a satisfactory relationship. The psychiatrist whom he marries for convenience's sake is the one person who is able to perceive the tremendous turmoil behind the man's alternately glacial and disdainful façade:

> El tiempo me ha hecho olvidar la pregunta o a lo mejor la he olvidado gracias a las respuestas imperfectas que me ayudaron a ir dejando de pensar en este trozo de mi vida, este año y medio cuando esperé pacientemente, casi confiada, que comenzase la felicidad, mi felicidad, y en cambio experimenté la severidad de la indiferencia de la persona amada. Creo que amé a Micky. ¿Por qué lo amé? ¿Qué me hizo amarlo? Creo que fue verlo perdido, algo confuso, buceando en su agua interior, sintiendo latentes posibilidades y no conociendo la naturaleza de esas posibilidades. Yo tampoco conocía la naturaleza de sus posibilidades pero estaba segura de que las tenía y mi seguridad fue el motor que provocó mi interés, mi afecto y mi amor hacia él. Los dos primeros sentimientos fueron retribuidos y por ellos le estoy agradecida. Mi amor, Micky prefirió ignorarlo. A lo mejor fue cruel de su parte darme interés y afecto sabiendo que yo quería amor. Fue cruel de su parte o boba insistencia de la mía, tan boba que, ya él en Caracas, yo lo llamaba por teléfono a cada rato, le escribía cartas, y seguía esperando bobamente que algún día él volvería a Nueva York o me pediría que yo fuera a Caracas, y que volviéndonos a reunir, él saturado de evitar enfrentarse consigo mismo y reconocido frente a mi lealtad amorosa, declararía querer estar conmigo.[11] (86)

Tina's words reveal her bewilderment in the face of someone like Micky, whom she mistakenly believes she can "save." As a professional psychiatrist she is able to discern the sort of virtually unresolvable tensions, which will in the course of the novel assume tragic proportions, that beleaguer her husband. There is little subtlety in Chocrón's execution of variations on the motif of the stranded seabird, and there can be no ambiguity for the reader that Micky is doomed never to achieve any sense of having found the proper "element" for his existence.

Tina is one of many individuals with whom Micky comes into contact throughout his via crucis in the various worlds of New York and Caracas. But she is one of the few to make any honest attempt to understand him and to ease the quiet despair they discover in him. However, it is obvious that they are merely imperfect human beings with their own problems who happen to be less cynically exploitative than the majority of those who are attracted by Micky's sexual magnetism. To be sure, Micky hustles their attentions, which is what allows him to survive in

New York and to gain a professional edge in Caracas. Yet he is sickened by the hypocrisy of these advances, particularly those that are hidden beneath a mask of conventional respectability. One of Micky's perceptions of the intentions lurking behind a charade of decency comes during a swimming party that echoes the novel's recurring ichthyc motif. Professor Bofors and his wife Elena have befriended Micky, who has done a cover design for one of the former's archaeological treatises:

> Bofors se hundió en el agua y salió agitando en el aire su pantalón de baño como si fuera una bandera, mientras gritaba: "¡Todo el mundo a desnudarse! ¡Todo el mundo a desnudarse!" Sonia y Adolfo corrieron hacia la playa, huyendo de la persecución de Bofors, quien entonces se acercó a Micky y de un solo tirón le bajó el traje de baño. Micky cayó debajo del agua y sintió las manos de Bofors sacándole el traje. Cuando Micky salió a la superficie, vio a Bofors gritando y mostrando los dos pantaloncitos a Sonia y Adolfo, quienes reían desde la playa. Entonces hubo un instante, un momento en que la mirada de Micky encontró la mirada de Bofors y la mirada de Elena. Fue sólo un instante, una milésima de segundo, un pelo de mirada, porque en seguida Bofors le tiró a Micky su pantalón, se puso el suyo y Elena se cubrió con el sostén.[12] (94)

It is not clear what sort of behavior from the individuals entranced by Micky's mere presence would constitute a strategy of sexual advance acceptable as nonhypocritical. Perhaps in a world in which one oppressive norm of decency crowds out any other pattern of human relationships, someone like Micky can never be approached with untainted disinterest. The fact that Micky himself does not know what he wants means, too, that no advance meant to appeal to him as a person can correspond to a coherent pattern of specific needs. Whatever the case may be, throughout *Pájaro de mar por tierra*, Micky is presented as constantly the victim of disingenuous hustles, and his basic response is a rush of disgust at perceiving yet one more crude assault on his sexuality.

Thus, the basic problem proposed by Chocrón in his novel is that of a homosexual's self-identity, particularly as it relates to an individual who, although he may not be very sympathetic as a human being (as a matter of fact, Micky is not especially lovable in his constant anger and withdrawal), cannot fit into either conventional heterosexual roles or facile homosexual parodies of them. Were Micky able to function as a carefree courtesan like his brother or accept one of the other many prefabricated functions contemplated by the structure of the homosexual underworld and the heterosexual world it in part serves, he could have something like a reasonably happy life, like the Cuban pick-up who befriends him early in his stay in New York. The fact that Micky is unable to construct an identity for himself in any sexual dynamic is the essence of his tragedy and what makes him a character of interest for Chocrón's novel.

Pájaro de mar por tierra assumes the form of a collection of reports that undertake in vain the recovery of Micky's story. As the editor of the text, the narrator has assembled chapters that alternate his own versions of Micky's life with documents that he has elicited, usually with a check for one hundred dollars, from individuals who have been a part of Micky's disastrous life. The result is a mosaic marked by the customary signs of unreliable narration, including pronouncements by hostile correspondents that serve only to confuse the clear lines of Micky's personality that Chocrón is ingenuously attempting to establish. Therefore, as an act of narration, Chocrón's text establishes a continuity between a life that can yield no pattern of significant coherence and a narrative effort that, in the end, is left with only fragmentary conjectures as to the details of Micky's life. Certainly, from the point of view of contemporary fiction, Micky's life can be no more meaningful than anyone else's in an absurd world that the conventions of decency and respectability ridiculously strive to belie.

However, Micky's problem is the special case of the homosexual for whom even the superficial explanations of conventional society cannot work. Thus, Micky must view his life as something that he must create like the design on a blank sheet of paper. When he returns to Caracas, it is not surprising to find that he experiences a certain sense of hope in this regard, which subsequent events will unfortunately gainsay:

> Recostado en su cama con los ojos cerrados, Micky vio todo blanco. Veía una página en blanco y sabía que pronto, mañana, comenzarían a llenarla incidentes y accidentes que como garabatos o excrementos de moscas irían cubriendo su superficie sin orden ni diseño. La página de Nueva York quedaba atrás. Aquí, frente a sus ojos cerrados, tenía la nueva, la expectante. Para ella quería un orden y un diseño. Se obligaría a tenerlo, tal como se obligaba cuando diagramaba un afiche o una carátula. Este sería su primer verdadero afiche, su primera verdadera carátula. Todo suyo.[13] (88)

Chocrón's narrative is a frustrated explanation of a life only in part an extension of the limitations of ordered discourse in the modern world. Micky's sense of personal identity is irremediably warped, and the outlines of his passage through the world are fundamentally unretrievable; at least, they cannot be reconstructed in any way that would satisfy the desire for the reasoned interpretation the narrator is apparently willing to pay so much money for. Thus, if Micky as an object of sexual desire can never be securely held by the many who attempt to hustle him, the inner dynamic of his personality becomes also an elusive fetish for a narrator who strives foolishly to possess him and is willing to pay good money in order to do so. "Chocrón's" narration emerges as an aggressive, if somewhat unique, form of sexual hustle in the quest for a sort of domination of another person via an act of interpretation. Several of his correspondents taunt him about his motives in being willing to pay them for their information, and Micky's Cuban friend makes it clear that his report is a kind of sexual favor given in return for money:

> ¿Comienzo? No me dí cuenta cuándo apretó el botón [del grabador]. Qué divertido es todo esto. Le juro que es la primera vez que me sucede, y eso que en mi profesión se ve cada tipo . . . Entiéndame, no es que quiera ofenderlo pero resulta raro que usted venga a buscarme aquí donde trabajo para ofrecerme cien dólares con tal de que yo le hable de Micky lo que quiera. Lo de la plata no me extraña porque frente a este bar me han hecho las proposiciones más increíbles que usted se pueda imaginar, casi siempre las hacen los americanos turistas, casi no; siempre las hacen los turistas y las turistas, poniéndome un billete entre las manos como carnada, pero nunca antes alguien me había propuesto pagarme para que yo recordara episodios prehistóricos de mi vida. Le juro que si usted no se hubiese sentado allí a recordármelo con pelos y señales, yo jamás me hubiera acordado de todo eso.[14] (43)

The extent to which the narrator's informants are remembering accurately and the extent to which they are attempting to match their stories with what they perceive to be the needs of his personal sexual fantasy is what gives *Pájaro de mar por tierra* its particular textual configuration as one interpretation of the features of homosexual identity and experience in Latin America. Against the backdrop of a society with fixed and unquestioned points of reference (Micky's father shouts to him as he departs for New York, "¡Cuidado con las maricas!"[15] [9]), the narrator's project of recovery and interpretation, as much as Micky's struggle to provide his existence with a design of meaning, must inevitably end in tragic frustration: "Así era Micky: todo un enigma"[16] (61) captures the situation, no matter how much the narrator may accumulate text upon text in the futile pursuit of something else that could never be there: "Aparte de lo anterior, lo único que queda para recordar a Micky son estas páginas. Ellas componen un recuerdo bastante tenue, sumamente inventado, sin pretensiones de ser un homenaje, escritas a lo mejor porque el ser vivo intrigó al autor lo suficiente como para crear una mentira, una invención, con visos de verdad, de realidad"[17] (183).

3

Organized around a counterpoint between a series of diary entries and narrative blocks that complement them, Miguel Barbachano Ponce's 1964 *El diario de José Toledo* (The Diary of José Toledo; claimed by Luis Mario Schneider to be Mexico's first homosexual novel) records the despair in unrequited love of the young bureaucrat, José Toledo, who commits suicide by throwing himself off the roof of a building. The daily diary entries, which cover a little over a month in time, all relate to the man's desire to revive his love affair with Wenceslao. However, Wenceslao is anxious to pursue new interests that involve, in addition to leaving his parents' home and seeking work in Guadalajara, abandoning José for another lover, perhaps even a woman. The complementary narrative blocks cover Wenceslao's actions during this time he is away from José's side, and the novel's primary interest lies in José's suicidal infatuation with a man who no longer even cares that he exists.

Additionally, José moves through his world so caught up in his obsessive passion that he is barely conscious of the life and death events around him, ranging from the beating his unmarried sister receives from their father, who demands to know who has "ruined" her, to strikes and protest marches going on in the streets. Although José is faintly involved with this world, his dominant form of existence comes through the brief diary he keeps, a practice that establishes the fundamental disjunction between his precarious identity and the world in which he lives.

Such a disjunction is appropriate, given the nature of his passion: although the diary allows free rein to the man's attempts to express the nature and extent of his love for Wenceslao, he finds that he and Wenceslao must be cautious not to manifest their relationship as anything other than that of good buddies. Since the complementary narrative blocks play an ironic role in the sense that they reinsert José back into the social world from which he attempts to set himself apart in order to pursue, at least on paper (i.e., via the fetish of writing), his love for Wenceslao, the futility of both his love and his fictional space are highlighted. Thus, we learn that his mother wonders about her son's sexuality, Wenceslao's father is fully aware of José's passion and only wishes José were in a position to maintain his son, several of José's office companions suspect why he has become so emotionally unstable since Wenceslao has disappeared, and various other men attempt to establish liaisons with José, only to be turned away because of the fidelity he professes to his absent lover.

The extent of José's unfortunate self-delusion is underscored on numerous occasions, but perhaps most vividly when he reports a conversation he overhears between two young men on the bus. He takes them for lovers and mentally cautions them to be careful about what they are saying out loud, seeing himself and Wenceslao in their place. But we subsequently learn that they are, in fact, only good friends (Barbachano Ponce 79–82). It is this clash between the diary entries and the narrative blocks that underscore the futility of José's erotic text.

The diary is written with an interplay between first and second persons, between José as the narrator and Wenceslao as the narratee. However, Wenceslao is a defective addressee in José's text. If his departure has been the occasion for the diary in the first place—that is, the diary substitutes for the dialogue that José cannot have with him in real life—Wenceslao cannot have access to José's written discourse. Therefore, the statements addressed to Wenceslao are pragmatically defective, and no communication can ever take place. Letters imply the possibility of their being sent, received, and read; but a diary is a personally secret, dead-end document never intended for an addressee (hence the traditional and often-lampooned practice of making the diary itself the narratee: "Dear Diary").

Significantly, José loses his diary on the bus immediately prior to his suicide, and the implication is that his suicide is as much as anything the consequence of the loss of the one remaining correlative of his dialogue with Wenceslao (126). In contrast to the form José's diary takes, the narrative blocks are a combination of both third- and second-person addresses. Where the narrator writes in the third person about the other characters, he addresses José directly, like a prosecutor summarizing the record of actions to be held as evidence against him. This is the narrator's comparison between what José writes about the conversation between the two boys on the bus and the information the narrator provides as the true facts: "Tú, al oírles hablar en el camión, juzgaste erróneamente su proceder, la intimidad que les unía"[18] (82). Just as José is fundamentally deranged in his interpretation of Wenceslao and in his ability to handle an affair that is now definitely over, his misreading extends to the larger world around him, which he, of course, has a tendency to read solipsistically in the terms of his own overwhelming preoccupations. José is "enfermo del alma"[19] (36), and this sickness both provides the stimulus for his gesture of text production and accounts for his pitiful errors in the reading of the social text in which he moves: "Aunque no lograste expresarlo en el diario, por la imposibilidad de racionalizar tus sensaciones, aquella mañana todo se te antojaba recién modelado, como si personas y objetos existieran por vez primera"[20] (88).

Certainly, Barbachona Ponce's novel, which was published at a time when gay issues were just beginning to acquire a definitive currency in Mexican fiction, belongs to the "tragic homosexuality" genre, where the social horror homosexuality generates and the need to hush it up is counterbalanced by the text's morbid fascination with chronicling in excessive detail the stations of the cross of the homosexual's martyrdom. Both in the accumulation of the diary entries and in the ironic antiphony of the parallel narrative blocks, the reader witnesses José's descent into an inescapable despair that cuts him off from the flow of the human world around him, an alienation that is confirmed by his "inexplicable" suicide (see the newspaper clipping that opens the novel, p. 7, a third, although brief, textual level that is useless because of the inherent inability of journalism to provide a reliable account, which at least the diary does).

From one point of view, Barbachona Ponce's novel might be accused of a homophobic stance, in that it portrays the acute character dissolution homosexual affairs are popularly alleged to result in, at least those built around torrid passion. Such a stance never gets around to considering how psychological problems might be not the consequence of homosexual passion, but the result of the humiliating persecution of it. From another point of view, one that takes into account how the clichés of sentimental love are part of a bourgeois concept of heterosexual love that one variety of homosexual identity unfortunately, if not pathetically, mimics (to be mocked in turn by an antisentimentalist concept of erotic relationships), one must acknowledge how *El diario de José Toledo* constitutes a complex elaboration of the difficulties of representation in writing of all-consuming passion and the attendant personal crises such a failure entails.

4

> Era esa capacidad de engañarme que en el fondo constituía lo único que podía ligarme a una clase especial de medida, de orden; un orden unido a mi simple proyección hacia las cosas, a mi posibilidad de dominio sobre un mundo que finalmente no me pertenecería.[21] (Wácquez 77)

> Un orden. La medida que el mundo ha rechazado y que yo no puedo darle. Porque el mundo . . . el mundo se olvida; el mundo no quiere equilibrio.[22] (162)

Toda la luz del mediodía (The Full Light of Noon, 1964), an equally early Latin American novel treating the issue of gay identity, could easily be labeled antigay, typical of a genre of writing somewhere between the virtually rigorous silence on the subject of homosexuality that continued to prevail until after World War II and the explicit and probing analyses that have become essential to contemporary explorations of all of the "hidden" aspects of the human experience. Mauricio Wácquez's novel must have seemed audacious twenty-five years ago. It concerns two childhood friends, Max and Paulina, who eventually marry. But before that decision, which finally affords the narrator Max some measure of emotional stability, if not a conventionally congealed personal identity, Max has had an almost paradigmatically disastrous affair with Paulina's son Marcelo. Although Marcelo never appears more than a shadowy figure in the novel (undoubtedly, this circumstance is a correlative of his elusive and evasive ties both to his mother and to Max) and although the details of the degree of actual sexual involvement between the two men are never given more than a suggestive reference (they do seem to have sex at one point, and Max on one occasion alludes to a brief erotic interlude of passionate hand-kissing), the object of Max's obsession is almost a caricature of the young lover who is wrenchingly cruel in his offhand refusal even to pay much attention to those around him and to the reaction his attitudes have on them.

However, at the end of the narrative, after describing the vicissitudes of his relationship with Marcelo, his decision to marry Paulina (who is even willing to suggest a ménage-à-trois in order finally to win her childhood friend), and the threat to his marriage to Paulina posed by the possibility of Marcelo's return, Max concludes his novel with an epiphany of realization, complete with an accompanying erotic flush, that some measure of happiness has not come to him with Paulina: "Seguramente el orden se puede encontrar en cualquiera parte"[23] (172). This apotheosized sentiment leaves hanging whether Max is happy with Paulina as second best, *faute de mieux*, whether he has discovered that his true sexual vocation can only embrace Paulina (during the course of his narrative he describes coming across an older man, now in decline, of whom he was once a protégé and feeling pity for him while realizing that he might in time also become a decadent has-been), or whether after all it really doesn't matter.

The last option has a good chance of being validated by the quotation from Max's conclusion. In any case, Max's sense of equilibrium involves a renunciation of Marcelo and a clinging to Paulina as the path to a sense of order open to him.

Beyond its being an example of a contemporary Latin American novel at least willing to explore homosexuality, even though it comes down on the side of the conventional morality's defense of heterosexuality as the only valid sense of a structured universe, is the relationship in the narrative between the act of writing and the search for meaning. As a first-person narrative, *Toda la luz del mediodía* involves the use of the act of writing, as much for the purpose of self-representation and the reconstruction of the individual's personal history, as for the attempt to encounter through the creation of text a meaning for the chaos of experience and feeling. If life is perceived as a chaotic jumble of emotions and events, the production of a narrative text involves both a discovery of meaning and the imposition of order through the reflective act of verbal elaboration. As a consequence, Wácquez's novel is built around a diary-like chronicle of Max's relations with Paulina and Marcelo and around his attention to writing as a means of coming to terms with the turbulence of those relations. Writing, therefore, becomes a leitmotif in the novel and a synecdoche of the narrator's compulsive quest for emotional order; when he believes he has found it—or at least one he can live with—in the company of Paulina, the novel concludes. But as an instance of narrative, Max's text refers strategically to the function of writing:

> Una y otra vez traté de averiguar lo que había de verdadero en mí, en Marcelo, en nuestras vidas. Anhelé terminar con nuestra historia; aunque fuera un libro que en muchos momentos pudiera llegar a su término, y que no obstante continúa hasta ese fin que no tenía nada en común con nosotros.[24] (61)
>
> El peso de todo este relato desarticulado deja una huella detrás de sí que no esperaba. Me abisma. Creo que la realidad era mucho más simple. Pero ahí está. Quemando.[25] (86)
>
> Eso es todo. Recién anoche regresamos del campo. En un momento más deberé vestirme y salir a comer con Paulina. Desearía, sin embargo, permanecer aquí, escribiendo, para reducir la impaciencia que siento.[26] (142)

An interesting intertextuality of Wácquez's novel is another recurring leitmotif, that of the *cuarto* or *habitación* (room), an unmistakable echo of James Baldwin's eloquent *Giovanni's Room* (1956), where the image of the room evokes the hidden space homosexual lovers have customarily had to create for themselves, a space easily shattered, as it is in

Baldwin's novel, by the self-satisfied triumph of conventional heterosexual morality. For Max, the various places he inhabits are both ordered refuges (like the summer beach home he occupies in a lover's idyll with Marcelo or his childhood bedroom in the old country ranch he shares with Paulina after their marriage) and threatening enclosures that attest to the crisis of emotional chaos the narrator experiences at certain disastrous moments in his quest for a structure to his existence and personal consciousness (for example, the apartment he gives up after having been abandoned by Marcelo for an older woman).

If Max's text is a space where order can be restored, as the written confirmation of the equilibrium that he attains with Paulina, the real-world spaces he traverses are signposts of his disordered feelings prior to that equilibrium and of false projections of stability that he must subsequently abandon in the face of the inevitable failure of his graspings at a satisfactory relationship with Marcelo. Although *Toda la luz del mediodía* only serves to reconfirm the cliché of homosexual love as melodramatic and its sense of a coherent life rests inevitably on conventional sexual morality, the image of the search for text makes it of some tangential interest for this study.

CHAPTER FIVE

THE SOCIOPOLITICAL MATRIX

I

From the concept of the noble savage in the writings of Jean-Jacques Rousseau and in Claude Lévi-Strauss's lamentation, *Tristes tropiques*, drawn from his experience as an anthropologist in Brazil, on the destruction of the observed by the observer (H. V. White), it has been widely held that the founding of Latin American culture meant a tragic conflict between *natura* and *cultura*. Although the *indianista/indigenista* component of Latin American thought maintains the more strictly anthropological view that pre-Columbian nature has been suffocated by the imposition of European culture, other translations of the conflict concern popular versus elite ways of viewing and experiencing the world and the disjunction between the New World as a new beginning for humanity and the New World as the rearticulation of the dominant ideologies of the colonizing powers.

Aguinaldo Silva's *No país das sombras* (In the Land of Shadows, 1979) is one of the author's several attempts to understand the conditions of the homosexual experience within the larger context of Brazilian social reality, in consonance with the prevailing Latin American view that issues like feminism and countercultural identities are essentially questions concerning a sociopolitical reality that affects everyone, not just feminists or gays and lesbians (Silva's *Primeira carta aos andróginos* [First Letter to the Androgynes] is discussed in Chapter 8). For this reason, Silva frames his novel in terms of two basic narrative axes: a homosexual "crime" as metonymic of a founding act of social repression and the typological echoes that exist between contemporary political experience and successive historical events. The narrator, as a journalist and historical researcher who stumbles upon an obscure event in early Brazilian colonial history that comes to assume for him the proportions of a master schema, ultimately reaches the unequivocal conclusion that "a única função do passado era explicar o presente e ajudar a modificá-lo"[1] (Silva, *No país* 96). Written against the backdrop of violent acts of social repression, the narrator's text, unfortunately, is unable to do much to modify the present and, at the end of the novel, the narrator becomes also a victim of police brutality.

Paralleling Carlos Fuentes's *Terra nostra* (1975), or, earlier, *Cambio de piel* (1967; *Change of Skin*), the novels of the Argentines Ricardo Piglia, *Respiración artificial* (Artificial Respiration, 1980), and Martha Mercader, *Juanamanuela mucha mujer* (Juanamanuela, Quite a Woman, 1980), or the Brazilian Haroldo Maranhão, *O tetraneto del-rei* (The Great-Great-Grandson of the King, 1982), Silva frames his novel as an exercise in historical research that will reveal the expanding synecdochic relationship between founding acts of violence and an abiding social code based on the hypocritical justification of repression and the cynical justification of social and political dissidence (see Trevisan, especially chapters 2 and 3).

Specifically, *No país das sombras* deals with two young soldiers who, during the first decades of the Portuguese occupation of the New World, enter into a homosexual relationship. One of them, however, is the object of desire of the chief of the military garrison, who apparently harbors behind the façade of his proper marriage and social rectitude a sexual preference for young men. Determined to separate the young man he desires from his lover, the *general-provedor* informs them that they will be posted to separate stations. Rather than accept this separation, the two men lure the *general-provedor* to a secluded spot and murder him. Seen leaving the jungle area where the body is later discovered, the two men are arrested, accused of murdering their officer as part of a plot to revolt against Portuguese rule, tortured to extract a confession to this effect, and hanged. Although the majority of the scarce remaining documents echo the allegations of sedition, Silva's narrator is able to ferret out an alternate reading of history whereby the official explanation is a smoke screen for a tawdry episode involving sexual jealousy and revenge.

One of the narrator's documentary sources is a diary, in bad Latin, by Tália, a Venetian courtesan who provides colonial Olinda with her versions of the glittering debaucheries of the European courts. Befriending the two lovers, Tália, who understands very well how her profession, working in tandem with the cynical Jesuit religious leader, fulfills an important function in the establishment of an extended Portuguese culture in the New World, and she recognizes how the two lovers represent a version of "natural" human destiny that is excluded from the cultural sign system of which she is part. She recalls witnessing their execution:

> Os dois tremiam e—como desejei que o fizessem—em nenhum momento se olharam. Para meu consolo, pensei que talvez já estivessem muito longe dali, tão adiante de tudo, e sempre juntos. Foi isso o que me fez suportar a execução (ah, a dança lenta do carrasco, seu capuz negro como a cara da própria morte), a certeza de que, ainda ali—e apesar de tudo o que lhes ocorrera—eles ainda se amavam. Foi nisso que pensei quando o alçapão se abriu repentinamente e os dois, durante breves segundos, se sacudiram no ar. E depois, quando todos já tinham ido embora e eu ainda estava lá, sozinha, diante dos seus cadáveres pendurados, era ainda sobre isso que eu meditava—eles, afinal, não haviam feito outra coisa senão obedecer ao que lhes ditara essa boa e poderosa natureza.[2] (55)

The "good and powerful nature" to which Tália refers includes, of course, the exuberance of the New World, the sights, sounds, and smells of which the European authorities distrust—along with the "uncivilizable" natives—as contributing to the corruption of soldiers and settlers. Control, by whatever means, becomes necessary in order to staunch the seemingly nature-inspired rebellion of the New World citizenry. Establishing a model that will, it is implied, become the official ideology of Brazilian society, first the *general-provedor* and then, after his murder, the Capitão-General inaugurate a text of lies that legitimates a multiplicity of persecutions in the name of Social Order.

The primary locus of Silva's narration thus becomes the discontinuities between historical and social reality and the disingenuous rewritings (or partial and ambiguous representations) of events in favor of a more compelling authoritarian imperative. Confronting successive layers of historical truth, the narrator works his way through ever-more revealing documents, watched over by the blind librarian of the Biblioteca Nacional, Luís Borges, who is a sly reincarnation of the celebrated Argentine writer and librarian, Jorge Luis Borges, who held an equally salutary view regarding the oppressive qualities of cultural constructs.

As an interpretation of the social role of homosexual love, Silva's novel offers the image of a profoundly natural and emotionally satisfying human experience that is both the object of a destructive jealousy hidden behind the cynical mask of public morals and a gesture of authentic social rebellion. In the first guise, the love affair between the two soldiers is the pretext for a spectacle of execution as an example to anyone who would subscribe to principles of social dissolution in defiance of the supremacy of the Portuguese king's authorities. From this point of view, the two men, falsely accused of the sedition that they acknowledge under torture, are sacrifices in an attempt to ward off any sort of challenge to the prevailing order. Silva thus presents two soldiers as inaugurating a gallery in Brazilian history of tortured and unjustly executed political prisoners as part of the authoritarian repression of "natural" forms of human dissent from a monolithic official culture that has its roots in the first vestiges of colonial control (concerning homosexuality in colonial Brazil, see Mott, *Escravidão* 19–47).

However, Silva's narrator discovers, almost by accident, that in reality the two men may not have been innocent of the charges against them. The narrator comes into possession of the memoirs of the Jesuit who was present at the proceedings against them (a document that the narrator has to "steal" back from an American historian who, in the continued tradition of the plundering of Latin America by self-serving imperial authorities, is about to spirit it out of the country). Thus, he is able to read the priest's revelation of the confession of one of the soldiers (this quote follows the priest's transcription of the Capitão-General's charge that the Church is under the obligation to cooperate in making the facts of the alleged crime fit the political exigencies of the moment):

> E na conclusão dos documentos ele reproduzia "para uma comparação também futura," a confissão do mesmo prisioneiro, que ajudara a forjar, e que foi a única citada no processo—aquela pela qual os dois soldados foram condenados:
>
> ". . . Após nossos encontros e as muitas vezes em que nossos corpos se enlaçaram passamos a ver que a vida fora feita para muito mais: cabe ao homem gritar suas razões e defendê-las. Pensando assim, partimos para observar o que nos cercava, e nos deparamos então com a mais cruel das injustiças. A colônia sofria os resultados da ganância desenfreada da Coroa. Aqui todos morriam, apenas este direito lhes cabia, enquanto lá vivia o Rei e tudo era faustoso. E ainda aqui, em meio aos infelizes, havia os que, cruelmente, contra eles trabalhavam. Daí partimos para conclusões sempre mais exatas e um dia, quando afinal nos demos conta, tinhamos feito um círculo em torno dos nossos pensamentos e concluído que era preciso lutar contra as forças que nos consumiam. Antônio Bentes me dizia que os soldados nossos irmãos tinham sido transformados em máquinas de conduzir a injustiça—e quem eram os culpados? Já éramos, então, dois místicos. Nossos encontros passaram do amor febril à condução febril das nossas idéias. Nem nos amávamos mais, porque éramos um só, havíamos formado uma maldita aliança. E nos lançamos então à conspiração final. Retomo a pergunta—quais os culpados? Foi a partir daí que nós e nossos amigos planejamos matar uma a uma as autoridades da Coroa . . ."[3] (95)

In this version of events, which must assumedly be taken at face value because they are the revealed sacred confessions of one of the accused, the outlawed sexual relations between the two soldiers evolve into a generalized revolutionary repudiation of Eurocentered military authority. Thus, the execution of the *general-provedor* is *both and together* the first step in the elimination of the agents of Portuguese domination and the elimination of a threat to the homosexual union between lovers. Love defined as immoral by the conventions of a dominant culture is transformed into a revolutionary solidarity against the exploitations of the riches of nature in the New World.

Silva's novel enjoys an inverted intertextuality with the utopian feelings of colonial chronicles of the Conquest that saw the New World as the opportunity to fulfill the Renaissance ideals of European culture. The executed lovers are the victims of a dystopian repression that judges them both for their outlawed sexual behavior and for the stimulus to social revolt it engenders in them. One conclusion of Silva's juxtaposition of sexuality and political history is that participation in outlawed sexual activity gives one a glimpse of what it could be like to engage in other forms of rebellion. As a founding act of Brazilian social history, the homophobic persecution of the soldiers the narrator recovers in his research (which he at first hopes will win him the support of the Instituto Nacional do Livro, only to realize that the story he has to tell cannot hope for official endorsement) installs a dynamic of social repression. The narrator himself, more than three hundred years later, inevitably falls victim as well to its projections into the modern day.

2

> ¿eso era también él? ¿esa era la imagen que todos se llevarían de él? ¿no habría escapatorias?, ¿no podría siquiera padecer con dignidad o discreción su desgracia?, no podía ser auténtico ni siquiera en el momento de manifestar su terror, condenado siempre a habitar un sitio donde sólo tienen sentido y lugar las frustraciones, donde no cabe más que el meneo o la burla [. . .]?[4] (Arenas 39–40)

> de pronto, reconoció que no había escapatorias, que todos sus esfuerzos habían sido inútiles, y que allí estaban las cosas, agresivas, fijas, intolerables, pero reales [. . .][5] (61)

Arturo, la estrella más brillante (1984; *The Brightest Star*), by the Cuban Reinaldo Arenas, is a novel of radical separation, of schizophrenic dissociation in the face of a social dynamic whose compact structures of exclusion for Arturo are so unchallengeable in their inability to accommodate his personal identity that the only options available to him are forms of madness and, eventually, suicide as a way of challenging the authorities of the prison where he is incarcerated for antisocial behavior to kill him for refusing to obey an order. The option of suicide as a desperate flight from an uncomprehending world or as a calculated determination to close a personal life cycle is not uncommon in writing about homosexuality—or, for that matter, in any cultural text about the radical disjunction between the higher moral nature of the individual and an inhumanly oppressive society.

Arenas's novel is of special interest within the spectrum of contemporary Latin American literature in that it locates this general question, manifested in terms of the specific issue of homosexuality, within the context of the Castro revolution and the social programs it created. The most controversial aspect of those social programs, because it has become widely viewed as an infamous transgression of human rights and because, as the direct consequence of this embarrassment, it is a taboo subject for leftists (who, at least, seem to eschew public discussion of antigay policies in Cuba out of a sense of loyalty to the revolution), is the treatment of alleged homosexuals after the revolution (A. Young; Argüelles and Rich; Rozencvaig; "Homosexuality in Cuba"; Montaner; see also Matías Montes Huidobro's 1988 play, *Exilio* [Exile]). It should be noted that the subject is also distinctly taboo among the anti-Castro right: the identification with an established Catholic morality makes it difficult to generate much sympathy for the concentration of homosexuals in work camps by the Castro government. The subject is a complex one, because it is fair to assume that the early Castro government was not particularly interested in repressing the personal dignity that the socialist revolution was interested in affirming, and that it did in fact enhance personal and social life in the case, say, of blacks, women, the rural disenfranchised, and the urban dispossessed. Yet Castro's government subscribed to the legendary (nineteenth-century social engineering) antipathy of Marxism-socialism-communism (and parallel revolutionary movements like anarchism) toward homosexuality as socially nonproductive behavior and toward homosexuals as paradigms of upper- and middle-class decadence that exploited poor youths as part of the overall disease of prostitution. Moreover, Havana was notorious for its public display of homosexuality, and homosexuality was an integral part of the extensive commercialization of sex in the Cuban capital, which mostly served the needs of local and foreign (i.e., American) exploiters and the raunchy tourism they serviced (at a time, to be sure, when a city like Havana was an easily accessible escape valve for Ozzie and Harriet America). Guillermo Cabrera Infante's novels recall, with a considerable degree of nostalgia, this Havana of a bygone era.

But whereas female prostitutes were "redeemed" by medical treatment and incorporation into a productive society as defined by the new social programs, male prostitutes and anyone suspected of being homosexual (one need not rehearse all of the tiresome classificational problems of distinguishing between forms of homosexual identity and their lack of comforting alignment with male hustling as a form of survival) were rounded up and sent to forced labor camps. It is questionable whether any attempt was made to "redeem" these men and to offer them the opportunity for social integration. Arenas's novel is grim in its depiction of the contrary: the *locas* are not only left to recreate, mostly undisturbed by the authorities, their former microsociety in the camps—to dress and make themselves up as they please, to have the social interaction they please—but they are also allowed to be readily available objects of exploitation for the camp guards. This exploitation takes two forms: the guards may use the prisoners as handy objects of verbal and physical abuse, and the guards may use them for sex as they wish, as long as they are not public about it.

Arenas's novel is noteworthy because it casts the well-established pattern of scapegoating and the rape of the publicly vilified queer within the context of a revolution that proclaims the establishment of a political and economic order that will respect the rights of individuals and accord them dignity and worth by incorporating them into a just social dynamic. Just as Edmund White said that one's attitude toward outrageous fairies is an index of the ability to take sexual freedom and its display seriously for oneself and others (51), the treatment of alleged homosexuals, whether fairies or simply nonconformists vis-à-vis the code of machismo, can be taken as an index of a socialist society's willingness to take seriously the question of human dignity. For this reason, Julio Cortázar, one of the most loyal of Castro's supporters among Latin American intellectuals and artists, in his essays on the Nicaraguan revolution, made an eloquent plea for the Sandinista government not to repeat the Cuban folly of the persecution of alleged homosexuals (*Nicaragua tan violentamente dulce* [Nicaragua So Violently Sweet]). To the best of one's knowledge, no attempt was ever made to identify and deal specifically with lesbians, and the safe assumption is that they were probably grouped together for a number of reasons with female prostitutes (Cuban lesbians are included in the study by Lourdes Argüelles and B. Ruby Rich).

What makes Arturo of special interest is that he is represented as something other than the stereotypical example of the screaming queen, the most overt manifestation of a putative gay identity, at least from the perspective of a straight world. Rounded up with others after a concert by a Soviet pianist whom the gay community turns out to hear in its best finery, Arturo is incarcerated with a group of men with whom he feels no personal affinity. Eschewing their pack mentality and their acquiescence to stereotypic behavior (which the guards seem to demand, reinforce, and reward, in order to engage in scapegoating and exploitation), Arturo is doubly an outcast within the concentration camp, a transparent synecdoche (like Solzhenitsyn's cancer ward for Stalinized Russia) for the new Cuban society. Automatically an object of degradation at the hands of the guards because he has been identified as a *maricón* (queer, fag) by being rounded up and incarcerated (i.e., social treatment has assigned him an identity, rather than merely acting in accord with a previously established identity), Arturo is subject to the same mistreatment at the hands of the guards that the other prisoners receive, including being required to sexually service one of them at least once a week. But because he prefers to withdraw within himself and to refuse the role of preening fairy, he is scorned and roughly abused by his fellow prisoners. Thus, "la eterna tragedia del sometimiento"[6] (12) comes from all directions, and Arturo becomes the scapegoat of scapegoats, as the prisoners accept and elaborate on the system of oppression of their oppressors, thus, in the time-honored logic of prison society (whether literal or metaphoric) reinforcing the efficiency of that system.

Arturo, la estrella más brillante is a novel of the forging of a self-identity within the circumstances described above. If Arturo is out of place in general society because of his sexual needs, the triumph of a social revolution, rather than affording him a new dignity, formalizes his degradation by making him even more of an outcast (homosexuality, while ridiculed, was widely tolerated in pre-Castro Cuba, as it tends to be in Latin American society in general, with the possible exception of Argentina [Whitam and Mathy]). The outcast victim of society's outcasts, Arturo engages in mutiple strategies to protect himself, and he becomes "la estrella más brillante" of the queens, beating them at their own game by performing as a witty cabaret star. Only when newer prisoners upstage him after he has been incorporated into the prison society of the *locas* is Arturo able to withdraw into himself.

This withdrawal impels him to literature. The most interesting aspect of Arenas's novel is that, in the pop-Freudian framework of literature as a form of psychoanalytical therapy, Arturo is finally able to establish some dignity for himself by the creation of an *él* (it is italicized in the text), an alter ego transcending the *él* of his daily persona that is an integral part of the system of humiliation and degradation. This *él* is also in opposition to the *ellos* of the other prisoners, who, as has been said, are part of the routine of submission. What is particularly ironic about all of this is that the need for escape into a fantasy, the need for a literature of evasion, comes within the context of a social revolution promising the full integration of the individual with dignity into society. Only by a strategy of opting out of the social dynamic as represented by the subworld of the synecdochal prison, can Arturo finally achieve any sense of personal worth: "esa misma noche decidió que para salvarse tenía que comenzar a escribir inmediatamente"[7] (42). Of course, writing in prison is a risky business. Aside from the possibility of being discovered and punished for transgressive conduct, the prisoner has the perennial problem of obtaining writing materials. Fortunately, because of the array of personal effects permitted the imprisoned *locas*, personal effects that encourage them to retain the antisocial identity for which they were imprisoned in the first place, justify their continued incarceration, and sustain them as functional elements in the prison economy (forced labor, scapegoating, and exploitation), Arturo has no problem hiding his writing. He solves the acute problem of paper, however, by stealing prison documents and posted announcements. These examples of writing transcribe the official versions of the new socialist society; Arturo literally covers that writing over with his own countercultural writing:

> las libretas traídas por Rosa [su hermana] se fueron saturando de una letra mínima, veloz, casi ilegible, ilegible para él mismo, había que darse prisa, había que darse prisa, había que seguir, rápido, y, tomando precauciones—se hacían registros, se prohibía llevar diarios, cosas de maricones, decían los tenientes como justificación oficial, irrebatible y reglamentariamente se violaba toda la correspondencia—, las libretas, las contratapas, los respaldos, los márgenes y forros de los manuales de marxismo leninismo y de economía robados de la Sección Política fueron garrapateados furtivamente, rápidamente, cuando nadie vigilaba, bajo la sábana, de pie en el excusado, en la misma cola para el desayuno, hasta los márgenes de los grotescos carteles políticos instalados en las paredes y murales para

> uso interno del campamento sufrieron la invasión de aquella letra microscópica y casi indescifrable en tarea interrumpida incesantemente y a la vez constante [. . .] había que seguir, había que seguir y Arturo continuó garabateando las cartas de sus compañeros robadas a medianoche, las consignas ofensivas y airadas del momento [. . . y] una noche descubrió en el Departamento de Fiscalía un baúl repleto de actas sobre consejos de guerra, sin titubear se apoderó de ellas y tuvo material para trabajar por varias semanas [. . .][8] (44–46)

However, rather than affording him a private world that would allow him to continue functioning without setbacks in the public realm, Arturo's writing becomes more and more lost in the realm of his other *él*, and he begins to have visions and waking fantasies. He escapes twice from the camp, and the second time he is shot for, it is alleged, resisting the order to give himself up; at the moment of his death, really a form of suicide, Arturo is able to feel that he is moving definitively into the realm of the complex fantasy he has created for himself. When the guards go through his effects, they find his reams of writing, the illegible countertext that he has created at the expense of the materials of both his fellow inmates and the prison officials—and, hence, the destructive reality of both their languages and their social codes:

> el primer teniente ordena un registro en los trastos de Arturo, y todo ávidos, pensando encontrar cigarros, dinero, alguna lata de leche, quien sabe si hasta joyas ("de un maricón todo se puede esperar"), registran, revuelven; cartas y fotos de maricones, dice uno, y las tira; potes de crema, dice otro y los lanza contra el suelo, y papeles, papeles, cartones, pancartas, afiches, actas de consejos de guerra, y todo escrito hasta los mismos bordes; las actas que se habían perdido, dice el teniente, qué haría ese verraco con ellas, y toma una y, con trabajo, lee, al instante, asqueado, mira al cabo y le entrega uno de los documentos garabateados, qué te dije, dice, con esta gente hay que tener mucho cuidado, éste no sólo no se conforma con desmoralizarse a sí mismo, sino que también nos desmoraliza a nosotros, al país, a la patria, mira lo que escribe, contrarrevolución, contrarrevolución descarada; y el cabo lee, trabajosamente, algunas palabras que no entiende [. . .][9] (76)

As a consequence, writing, the creation of a radically private text, becomes Arturo's only form of salvation and, yet, paradoxically, also the confirmation of his need to escape through an induced suicide from the prisonhouse of his oppression as a human being. Writing is a form of definitive, if pathetic liberation for Arturo. In his colophon to the novel (93–94), Arenas explains that it is based on the story of his friend Nelson Rodríguez Leyva, who was shot in 1971 while attempting to hijack a

Cuban plane. Rodríguez Leyva's own writings during his stay in a *campo de concentración* like the one described in the novel were apparently destroyed by the authorities.

3

La otra mejilla (The Other Cheek, 1986) by Oscar Hermes Villordo concerns the intersection of a love story and the account of a political murder. Like other Latin American works that deal with renovation based on the restructuring of official societal values, Villordo's novel has an explicitly Biblical title and overt religious references (one of the most famous examples is the Paraguayan Augusto Roa Bastos's *Hijo de hombre* [Son of Man, 1960]). In this fashion, the murder victim, Víctor, assumes Christological dimensions that must surely be the source of discomfiture and bemusement for readers uneasy about the conjunction of the cause of sexual liberation and the repression often associated with Christianity, at least through its institutional hierarchies and conventionalized moralities. However, the sense of Villordo's novel is clear: as one of the major spokespersons for the gay experience in a recently redemocratized, post-military-dictatorship Argentina, Villordo has in this, as well as in his 1984 novel *Con la brasa en la mano* (With the Burning Coal in His Hand), a message of a social regeneration that accords the same dignity to the homosexual quest for identity and recognition as it must strive to do for an entire range of formerly proscribed and repressed political convictions and individual forms of behavior (D. W. Foster, "Narrativa testimonial").

The love story told within the three-day frame of reference of the narrative is the conquest by the narrator of a young man, Lucio, who seeks his assistance in finding work. Almost ridiculously successful in his conquest (which, in its outlines is reminiscent of magazine romances; cf. Villordo's 1985 novel, *Consultorio sentimental* [Miss Lonely-Hearts]), the narrator describes the perfect meeting of mind and body between himself and Lucio, in what surely ought to be a figure for the sort of star-blessed union possible in a society that has transcended mindless prejudices against homoerotic love.

Unfortunately, the Argentina of the narrative hasn't achieved this degree of transcendence, and the narrator's liaison with Lucio is intersected strategically by a series of persecutions of increasing seriousness that culminate in the assassination of Víctor, the narrator's friend, the prototype of the perennially abused Romeo. First in the form of a generalized queer-baiting in the context of workplace jealousies, these persecutions grow in intensity to include harassment and exploitation by the police (who may require prisoners to have sex with them, as in Arenas's novel), the intimidating violence of anonymous hit squads, to culminate in the murder of Víctor by unknown agents who will, of course, never be identified and never brought to justice.

There is little question that the essential social backdrop for *La otra mejilla* is the Argentina of the military dictatorships of the mid-1970s and early 1980s that made police persecution of homosexuals by gangs of thugs condoned by authorities an integral part of a policy of social control that sought to extirpate all vestiges of countercultural defiance. By the same token, for the middle-aged characters in the novel, such violence is an encoded sign of a collective experience of anonymous but systematic violence. Ernesto, whose birthday celebration is the point of reference for the second half of the novel, recalls a traumatic childhood act of witness:

> Pero para entender el porqué de esta manera de ser—de los estallidos que no podía contener en momentos como éstos—tal vez haya que recordar el episodio de su infancia, lejano y perdido en su memoria, pero claro y preciso cada vez que lo evocaba, de los muertos en la plaza de pueblo, contemplados, por dos niños inocentes, uno de los cuales (él [Ernesto]) develaba al mirar la escena el misterio del amor acabado violentamente. "Yo era muy chico cuando vi por casualidad el primer crimen contra homosexuales—me contó—. Vestidos con nuestros guardapolvos blancos y con nuestras carteras de escolares golpeándonos las espaldas, mi amiguito y yo corrimos hasta el lugar donde se amontonaba la gente. El quedó atrás y yo me adelanté. Vi, mudo de asombro, que el muerto tendido boca arriba en el cantero, bajo los naranjos agrios [. . .], era Fernando, el muchacho del aserradero que yo conocía y que, según los mayores, tenía 'malas costumbres.'"[10] (Villordo, *La otra mejilla* 183)

The death of Víctor, just like the death of Fernando that Ernesto relives in his memory, is an act of political assassination. Paralleling the violent arrests, often in public during the height of the military's so-called dirty war in the late 1970s and the subsequent permanent disappearance of the many thousands detained both by the regular police and by unidentified agents, the victims of antihomosexual persecution in *La otra mejilla* are designed to be read as synecdoches of an issue of sociopolitical intolerance of far larger proportions than the right to a personal life style of a specific sexual minority.

In this way, Villordo inscribes his novel within a specific Latin American tradition that sees that the quest for gay liberation not only as the generalized struggle against a variety of self-serving intolerances, but also as an effort to counter forms of political repression that define deviance in many but ultimately confluent ways. This explains why the enormous success of the 1981 Argentine production of Martin Sherman's *Bent*, which deals with the persecution of homosexuals in Hitler's Germany, was due in great measure to its perception as an allegory of Nazi-like campaigns of extermination under the Christian moral order touted by the military tyranny.

But *La otra mejilla* is more than a sensational account of Víctor's murder and the romance magazine detailing of an exemplary falling in love. Both of these narrative nuclei are essentially stereotypes, despite the legitimate—and antithetical—poles of experience, success versus defeat, love versus death, fulfillment versus destruction, that they represent. These nuclei are foregrounded as specific references to homosexual identity. But they also form part of a process of storytelling that refracts them into a multiplicity of individual experiences.

Villordo's novel, like *A Thousand and One Nights*, is a narrative about narratives, and in some instances it is a narrative about narratives about narratives, as a mosaic of personal stories crisscross in a complex network of intersecting identities. While the narrator is engaged in telling his own story of falling in love with Lucio, he is also occupied in repeating the stories of others, as well as their stories of others. These stories, particularly as regards the street-wise Ernesto and the repeatedly abused Víctor, constitute a selective typology of gay experiences in the context of an Argentine society seen as repressive and hypocritical in its public morality. Significantly, key acquaintances reappear in these personal histories, providing a panorama of the countercultural world that exists on the fringes of Argentine social life.

Through the telling of these interwoven stories, the narrator seeks to complete for himself a sense of the proscribed underworld of which he is a part. As a consequence, he is preoccupied with the difficulties of grasping the elusive meaning of what he is being told and of specifying the nature of the individuals whose stories he repeats. Tags referring to understanding, to the discovery of meaning, and to the postponement of comprehension abound in the narrator's discourse, as do references to events as a theatrical *escena* that requires an act of interpretation:

> Detuve la mano que iba a golpear con los nudillos sobre el vidrio porque, aunque estaba acostumbrado a las sorpresas de Víctor, la escena no podía dejar de llamarme la atención. Como Ernesto sus encuentros, yo solía contar las andanzas de Víctor. Lo hacía de modo que los hechos resultaran graciosos en la sucesión disparatada, a falta de explicación, como él narraba sus aventuras exagerando el cuento para que causaran risa. Pero mi manera de contar era sólo la forma de decir la extrañeza ante lo inexplicable. Podía entender, sí, las razones—ya me las contaría—por las cuales ahora estaba hablando con la guardia en pleno hospital, pero que eso sucediera con tanta naturalidad y después de escenas como las que acabábamos de vivir hacía unas horas, no. Porque me preguntaba: ¿Cuál es Víctor? ¿El de la comisaría que siembra billetes en el piso para que los recoja un preso que los necesita? ¿El del departamento del portero que cae de rodillas y transforma con su rezo a quienes lo rodean? ¿El robado? ¿El engañado que se deja engañar? ¿Ese que pide que venga—porque sabe que iré—y está riéndose y haciendo reír a los médicos mientras habla? Golpeé.[11] (162)

In the search for a language capable of characterizing crucial human experiences that are aggressively persecuted by the police and the public that supports it, *La otra mejilla* opts for an assertively colloquial register. This register derives from the fact that its readers will know that organized police oppression of homosexuals has been suspended in redemocratized Argentina, along with the official censorship of culture, while at the same time these readers are to understand that homophobic attitudes continue to prevail among the majority. Thus, as a novel that conjugates texts that read like personal diaries, romance-magazine fictions, crime news, and a Spanish translation of *The Joys of Gay Sex, La otra mejilla* is written with a nonchalant colloquial register that runs counter to the highly metaphorized language of sexuality to be found in novels published during periods of military repression and in conformance with cultural taboos circumscribing the transcription of frank discussions on the subject. Eschewing both the "poetic" encodings of writers like Manuel Mujica Láinez and the sort of inverted modernism of a William Burroughs (a form of sexual writing brilliantly developed in Spanish by the Cuban Severo Sarduy), Villordo turns to a documentary literalness in the style of Edmund White. The result is a narrative texture that is, in comparison with previous narrative treatments of the subject, strikingly unmediated by any form of euphemism, and it is accompanied by a commitment to the narrator's recording of his stories with admirable explicitness.

4

Like Manuel Puig, the Brazilian Darcy Penteado (who died of AIDS in 1987) was committed to a belief that sexual liberation and political liberation are one and the same process, that any movement of political freedom that does not take into account the sexual rights of the individual cannot in good faith promise release from tyranny, and that the struggle for the right of individuals to satisfy their individual sexual needs is continuous with the struggle for social and political revolution. Thus, it is an internal contradiction for individuals to be asked to suppress personal rights in the name of a political movement, since the latter is meaningful only to the degree that it can respect the dignity of individual needs.

Jerônimo, in Penteado's *Nivaldo e Jerônimo* (Nivaldo and Jerônimo, 1981) is a man in his early thirties involved with a group of political revolutionaries who combine urban guerrilla operations with a movement on behalf of the rights of farm workers, alongside whom they work in the attempt to raise their consciousness of their collective rights. An ex-teacher, Jerônimo falls in love with Nivaldo, a student in his early twenties whom he meets on the street in São Paulo almost on the eve of a guerrilla operation. As a consequence of this operation, Jerônimo disappears from São Paulo, and Nivaldo's life revolves around finding Jerônimo and resuming their love affair. He first nurses Jerônimo as he recovers from a bullet wound in a cabin in the mountains. After they are again separated for over a year, Jerônimo summons Nivaldo to join him in the outback, where he is working alongside the peasants. But before Nivaldo can join Jerônimo in his commitment, the latter is arrested, tortured, and imprisoned. Incorrectly believing his lover has been killed by the military repression, Nivaldo enters a spiral of decline, attempts suicide, becomes a male prostitute and kept boy, and ends up as Viviane, a transvestite nightclub performer. When Jerônimo, who has not been killed and is eventually released from captivity, happens to visit the nightclub where Nivaldo is working, the latter recognizes Jerônimo but is too ashamed of his decline to identify himself, and their separation now appears to be definitive. The destruction of the personal affair between the two men is almost inevitable, given the larger context of the social and political tensions of Brazil in the early seventies. The novel is the chronicle of this affair from initial meeting to final disastrous parting of these two star-crossed lovers (cf. MacRae, passim).

The melodramatic term is well-advised. For, aside from subscribing to an ideology of gay rights that has seriously challenged the homophobic element of leftist political liberation movements of the 1960s, Penteado's novel does not aspire to go beyond comic-book stereotypes of a pure and simple romantic love destroyed by the incomprehension of the world at large. Despite the fact that the two lovers are supported by other individuals—an Austrian priest and a hotelkeeper whose husband was killed by the police—Nivaldo and Jerônimo pursue a course of personal sexual liberation that cannot withstand the circumstances of a military tyranny that sustains its power through the emotional and physical destruction of the individual. By calling Nivaldo to his side, Jerônimo exposes his lover to the dangers of the struggle, and Jerônimo himself ends up paying the price of his commitment through his physical torment.

Thus, the backdrop of the novel is the sustained pattern of official terror that existed in Brazil during the early years of the military dictatorship that lasted from 1964 to 1985. The threat posed to the union between the two men does not come directly from a prevailing heterosexual code of Brazilian society at large but immediately from the right-wing ideology of the military tyranny. While the former does represent a sustained threat to individual sexual deviation, urban Brazilian society is notably tolerant of homosexuality, although social practices and legal considerations are often equally tolerant of economic extortion and the physical abuse of homosexuality (Lima). The military governments that came to power in Latin America beginning in the mid-1960s were committed, among other things, to a moral cleansing of the body politic that included a reform of sexual mores, most specifically the homosexual presence (Pinochet has been a notable exception, and Chile has not seen the stridently repressive moral pogroms found elsewhere in the Southern Cone).

Yet, Penteado does not portray Nivaldo and Jerônimo as victims of social condemnation or right-wing moral crusades. Nivaldo's mother quietly resigns herself to her son's following his lover into the backlands, and, although the two are careful not to make a public display of their passion, people who know them accept the nature of their involvement. In this sense, Penteado's novel is quite utopian in nature, since the two lovers are able to explore their passion with little immediate concern about being condemned as perverts or sinners. Indeed, beyond the cocoon of their private space in the urban jungle of São Paulo, the two men find a utopian refuge in the mountains during Jerônimo's convalescence, in the river town in the outback where they are reunited, and, tentatively, in the rural farm camp where they go together for Jerônimo to resume his revolutionary activities and Nivaldo to take up a commitment to them alongside his lover. (The guerrilla campaign in the tropical Brazilian outback inevitably recalls the paradigmatic image of Che Guevara in the Bolivian jungle.)

It is in this third context that their utopian ideal breaks down with the government sweep against the guerrillas, and the novel makes clear that the persecution of Jerônimo has nothing to do with his sexuality but involves, rather, the generalized destruction of any utopia at the hands of political oppression. The narrative explores Jerônimo's doubts over the wisdom of having called Nivaldo to his side and his growing reservations about the legitimacy of the revolutionary cause to which he has committed himself, a cause that may end up imposing on him a tyranny as destructive of his personal dignity as the oppressions of the military dictatorship. Moreover, Penteado's novel draws the outline of their story with the sharp contrasts of black and white. As a consequence, the two characters never speak or feel in terms other than romantic clichés, and the agony of their initial separations is a clear-toned foreshadowing of the inevitable defeat of their love by the actions of a military dictatorship destructive of a vestige of human dignity, represented here by the demands of personalized sexual needs. The following passage is typical of the midpoint foreshadowing of the impossibility of the purity of passionate love between the two men:

> Abriu [Nivaldo] a cortina na esperança de que talvez Jerônimo estivesse visível logo ali, talvez voltando. Mesmo sem poder gritar o seu nome, precisava que ele aparecesse para, olhando-o, fazer com que sentisse o quanto o amava. Esse amor ganhava agora proporções tão grandes que já não cabia mais dentro dele, pedi espaço aberto para continuar crescendo. Então ele subiria, flutuando no ar e lá de cima gritaria bem alto para que todos na praça na ancouradoura, nas lojas, nos bares, nas escolas, nos prostíbulos, ouvissem o seu clamor sôfrego de paixão: "Jerônimo, eu te amo! Jerônimo, eu te amo! Jerônimo, eu te amo! " [. . .] Mas o excessivo e súbito gosto da liberdade faz com que as pessoas às vezes se sintam momentaneamente perdidas. Foi o que aconteceu a Nivaldo, naquele momento. O sol entrou de uma só vez no quarto trazendo-lhe uma visão exatamente igual à do dia anterior: a escaderia por demais pretensiosa para o lugar e para a simplicidade da fachada da igreja: o

> posto Shell com a placa reluzente oscilando levemente, a delegacia de polícia recém-pintada em duas tonalidades de azul, as casas de comércio do outro lado da rua, e o espaço de terra vermelha e sem árvores defronte à igreja, com algumas raras pessoas passando, indo ou subindo da rua principal—e Jerônimo não estava entre elas. Sentiu-se traído por aquela paisagem a quem desejava transmitir a sua felicidade e que no entanto permanecia indiferente e adormecida.[12] (Penteado 108–109)

The narration continues in this vein for another page, culminating in a nightmarish vision for Nivaldo of Jerônimo being crushed to death: "era uma ordem dominadora contra a qual qualquer voz era castrada na própria garganta"[13] (110).

Where Penteado's novel is of some interest, despite the portrait of Nivaldo and Jerônimo's relationship in stereotypes of *fotonovelas*, is in the narrative strategy of naturalizing a homoerotic love affair within a social and political context that would conventionally be seen as tragic. The rhetoric of the novel takes for granted, of course, the legitimacy of their passion and it legitimates it within their specific personal and social setting. By contrast to the legion of novels—gay or otherwise—where pathos and tragedy flow from the conflict between passion and the social norms it transgresses, Penteado's novel assigns the clichés of romantic love destroyed to the effects of a dynamic of social oppression unconcerned at all with the lovers' sexuality. By representing the two men's passion as a disruption of the discourse of political oppression, Penteado's novel denounces the overall destruction of the individual under military governments. The "*tudo isto*" ("all this") of the following quote is both the dominant social text and the revolutionary struggle that is shown, as far as individual sexual rights are concerned, to be disastrously homologous with it:

> —Então aprenda [Nivaldo] desde já a só ter medo das coisas perigosas, as que realmente existem e que . . . ("convinha continuar mentindo ou não?", ele pensou no meio da frase, decidindo-se pela resposta positiva) . . . você terá que enfrentar de agora em diante: malária, cobras, escorpiões, moscas varejeiras, injustiça e gente—os federais, Nivaldo!, que você vai ter que ajudar a combater comigo; e nós vamos lutar duro, você vai ver, como fé na liberdade que, para nós, inclui o direito ao nosso amor e a paz para continuarmos vivendo juntos, quando tudo isto terminar.[14] (112)

Nivaldo shields himself from a social reality (concentrated in the circumstances of his loss of Jerônimo) behind the mask of his transvestism (199, 217–218), and he does it so successfully that when Jerônimo suddenly reappears, Nivaldo can no longer emerge from behind that mask, which has become, in effect, his new private identity.

Penteado's novel, in attributing the pathetic story of the separation of the two lovers to the machinations of military dictatorship, succeeds in naturalizing homoerotic love within the social context of everyday Brazilian life. But in the process the novelist fails to address the ways in which the "they" of military repression are part of the same society as the "we" who are persecuted. This stark disjunction between "they" and "we," which may be considered reactionary by those who speculate on the ways in which authoritarian governments are often legitimized, if only temporarily, by the very citizenry whose dignity they threaten, is another facet of the comic-book or *fotonovela* conventions Penteado's novel employs.

5

The discovery of the world has always been one of the major motivating impulses in narrative fiction. Through the movement of the characters through a specific space and through the order of events that befall them, the narrator lays before the reader something new in the way of a vision or interpretation of the world. And, whether in the fashion of Bunyan's *Pilgrim's Progress*, Cervantes's *Don Quijote*, Twain's *Huckleberry Finn*, Kerouac's *On the Road*, or in one of its many other guises, the tripartite combination of characters–events–spatial movement is particularly suited to the revelation of panoramic features of the world and the human experience that has the world as its stage. This revelation may be a heightening of features already assumed to be part of society's general knowledge (the aspects of Sin and Grace in Bunyan's allegorical narrative). It may be a particularly subtle interpretation of values that a usually superficial society does not customarily consider in all of their complex ramifications (the questions of idealism and realism in *Don Quijote*). Or it may be the occasion for the relentless unveiling of features of human life that (essentially sheltered) readers wish to deny.

The latter equation is certainly operant in all that extensive inventory of modern literature, beginning at least with Naturalism, that insists on tearing the blindfold from the eyes of polite or decent bourgeois readers in order to give them an idea, often by bludgeoning them with various combinations of the explicit representation of facts and the graphically sociolinguistic document of noneuphemistic speech, of what it is like in the realms of life not hitherto recorded or that have been transcribed deceptively.

In the ample inventory of such representations of life as sociological document, lesbian and gay experience has come to constitute almost one of the last truths to be so "unveiled." The record for Latin American literature is incredibly scant until recent years, and the few representations of homosexuality in earlier texts ring very false, if not directly disingenuous, by current standards. Despite the extent to which the Argentine Roberto Arlt (1900–1942) was able to understand the dynamics of existence on the fringes of decent society of the cast of misfits and outcasts that populate his theater and his fiction, individuals identified with homosexuality are portrayed as loathsome outcasts even in Arlt's writing. This is undoubtedly due to Arlt's irreflective acceptance of the vampire theory of homosexuality and the extent to which the anarchists and Marxists of the period of Arlt's writing during the first half of this century adhered to the idea that homosexuality was one of the many degeneracies visited on the pure and noble natural man by the oppressors (see Chapter 2).

"Rodolfo Carrera: Un problema moral" ("Rodolfo Carrera: A Moral Problem") is one of three novelettes that make up the Argentine Carlos Correas's *Los reportajes de Félix Chaneton* (The Reports of Félix Chaneton, 1984). Written in the first person, these narratives are ostensibly the previously unpublished papers of a man who moved in the homosexual underworld of Buenos Aires during the late 1950s and early 1960s, a period marked by a certain amount of social and intellectual openness, but quite a bit of moral hypocrisy, in the name of the new Argentine to meet the challenge of the post-Peronist return to constitutional democracy (Goldar). In fact, historically, this is a period of considerable social, political, and economic shambles, leading to the rise of military fascism in 1966, inaugurating a round of repressive dictatorships that would last essentially uninterrupted until 1983. Published just after the end of this period of military tyranny, Correas's novel contains an ironic subtext that underscores the disingenuousness of the post-Peronist phase and the undercurrent of bourgeois morality that was to become a major ingredient of the 1966 coup. If the late 1950s and early 1960s permitted a certain amount of libertarian enthusiasm (in fact, this is one of the most intellectually exuberant periods in Argentine cultural history) that included a more public display of homosexuality, the general contemporary news was that such a display posed a direct threat to the moral fabric of society, and indeed this is the image to be found in prominent works of the period like H. A. Murena's *Las leyes de la noche* (1962; *Laws of the Night*). It is true, however, that David Viñas was already able to write about military officers who masked their own "homosexual tendencies" while exploiting them in their subordinates, against whom homosexual rape is a form of exercised power (e.g., *Dar la cara* [Facing Up, 1962] and *Los hombres de a caballo* [Men on Horseback, 1967]).

Introduced by a presumably fictitious prologue signed by Juan Manuel Levinas, Félix Chaneton's three narratives are attempts to portray, in terms that are reminiscent of Arlt's most caustic *aguafuertes*, the marginal world of Buenos Aires homosexuality. In this regard, "Rodolfo Carrera: Un problema moral," which is the lead novelette, is especially interesting because of its use of the pilgrim's progress motif to sketch a panoramic mosaic of one of the most outcast of the city's many outcast lumpens. Carrera, a policeman who heads the security operations of a football stadium, enlists the aid of Chaneton in the search for his missing stepson, whom he suspects of having disappeared into the homosexual underworld. Chaneton leads Carrera on an exploration of various haunts—plazas, amusement parks, bars, cabarets, movie houses—frequented by the men Carrera's son, Mili, may have taken up with. At the end of the story, Carrera finds his son and murders La Mejicana, the *marica* (fag/swish/fairy) he is with. Although his son once again escapes from his stepfather, Carrera feels that his masculinity has been vindicated, particularly when he proves that La Mejicana is a cheat. Carrera, therefore, feels justified in robbing the dead body of La Mejicana, and he invites Chaneton to help him spend the money in an evening of fun. Significantly, he invites him to go with him to the Trinidad cabaret, where they both know that the women available are in reality transvestites.

What makes Correas's novel of interest as a representation of a variety of homosexual identity and experience is the deconstruction of social reality that is at the heart of Chaneton's description of his and Carrera's movement through the spaces inhabited by the *maricas*. The prologue calls attention to how Chaneton's narratives will essentially deal with a question of the reality they seek to portray: "Los autorreportajes novelados de Félix Chaneton serán construcción de literatura si son aniquilación de la realidad dada"[15] (Correas 12). The *realidad dada* (given reality) of these narratives is the underworld of the *maricas* and the aggressive attitudes toward it by standard-bearers of morality like the policeman Carrera.

In the first place, this reality must be questioned as regards the identity attributed to the homosexual as such. Quite aside from the issue of who is and who is not a homosexual is the now fairly widely accepted, although rather studiously limiting, wisdom that "homosexual" is only an inanimate adjective (because it describes acts, not persons), and never an essential noun. The problem, to be sure, with this position, which has the merit of repudiating ominous attributions, is the disadvantage of also denying the various legitimate forms of self-attribution that characterize many of the works examined in this study. While Chaneton, who is telling a story set in the Buenos Aires of the 1950s, does not address the semantic issue directly, his portrayal of Carrera is one of the many implied assertions in the novel that the black and white moral vision loudly ascribed to by someone like Carrera is an ideological construct and not social reality.

Such a circumstance extends also to the belief in an identifiable homosexual underworld, with identifiable members and identifiable patterns of behavior—the fantasy that gay men are exclusively to be found in such exotic habitats. While there is no denying a certain range of behavior that is called in Spanish *marica*, such behavior, generally defiant of bourgeois identities and proprieties, is not coextensive with homosexual acts in any meaningful way. Who does and does not engage in homosexual acts cannot be determined by circumscribing an underworld of *maricas* and those who hang out with them (the *chongos*, English "butches"). Rather, Chaneton as narrator summarizes the several fragmentary glimpses of the realm of those whom Carrera calls *maricas* by challenging the reader to accept the ways in which this so-called underworld is a construction of the dominant social ideology which finds it convenient to have a scapegoat in the form of a marginal subsocial set which it can then denounce as immoral and dangerous ("la desdicha, la sordidez, la mariconería y hasta la homosexualidad eran y son efectos de la opresión"[16] [117]):

> Si con respecto a las maricas, que, como ya habrá advertido el lector, son la clase más baja, la más grotesca, dentro de la homosexualidad; si con respecto a las maricas, digo, lográramos aislar y luego reunir en su desnudez extrema las cualidades propias de las mismas (la temeridad, el ansia de vencer el bochorno, la inversión también de la moral, la bruma y el turbio resplandor, la magnificación del ridículo, el refocilo en el desqui-

> cio, el sueño de la más grave descalificación y condena), tendríamos ante nosotros, por un imposible, el universo absoluto de las maricas. Este universo excluye radicalmente a las mujeres, pero a la vez las contiene en el modo de negarlas por identificación con ellas o, mejor, con cierta idea de mujer. El lenguaje que aquí se habla está asediado por la pornografía victoriosa; sus imágenes florecen entre la mayor suciedad que saben segregar los machos; sus costumbres se orientan por el fanatismo de las masturbaciones que tienen que adorar y destruir en el propio cuerpo el sexo que se desea. El que ha saboreado este lamentable, es decir, este compadecible y asolado universo donde la muerte no es sorprendente, ha preparado su paladar para la atrofia, la mutilación, la agonía de la desnutrición, la peor desazón. Sin duda es un universo aberrante, y sus habitantes son enfermos, pero sólo porque en la base de este *pathos* se encuentran la rabia y el pavor en mezcla inextricable. Mientras haya hombres rabiosos o espartados este universo estará *ahí*. Yo te invito, lector, a que lo tomes a tu cargo.[17] (122–123)

Edmund White remarked in *States of Desire: Travels in Gay America* (51) that the ability to accept the "fairy" is the true test of an individual's humanity, since the individual who so extravagantly and openly displays his deviance often tries the patience of the respectable homosexual concerned to allay the homophobic anxieties that the fairy insists on challenging openly. Chaneton's narrator does not explain what he means by *aberrante* (aberrant) and *enfermo* (sick). It may either refer to the prevailing gay liberation belief that such individuals are "sick" with a medical and/or psychological definition. Or it may mean, as perhaps suggested by the rest of the sentence and the one that follows, that there is a social sickness that manifests itself in the need to achieve this form of *desnudez extrema* (extreme nakedness). If the *marica*'s identity may be viewed as an ideologically charged discourse created to challenge decent society, the latter's identification of the *marica* through its many strategies of humiliation and degradation is also a discourse based on ideological premises.

In Chaneton's narrative, it is Carrera who both articulates the latter discourse and subverts it in his own relationship with the *maricas*. Carrera views himself not only as a real man, but also as a member of society, a policeman, charged with enforcing public morality. On several occasions, the narrator remarks on his virility, on his swaggering masculinity, and on his Jehovah-like self-image (35, 43, 80). Carrera is an enforcer, and his quest for Mili is as much the enforcement of conventional social morality in the case of his wife's son as it is a series of aggressions against the circles in which he expects to find Mili. The narrator is admittedly fascinated by Carrera. He is both attracted to his powerful masculine presence and morbidly fascinated by his attitude toward the *maricas*, an attitude within whose parameters he contemplates his own self-identity:

> La angustia me cierra la garganta, me impide pensar. Carrera es GUASO, pero si yo me separo de él, pierdo la seguridad y me convierto en un gusano. Este es el precio de mi pasividad: no soy nada más que un espectáculo lamentable que me avergüenza.[18] (106)

By agreeing to accompany Carrera, and by accepting both the humiliation of abetting Carrera's ferreting out of Mili and Carrera's verbal abuse of his guide for his own lack of manliness, the narrator accepts subjecting himself to an (obviously quite clumsy) analysis of his own homosexual identity. This self-analysis, hardly a uniformly productive process at the side of a lout like Carrera, is presented as the principal motive for serving as the latter's guide. The narrator is not concerned with rejecting a segment of society within which he has moved himself; rather he wishes to discover it through the eyes of a "decent citizen" like Carrera in order to attain a better understanding of its complexities and, precisely, its relationship to the ideology embodied by Carrera: "(No he escrito estas metáforas para hacer vislumbrar una confabulación progresiva, sino para indicar, con ese fraseo sin fundamento real, los huecos que se abrían entre Carrera y yo)"[19] (72). The abyss between the two, despite the narrator's fascination with Mili's father and the sexual game that develops between the two of them, is the principal occasion in the novel to chart the ways in which the *maricas* are an element in the violent aggressions of the morally decent:

> Los espectadores del *Pablo*, si bien no abominables—lo que sería excesivo—, eran obviamente personas desestimadas, de ideas y acciones desestimadas. La mirada de control de Carrera los desconcertaba, y a la vez los hundía en la butaca. Carrera contraía la nariz, como si aspirara el olor de los basurales o el olor de la muerte. Además tendía el oído como escuchando los susurros por los que algo o alguien le revelaba las mentiras y dobleces de los lamentables exponentes barridos por su mirada.[20] (80)

Carrera never questions the right to exercise his "mirada de control," and it is as a function of that *mirada* that the *maricas* are identified and Chaneton as narrator accepts that definition. Carrera, through his brutal moral righteousness, brings that world into focus for the narrator, who is then able to consider for himself why it exists as a phenomenon of the social marginalization of those who cannot accept the phallocentrism of the dominant society of the Carreras and what his own place is in it.

Like Quijote and Sancho, Carrera and Chaneton end up inextricably intertwined. But if for Chaneton this means the bringing into focus of his own identity, with its ingredient of seduction by Carrera's brutal sexuality, for Carrera it means the manifestation, but not the acceptance, of his own homosexual motivations. Although the narrative does not specify how Carrera and Chaneton became teamed up in the first place, the narrator perceives throughout their relationship a series of tentative sexual advances toward him by the acknowledged homophobe he is guiding. If the reader is at first inclined to dismiss the narrator's references to wishful thinking, there are two clear episodes to confirm Carrera's advances on Chaneton. The first occurs when they take a modest hotel room to rest before visiting the late night bars. It is the middle of the hot and muggy Buenos Aires summer, and Carrera strips in front of Chaneton, and then motions for the latter to do the same. He not only parades his nude masculinity before Chaneton, but asks him to compare his genitals to those of other men he has been with. Although no direct sexual contact takes place, the narrator notes that a complicated story Carrera has given him about having recently developed a deformity in his penis making intercourse with his wife impossible and explaining why he readily masturbates in one of the movie houses where they go looking for Mili appears to be a lie. And there is no mistaking Carrera's invitation at the end of the narrative for Chaneton to accompany him to the Trinidad cabaret (154–155). Carrera knows that the women there are transvestites and that his companion for the evening engages in homosexual acts. It is the final affirmation of his concept of masculinity, necessary to deny any possibility that he is attracted to gays, that he wishes to spend money stolen from a *marica*, whom he has killed at the same time he has failed to "rescue" his son, in a further exploitation of the very world of sexual subculture he is devoted to exterminating:

> Hasta aquí Carrera y yo habíamos sido dos individuos fascinados por el espectáculo del mundo. Y me dije, una vez más, que yo todavía era joven, que *sólo* tenía veinticinco años. Más allá, en el tiempo, me esperaba el Bien. Más allá de mi soledad, de la sordidez de mi ignorancia, de Carrera, de mi odio rabioso, yo me reservaba el Bien: estudiar, ser algo, alguien.[21] (155)

However, it is not likely that the narrator will be able to find the *Bien* (the Good) in the world dominated and exemplified by Carrera. Rather, through his contact with the policeman, he confirms the sordidness of a dominant society that exploits its marginal sectors while at the same time committed to destroying them in the name of a higher moral order. Throughout "Rodolfo Carrera: Un problema moral" the various strategies to deconstruct the languages of both neutral description and moral interpretation (italics, quotation marks, parenthetical definitions, ironic asides) reveal a hypocritical and repressive vocabulary of containment. But it is a social reality that someone like Carrera seeks to contain in order to exploit while reaffirming his own sense of moral superiority. Like Viñas's corrupt military officers, whose need to dominate the weak assumes the form of rape of homosexuals whom they victimize violently in order to exorcise their own demons, Carrera synthesizes the practices of a terrifyingly corrupt social order. In the process, Chaneton's analysis of this order and his own relationship to it provides the occasion for a meditation on the duplicitous language and the ideologized discourses of Argentine society: "No sé si esas palabras debían tener poder para luchar contra el aplanamiento de ese mediodía, y, a partir de aquí, de Buenos Aires y de la Argentina"[22] (73).

6

> Que venga. Me quiero reír. No puede ser todo así tan triste, este pueblo que don Alejo va a echar abajo y que va a arar, rodeado de las viñas que van a tragárselo, y esta noche voy a tener que ir a dormir a mi casa con mi mujer y no quiero, quiero divertirme, esa loca de la Manuela que venga a salvarnos, tiene que ser posible algo que no sea esto, que venga.[23]
> (Donoso, *El lugar sin límites* 123)

La Manuela, in José Donoso's *El lugar sin límites* (1966; *Hell Has No Limits*), is an aging transvestite who shares ownership of a broken-down whorehouse with La Japonesita, a woman whose frigidity has kept her from exercising the profession of her employees. La Japonesita inherited the establishment from her mother, La Japonesa Grande, a woman of formidable sexual talents who at one time had been the lover of Don Alejo, the local landowner and political boss. During the revelry the night his election as senator is being celebrated with La Japonesa Grande's girls, Don Alejo challenges his protégée and former lover to demonstrate that her talents have not waned by seducing La Manuela, a skittish fairy who has arrived with reinforcements from a sister establishment in Talca. La Japonesa Grande rises to the occasion, demands that Don Alejo deed to her the house she has been renting from him, and convinces La Manuela to engage in a *cuadro plástico* (tableau) of sexual intercourse in exchange for half ownership of the house. La Manuela accedes to this deal, discovers that La Japonesa Grande in effect has raped him, and, in time, finds that he is the father of La Japonesita, who inherits her mother's clientele and Don Alejo's protection. Although La Manuela can never accept this misfortune of paternity, he makes his life alongside La Japonesita, grateful that he no longer has to suffer the indignities of being the butt of ridicule and drunken aggression in one whorehouse after another. Employees like La Manuela are common brothel retainers (La Manuela serves La Japonesa Grande as a loyal right hand); if they are lucky enough to have their own clients, they may be as much abused by the latter, because of the challenge they represent to their manhood, as they are by customers who simply resent their presence.

Pancho Vera, a truck driver who arrives in the company of his *compadre* Octavio, fits both categories. Although he was raised on Don Alejo's property and favored by him, Pancho, goaded on by Octavio, rebels against Don Alejo's authority. His pursuit of La Manuela, now protected by Don Alejo for obscure reasons that have in part to do with "her" ties to La Japonesa Grande (and the fact that she may have been tricked into accepting a paternity that in reality belonged to Don Alejo), is part of his rebellion against his master, who has forbidden him to visit La Japonesita's house. But Pancho finds himself strangely attracted by La Manuela who, although over fifty, still prides herself on her Spanish dance routine. The drunken Pancho makes up to the pathetic La Manuela until he is brought up short by Octavio's taunting accusations that he is lapsing from his manhood. Infuriated by the truth of this allegation, he turns on La Manuela and, abetted by Octavio, he chases the fleeing "woman," beats her senseless, and leaves her to be mauled to death by Don Alejo's ferocious mastiffs.

In the process of working through this complex scheme deriving from Don Alejo's power and the shifting patterns of loyalty and rebellion of those dependent on it, Donoso's novel provides a compelling interpretation of an infernal social dynamic in which individuals destroy themselves and each other in the struggle for access to the influence of Don Alejo, who is alternately a distracted and a scheming Jehovah. La Japonesita senses her world as immutable, presided over by the omnipotent Don Alejo in his "lugar sin límites": "No quedaba ni una esperanza que pudiera dolerle, eliminando también el miedo. Todo iba a continuar así como ahora, como antes, como siempre"[24] (59).

However, La Manuela is a disruptive element within this eternal structure. Don Alejo subscribes to a world of immovable patriarchy, which he sustains within his own household and domain. The local whorehouse is merely a microcosm of this system, and physically present or absent, Don Alejo is the nuclear force behind La Japonesita's marginal world. If the whorehouse reduplicates in harsh terms the male-female relationships that dominate Don Alejo's social world, La Manuela's presence, as she is both tolerated by Don Alejo and victimized by the house's customers, is a defiance of those relationships. Although the novel leaves in suspense whether Don Alejo's tolerance of La Manuela derives from his acceptance of her sexual "deviance" within an unquestioned patriarchy or whether she is only some perverse fun on his part at the expense of the men under him, a bit of playfulness allowable precisely because the patriarchal edifice is unshakable, the presence of the transvestite is a constant provocative presence within this world, and the ultimate assault to which she falls victim is the propelling element in the novel's plot.

The conflict deriving from a social structure that pretends to accommodate La Manuela (whether as a consequence of Don Alejo's whim, his gratitude, or his own secret sexual needs, as evidenced by the disastrous *tableau vivant* he is willing to pay La Japonesa Grande handsomely to execute) and the constant scandal of La Manuela's existence as a contradiction of that structure generates a violence of sentiment within Pancho that is transferred to La Manuela in order for her would-be swain to reassert his masculinity within the very patriarchal system he pretends to defy by pursuing La Manuela in the first place. This unresolvable clash of acceptance and repudiation produces the novel's dénouement:

> Pancho, de pronto, se ha callado mirando a la Manuela. A eso que baila allí en el centro, ajado, enloquecido, con la respiración arrítmica, todo cuencas, oquedades, sombras quebradas, eso que se va a morir a pesar de las exclamaciones que lanza, eso increíblemente asqueroso y que increíblemente es fiesta, eso está bailando para él, él sabe que desea tocarlo y acariciarlo, desea que ese retorcerse no sea sólo allá en el centro sino contra su piel, y Pancho se deja mirar y acariciar desde allá . . . el viejo maricón que baila para él y él se deja bailar y que ya no da risa porque es como si él también, estuviera anhelando. Que Octavio no sepa. No se dé cuenta. Que nadie se dé cuenta.[25] (126)

But, of course, Octavio does quickly realize what is going on, and his challenge to Pancho to reassert his manhood by punishing La Manuela for her advances restores the patriarchal order. This restoration is confirmed by Don Alejo's mastiffs, which he has deliberately allowed to run loose as though sensing the need to contribute, despite his warning to Pancho to stay away from La Manuela, to the latter's destruction. With La Manuela's death, the world of Estación El Olivo returns to the unequivocal primacy of untransgressable male-female identities.

La Manuela's perturbation of the social text, permitted by Don Alejo for his own casual enjoyment during a period that he arbitrarily both opens and closes, evidences itself in a linguistic aporia underscored by Donoso's narrative. This aporia involves the grammatical identity of La Manuela as masculine or feminine. In La Manuela's mind, she is feminine and refers to herself with the corresponding morphology. Don Alejo and the other whores go along with this self-identity. However, La Japonesita insists on reminding La Manuela that the latter is her father, and her address is based on masculine markers. Men like Pancho also view La Manuela as a man, and her perverse assertion of femaleness is the source of their aggressive stance toward her. In terms of real-world referents in the novel, the conflict between maleness and femaleness is underscored by details, on the one hand, of La Manuela's transvestism and accompanying mannerisms and, on the other, of specifics of her biological maleness, beginning with her hairy legs and absence of breasts and culminating, quite insistently, in the nature of her relationship to La Japonesita. While La Manuela doggedly insists on her feminine identity, La Japonesita is constantly there to belie the sexual and linguistic discourse she projects by treating her as a man and her father to boot:

> Cuando la Japonesita se ponía a hablar así a la Manuela le daban ganas de chillar, porque era como si su hija estuviera ahogándolo con palabras [. . .].[26] (60)
>
> —¿Y la Manuela?
> La Japonesita no contestó.
> —¿Y la Manuela, te digo?
> —Mi papá está acostado.[27] (122)

The grammatical solecisms that derive from the conflicting treatment of La Manuela as a man or as a woman provide a jarring textual trace of the fundamental conflict in the world of Don Alejo's Estación El Olivo with respect to sexual roles. La Manuela refuses to accept the masculine role assigned to her by her society's reading of her biology, even after that biology has been tested by the fathering of La Japonesita. It is a refusal confirmed by those who either treat her as a woman (the other whores) or pursue her as a woman (Pancho and, with less drunken openness and more ambiguousness, possibly Don Alejo). But in so doing, she endorses the sexual codification of her society: her insistent self-attribution of the feminine gender calls attention to the sexual code and emphasizes it in numerous ways. This she does by the sheer necessity of her act of defiance, resulting in the confirmation that comes from those who decry her transgression and punish her for it by subjecting her to repeated acts of corrective violence and then, through Don Alejo's tenebrous complicity, by killing her. La Manuela speaks of accepting her brutalization: one could even venture to say that it is a necessary part of the dynamic of her sexual fulfillment, although such an interpretation borders on the oppressive caricature of the fairy as a victim deliberately courting self-destruction. Along with any such acceptance, La Manuela is perceptive enough to grasp that somehow her sexual persona is a threat to the code of gender identity:

> Lo sintió tiritar junto a las brasas. Mojado el pobre, cansado con tanta farra. La Japonesa se fue acercando al rincón donde sintió que estaba la Manuela, y lo tocó. El no dijo nada. Luego apoyó su cuerpo contra el de la Manuela. [. . .]
>
> —Son tan pesados . . .
>
> —Brutos.
>
> —A mí no me importa. Estoy acostumbrada. No sé por qué siempre me hacen esto o algo parecido cuando bailo, es como si me tuvieran miedo, no sé por qué, siendo que saben que una es loca.[28] (84)

For the purposes of Donoso's narrative and the narrator's interpretation of her, La Manuela does not rise above being a stereotypic *loca*: hysterical, ludicrous, alternately sentimental and viper-tongued, coquettish with men she knows will likely end up beating her half to death when they are no longer satisfied with shouting insults at her at the same time that they are strangely attracted to the tattered eroticism that she can still manage to project. Pancho recriminates La Japonesita for her frigidity (i.e., the way in which she belies her femaleness by not showing arousal in the presence of men, as a real woman presumably must), as he shouts for La Manuela:

> —¡Qué va a estar enferma esa puta vieja! ¿Crees que vine a ver tu cara de conejo resfriado? No, vine a ver a la Manuela, a eso vine. Ya te digo. Anda a llamarla. Que me venga a bailar.[29] (123)

Pancho is both attracted to and repulsed by La Manuela. The transvestite understands this manifestation of sexual ambivalence and the ritualized games it engenders, for she is as accustomed to "dancing Spanish" for the men who court her as she is to being sexually used by the *brutos* when they come to realize the threat she poses to the codified versions of their masculinity. Only the focal point of these versions, Don Alejo, is able to countenance with some equanimity La Manuela's transgressive and affirmative role, and only because it enters into his manipulation of the system of power by which he exercises his authority over Estación El Olivo. In this way, La Manuela is crucial to sustaining that power because both her transgressions and her victimization serve to confirm its perpetuity as it is translated into the code of the sexual text.

The ineffectualness of Pancho's rebellion, encouraged by Octavio, lies in how Don Alejo (who constantly "unmans" his former protegé by taunts that, within the conventions of their shared society, are insults to his masculinity, beginning with the threat to turn his dogs loose on him) is able to shift the anger of rebellion from against himself to against La Manuela, whom Pancho both courts and punishes for the transgression she embodies. This transferral is underscored by the way in which La Manuela, rather than Pancho, is torn to pieces by Don Alejo's mastiffs, metonymies of his brutal power (118).

By projecting La Manuela as a stereotype, Donoso's narrative can hardly be said to be concerned with an analysis of her transvestism, and the only allusion to her biography beyond the time frame of the novel is to a commonplace story of being caught as a youth having sex with another boy and running away from a father's wrath (87). Indeed, the extent to which La Manuela's sexual persona serves as a linguistic shifter in the microcosm she inhabits is conveyed by the narrative discourse, which adjusts the third-person references to La Manuela in conformance to the differing identity attributed to her by the other characters. Thus, in *El lugar sin límites*, La Manuela's sexuality is a coordinate of a system of power relationships that are the principal concern of Donoso's novel, as they are indeed of all of his fiction. Those coordinates, as they function to confirm a specific version of feudal power, are translated into a sexual text mediated through the transgressive role La Manuela must play out until her final punishment for its violation of the social code:

> [Ella] es la única capaz de hacer que la fiesta se transforme en una remolienda de padre y señor mío, ella, porque es la Manuela. [. . .] Esas no son mujeres. Ella va a demostrarles quién es mujer y cómo se es mujer.[30] (111)

The pathos of La Manuela's situation and her ludicrously deluded self-image are of a whole with how Donoso's novel fixes her as a stereotype whose primary function is to create a disturbing change within the social structure she highlights. Moreover, the fact that this structure is seen as immutable, both as echoed by La Japonesita's sense of despair and futility and by La Manuela's violent end in order to reaffirm a pride of masculinity, places *El lugar sin límites* within the realm of tragipathetic homosexuality more than it reveals an interest in sexual transgression as a version of social restructuring. Nevertheless, among those narratives that present figures like La Manuela doomed by a sociohistorical matrix that cannot accommodate them, Donoso's novelette is especially noteworthy for the decision to use transvestism as a point of reference for the interpretation of the patriarchal code that underlies that matrix.

CHAPTER SIX

OPTICAL CONSTRUCTIONS

I

In Márcia Denser's story "Ladies First" (1986), the first-person narrator describes how she allows herself to be invited to the lesbian bar of the title. From drinking alone in a restaurant to falling in with a group that includes individuals of diverse sexual interests, to visiting Ladies First, the narrator is hardly an innocent who has been deceived by the hard sophistication of people who take advantage of her. Yet, when she finds herself a spectator in a setting where reality—at least a comfortably familiar public sexuality—has suddenly become ambiguous and startlingly confusing, she describes how she is at a loss either to tell who is what or, more significantly, to identify her own disoriented feelings. Her uncontrolled reaction is suddenly to begin behaving incoherently. Her would-be partner slaps her to oblige her to cease making a scene, provoking within the context of the self-reflection of the narrative act the following assessment:

> —Diana, você está bêbada! Das Graças estava quase gritando e continuava a me sacudir tão forte que meus dentes rangiam.
> —Olha ali! Olha ali! apontei um vulto.
> —Ali o quê dirigiu um olhar alarmado para a direção indicada. Algumas pessoas começavam a nos observar.
> —Corto o meu saco se aquele não é um velho usando calças com suspensórios, juro que eu corto . . .
> —Corta o quê?
> —Meu saco. Ali! Pera aí que eu vou lá. Aposto que tem também uma garotinha debaixo da mesa . . .
> —Diana! Pára com isso!
> —. . . brincando de pique. Quer apostar? Eu corto meu sa . . . A bofetada que levei naquele preciso momento realmente cortou-me a palavra. Mas agiu como um santo remédio. A náusea desapareceu, fulminada pela consciência da dor, da raiva e da vergonha. Encarei estupidamente Das

> Graças plantada na minha frente, sua expressão preocupada na face morena e sofrida, seus olhos que me fitavam com doçura e piedade. Podia ter sido minha amiga, ainda pensei. De repente, compreendi. Uma dor que até então estivera represada, uma dor de criança, veio subindo, subindo e explodiu em soluços altos, violentos e as lágrimas escorreram boas, livres e um profundo, um imenso alívio era agora poder olhar o rosto bom de Das Graças por detrás da cortina de lágrimas e fumaça, e poder lhe pedir perdão algum dia, quando então ela tiver se esquecido de mim de das outras de todas e da si mesma, quando ela tiver esquecido tudo então eu poderei lhe pedir perdão e compreender e aceitar dançar com ela e permitir que me enlace e que se console e que esqueça quem sou eu que não sou ninguém e que aceite meu braço e que, mais uma vez, me perdoe por tudo.[1] (Denser 92–93)

The anagnorisis that the narrator describes after the fact is neither a sense of pity for Das Graças nor even any sense of the narrator's really belonging, after all, to the world that her hysterical charade seemed to want to block out. Although there may be elements of both pity and self-recognition in her ability to "see beyond the curtain of tears and smoke," the recognition that is involved has suddenly become the ability to see, in something like its legitimate proportions, the world that throughout the narrative she has sought to suppress, despite (or perhaps because of) her acceptance of Das Graças's invitation to accompany her to Ladies First.

Denser is responsible for one of the most rigorously feminist discourses in Brazilian literature, at least in terms of a group of texts that mercilessly deconstruct the principles of sexual relations that prevail among Brazil's putatively carefree high bourgeoisie. Characteristically told as first-person narratives by her feminine protagonists, Denser's short stories are a mosaic of the hypocrisy, manipulation, and exploitation that characterize the devastating personal experiences, both directly sexual and simply interpersonal, of women who by any metric of middle-class values are effective and in control of their own mind and bodies (Hohldfeldt).

The recurring protagonist of Denser's *Diana caçadora* (Diana Huntress) is, in fact, a highly successful writer who believes herself, in the tradition of her mythological namesake, to be a relentless huntress of self-important machos. Yet her vengeful, predatory stance is also her weakness, and her self-confident analysis leads her to assume compromising postures vis-à-vis men whom she wishes to scrutinize and to humiliate. Diana, however, falls victim to the sexual hunt she wishes to control from the exteriority of her analytical stance as represented by the textual form she is able to give her adventures. In this collection, as in other of

Denser's books, the failure of the stern critique of Denser's participant-witnesses is less a criticism of feminism than it is a reflex of the degree to which the structures of sexism that feminism proposes to address are considerably more resistant to both analysis and deconstruction than initially believed.

In the case of "Ladies First," Diana makes the mistake of extending to lesbianism (and Das Graças clearly is seen as intending to play the stereotypic masculine role) her feelings about machismo. Such an extension is a mistake in two ways. In the first place, Das Graças's moves on Diana are not simply a replay of macho stereotypes. This is made clear by the fact that Diana cannot recognize in the microcosm of Ladies First simply a projection of the heterosexual bar scenes with which she is amply familiar and which she prides herself on being able to handle skillfully. The world into which Das Graças leads her is fundamentally alien, which is what provokes Diana's outbreak.

Second, Diana makes the mistake of believing that she can come to terms with the alien setting by mocking it, and Das Graças's blow brings Diana up short enough to begin to assess Das Graças's world not as a continuity of the degraded world centered on the macho with which she is familiar, but as an alternate space of human aspirations. Diana's rhetorical begging of forgiveness (rhetorical because it is uttered in the context of the narrative and not in the extratextual world itself which occasions the text) is a metonymic gesture toward coming to terms with a reality that must be assigned its own vocabulary and examined in terms of its own internal processes of meaning. Such an examination is the project the narrator assigns to herself through the text, after which she will actually be able to "lhe pedir perdão algum dia" (ask her forgiveness one day) after she has attained some level of descriptive adequacy toward the alien social text.

Denser's story, therefore, is the portrait of a writer who discovers the need to struggle to assign meaning to an alien social text that, in this case, happens to belong to what for the narrator is an unfamiliar (but, the story ironically insinuates, not totally ungermane) sexual domain. Diana endorses the imperative to assign meaning to that domain, not via a mocking scrutiny that underscores its members' parody of familiar patterns of clothes, manners, and actions, but in an analytical account of the sexual and interpersonal arena of urban Brazilian life. It remains to be seen if that posture, which elsewhere, when applied to male antagonists, often leads Diana into being the hunted rather than the huntress, can render a useful portrait of Das Graças's alien world. Denser has yet to publish what might be Diana's fully rendered examination of the world to which she initially is at such a loss to give adequate textual form.

2

La condesa sangrienta (1971; *The Bloody Countess*) by the Argentine Alejandra Pizarnik (1936–1972) has become something of an underground classic of Argentine literature, aided in large part by the author's suicide the year after its publication (Peri Rossi; Malinow; Beneyto; Running; Perla Schwartz). In addition to the limited number of copies that were printed, the text is a chillingly clinical account (and for that reason all the more fascinatingly poetic) of the sadistic career of the early seventeenth-century Hungarian Countess Erzébet Báthory (born ca. 1560). Accused of the death by torture of over six hundred girls between the ages of twelve and eighteen, Báthory was confined until her death in 1614 to her personal chambers in order to prevent a peasant uprising over the growing rumors concerning the disappearances of girls who were invited to be handmaidens at her castle and the fate that befell them there (apparently upper-class girls were also her victims). Protected by the Hapsburgs and abetted in her erotic pursuits by an old crone, Dorkó, who disappeared as the countess was being investigated by an emissary of the king, the widowed Báthory seems to have indulged in a calculated program of seduction, torment, and murder of her victims in part in order to fulfill erotic fantasies and in part in the pursuits of rites of rejuvenation through the use of the blood of the young women (Penrose).

Pizarnik recognizes the 1962 account of the Countess by Valentine Penrose, *Erzsébet Báthory, la comtesse sanglante*, and it is obvious that she has even used Penrose's title. Thus, Pizarnik's slender book, a series of eleven vignettes that are mostly two to three pages in length, is a Spanish-language version of Penrose's account, itself probably based on legendary and archival material. In her vignettes, Pizarnik presents cameos of Báthory's activities; the concluding segment describes the countess's immuration for her crimes.

In contrast to extensive narratives recognizable as conventional novels where the homosexual motif is developed within the context of a system of social and personal relations, such as all of the other texts treated by this study, *La condesa sangrienta* is notable as a mosaic of prose vignettes that are related to one another strictly by virtue of their dealing with some aspect of Báthory's indulgence of her erotic interests. Only in the concluding paragraph of her text does Pizarnik state an interpretive hypothesis that could have been used to develop a conventional novel:

> Como Sade en sus escritos, como Gilles de Rais en sus crímenes, la condesa Báthory alcanzó, más allá de todo límite, el último fondo del desenfreno. Ella es una prueba más de que la libertad absoluta de la criatura humana es horrible.[2] (Pizarnik 65–66)

Rather than functioning as a thesis sentence for Pizarnik's portrayal of the countess, this declaration is an unexpected coda that colors, in retrospect, the reader's assessment of Báthory's compulsions. Such an interpretive statement, particularly when read in the context of the moral vision of the reconstructive dictatorships successive military tyrannies in Argentina have attempted to impose, makes it easy to understand the countercultural enthusiasm for *La condesa sangrienta* as a version of the abyss of human cruelty behind the façade of gentility and the sadistic abuse of power permitted those protected by the agents of established order. This is even more the case when one realizes that Pizarnik's text prefigures the worst abuses of power in the name of moral reconstruction of the 1970s.

The revelations concerning Argentina as "el estado terrorista" and the horrifying inventory of persecutions and tortures that have been made as part of the return to institutional normality and the analysis of recent national history in the spirit of "Nunca Más" (Never Again)—the rallying cry of the trial by the democratic government of those implicated in human rights abuses and a deliberate echo of the Jewish post-Holocaust consciousness—over ten years after the publication of Pizarnik's book add to its intercultural resonances among the present generations of readers, who have made it a classic and Pizarnik an emblem of the poet as a marginal individual in society (Piña; Vela).

Read in these terms, the figure of Báthory speaks more to the abuse of power through the physical torment of her victims than to the issue of a legitimate homosexual erotic. Although Pizarnik is associated with lesbianism both in her personal life and in specific aspects of her poetry, Pizarnik's Báthory, unlike contemporary versions of Sade which see him freeing the Western discourse on sex from its encrustations of moral hypocrisy (Carter), cannot, in view of the aforementioned coda, be viewed as an example of sexual liberation, unless one can view the author's closing affirmation as devastatingly ironic: ironic in the sense of belying the conventional morality that would be quick to agree that Báthory's actions were inexcusably, unredeemably horrible and that we can take comfort in a shared belief that they constitute an unacceptable program of erotic fulfillment; devastatingly so in the sense that to accept the plausibility of Báthory's dramatic executions of her sexual fantasies would be to go beyond the rather jejune and blithely accumulated hyperboles of Sade's "philosophy in the boudoir" to accept the most calculatedly cold-blooded forms of torture as a legitimate erotic.

Yet, Pizarnik's discourse does in fact reasonably allow such a reading of her coda, which as an ethical statement (ironic or otherwise), is appended almost as an afterthought to a series of vignettes recounted in a noninterpretive, clinically expository prose. Consider, for example, the following vignette, "Muerte por agua" ("Death by Water"):

> El camino está nevado, y la sombría dama arrebujada en sus pieles dentro de la carroza se hastía. De repente formula el nombre de alguna muchacha de su séquito. Traen a la nombrada: la condesa la muerde frenética y le clava agujas. Poco después el cortejo abandona en la nieve a una joven herida y continúa viaje. Pero como vuelve a detenerse, la niña herida huye, es perseguida, apresada y reintroducida en la carroza, que prosigue andando aun cuando vuelve a detenerse pues la condesa acaba de pedir agua helada. Ahora la muchacha está desnuda y parada en la nieve. Es de noche. La rodea un círculo de antorchas sostenidas por lacayos impasibles. Vierten el agua sobre su cuerpo y el agua se vuelve hielo. (La condesa contempla desde el interior de la carroza). Hay un leve gesto final de la muchacha por acercarse más a las antorchas, de donde emana el único calor. Le arrojan más agua y ya se queda, para siempre de pie, erguida, muerta.[3] (17–18)

The reader is immediately struck by the sparse poetry of this description: the polymembrational syntactic structures, the alternation of short and long clauses, the sudden pathetic image of the girl's frozen grasping toward the sole glimmer of heat. This mode of poetic diction predominates in *La condesa sangrienta* until the closing coda, and it bears a close continuity to the poetic diction in verse of Pizarnik's lyrics as a whole (Lasarte V.; Lagmanovich; Amat). And it is undoubtedly this mode of poetry in prose that accounts for a good measure of the more specifically aesthetic recognition this text has been accorded in contemporary Argentine writing, along with similar writings by Osvaldo Lamborghini like *Sebregondi retrocede* (Sebregonde Retreats, 1973).

But in the construction of its discourse, "Muerte por agua" shares another feature with the other vignettes of *La condesa sangrienta*, the reduplication of a process of contemplation, of sexual voyeurism (Kappeler). The controlling point of reference of the act of seeing is the parenthetical, and therefore underscored, statement, "(La condesa contempla desde el interior de la carroza)" (18). Her contemplation of the erotic spectacle she has commanded, the death by hypothermia of a girl she has ravished and tormented, is shared by her unflinching lackeys ("apasibles") and, presumably, by the other members of her cortege, from among whom we assume she has drawn the victim whose physical suffering will alleviate Báthory's boredom. Concomitantly, the girl sees her own fate at the hands of the countess (which is why she attempts to flee), as perhaps she has seen the sacrifice of other girls to their mistress's unrelenting erotic needs. Turned into an ice sculpture, the girl constitutes a public monument, for all to see, of the passage of the noble Hungarian "Dama de la Muerte."

From the perspective of this vignette as text, the most immediate witness to the girl's martyrdom and the most relentless viewer of the ice sculpture added to the Hungarian landscape is the reader, whose gaze is sustained infinitely through the medium of textual permanence. Pizarnik converts her readers, to the degree that they are willing to persevere through all eleven vignettes, into voyeurs whose look outlasts immeasurably the contemplation of the countess who died immured in 1614. Like a certain form of pornography that pretends to justify itself with intellectual pretenses to satisfy the needs of readers made squeamish by so much attention in pornographic texts to bodily details, Pizarnik's text embodies a chal lenge to the reader to accept one of two conflicting but equally immoral postulates: (1) Báthory's elaborate erotic tableaux bespeak the basest in human nature, yet we learn about them through a carefully crafted poetic prose (as opposed to the "straightforward" journalistic chronicle that characterizes the aforementioned descriptions of the systematic abuses of the Argentine military tyranny that basically held sway between 1966 and 1983, with the exception of the brief parenthesis around Perón's return in 1973); (2) Báthory's fulfillment of her erotic needs through the torture and murder of nonconsenting girls fascinates the reader precisely because it offers one sublimely terrifying version of human sexuality that can be indulged through the pornography of the poetic text.

If pornography is a culturally determined mode of writing that legitimates within the putatively closed realm of the text what is accepted to be necessarily forbidden in the real-world realm beyond the text, but which the text supplements by legitimizing in a fictionally staged real world, *La condesa sangrienta* is an example of lesbian pornography. Although Pizarnik does not explore Báthory primarily as the locus of a lesbian matrix, the descriptions of her dramatic representations of erotic fantasies through the martyrdom of victims of the same sex necessarily signifies Báthory's programmatic pursuit of an evil lesbian erotic (Faderman 277–294).

Certainly, one cannot lament the fact that Pizarnik did not choose to write a conventionally recognizable novel. Nor can one object to her choice to deal with a woman motivated by lesbian sexuality in terms of the unsettling challenge to the reader brought about by the real-life fulfillment of her most horrifying erotic needs rather than with the legitimation of homosexuality in the modern world which is the interest of the majority of the texts dealt with in this study. Where *La condesa sangrienta* is of direct pertinence to this study is in the quandary posed to the reader both fascinated and horrified by the countess—fascinated because of the margins of erotic sadism inherent in Erzébet Báthory's story and horrified because her sexuality resists virtually any strategy of accommodation within a scheme of "legitimate" sexuality, heterosexual or homosexual.

For Argentine readers familiar with the rigorous code of Catholic sexual morality as reinforced sporadically by censorship and other forms of repression, Pizarnik's text is all the more a challenge, and its coda is all the more devastating if read ironically. By encoding in the vignettes a discourse of voyeurism, whereby the countess, her accomplice Dorkó, and her lackeys and handmaidens (each one of whom can and will in turn become an object of contemplation in her erotic martyrdom), *La condesa sangrienta* mocks an implied "moral" reader who might nevertheless experience along with Báthory the sexual response of voyeurism through the displaced medium of the text. Ostensibly a cautionary access to a forbidden realm of sexuality, which happens to be lesbian in the case of Báthory's erotic program, like all pornography *La condesa sangrienta* pretends to legitimate what it in fact holds up for our fascinated contemplation. What moves Pizarnik's text beyond the realm of pornography as a cynical and hypocritical form of discourse about sexuality, is the ironical stance offered as a challenge to her readers-voyeurs in the form of the suddenly intrusive ethical coda that purports to decry precisely what it has evoked with a sparse prose poetry up to that point:

Ella no sintió miedo, no tembló nunca. Entonces, ninguna compasión ni emoción ni admiración por ella. Sólo un quedar en suspenso en el exceso del horror, una fascinación por un vestido blanco que se vuelve rojo, por la idea de un absoluto desgarramiento, por la evocación de un silencio constelado de gritos en donde todo es la imagen de una belleza inaceptable.[4] (65)

CHAPTER SEVEN

NARRATIONS ON THE SELF

I

One of the essential principles of narrative is the maxim of perspicacity, by which it is meant that a story should have sufficient insights to warrant its telling and to justify the investment of effort demanded from the reader by the act of narration. Part of a network of narrative conventions (Pratt), this maxim is part of our intuitive understanding that narratives must have something unique to say that we might not otherwise have access to, and that they will provide this information to us in a particularly perceptive and informative fashion.

Originally published in 1969 and claimed by John S. Brushwood (83) and Luis Mario Schneider to be the most influential homosexual novel of Mexican literature, José Ceballos Maldonado's *Después de todo* (When All Is Said and Done) addresses itself to satisfying the maxim of perspicacity in two ways. In the first place, it is essentially an album of narrative snapshots in which the middle-aged first-person narrator describes his many experiences in active and generally very successful pursuit of teenage male lovers: "Esta foto de Gastón es la que aparece en la primera hoja de mi álbum. En rigor debería encabezarlo la foto de Jaime; pero la perdí"[1] (Ceballos Maldonado 90). Only a few of the almost two dozen boys collected by Javier Lavalle acquire any dimension of personality in the narrative, and the overall result is a series of brief, blurred images that constitute a lifetime sexual activity at the core of the narrator's self-identity. Like a catalog of sexual images at an exhibition, Ceballos Maldonado's novel engages the reader in the first instance because of the candidness of the narrator's chronicle, the unabashed specifications of his sexual interests, the frank treatment of the interplay between artful conquest and material remuneration that characterizes Lavalle's pursuit of adolescent lovers, and the overall honesty of the narrator in presenting himself with neither self-pity nor self-righteousness:

> Me pregunto a veces, con un melancólico temblorcillo interior, si no me habré equivocado en todo. Pero entiendan ustedes: es sólo en raras ocasiones. Porque en general, bajo un dilatado cielo de condenación, pero a la vez renovada promesa, he vivido de acuerdo con lo que quiero y lo que soy. Es cierto, desde luego, que no he triunfado en el sentido común y corriente, ni en el que yo mismo me proponía antes de que apareciera Leonardo. (El está allí, como fin y principio.) Pero en cambio, he vivido sin inhibiciones. ¿Pueden entenderlo? No durante algún tiempo, que es por lo que opta la mayoría de ustedes, sino eternamente. He vivido así y no me siento amargado a pesar de los numerosos reveses. Porque, después de todo, es lo que importa.[2] (195)

These closing words of the novel underscore Ceballos Maldonado's interest in presenting a narrative of homoerotic love that abandons the time-worn pattern of the pathetic chronicle of disastrous encounters, persecutions, and emotional and physical destruction. Certainly, there are elements of these passages of life in *Después de todo*: the narrator writes about his sexual life from a present in which he is being abandoned (for a woman) by his most recent lover, Rolando, who has lived with him and whom he has supported by paying for his studies and obtaining a job for him. We learn that Lavalle's past includes losing his job as a chemistry professor at the university in Guanajuato because of a denunciation of him published in the newspaper; we also learn that his liaisons have included the usual inventory of betrayals, insults, and violence. Yet all of this is relayed in quite a matter-of-fact tone by a narrator who is proud of the degree of success he has had in his conquests: "En el arte de fraguar tretas para abordar a los chamacos me considero realmente extraordinario; fallo muy rara vez"[3] (122).

The narrator expresses considerable pride in being able to satisfy his sexual needs, needs that, although they may run counter to public morality in Mexico, are described as very easily met in a setting in which the seeker has emotional and material goods to offer, confirming Whitam and Mathy's research finding that, in a society like Mexico, homosexual acts serve as marketable goods that do not impinge on the seller's sexual self-identity, which is why Lavalle often loses his lovers to women as they reach the age for heterosexual mating in their society. As a consequence, *Después de todo* establishes a narrative relationship with readers based on the willingness of the latter to accept the details of these conquests, while at the same time realizing that such details of male homoeroticism go beyond their presumed average range of information about sexual passion. That is, the narrative contract underlying *Después de todo* assumes readers do not belong to a circle sympathetic to homoeroticism and that they are unfamiliar with the details specific to homoerotic conquests and, more especially, with the reasons why such relationships are frustrated and terminate. It is reasonable to assume that any novel writing against the grain of the cultural repression of sexuality and eroticism will find itself obliged to assume a stance of having to tell it all and in considerable detail, which may be one point to begin to explain the (perhaps quite viciously ironic) rhetoric of hyperbole and accumulation in Sade's writings and pornography in general. Given the generalized silencing of homoeroticism in Western society, a measure of the rhetoric of accumulation, if not hyperbole, is especially called for.

Written on two narrative levels, *Después de todo* describes both the growing distance between the narrator and Rolando and the lovers he has had from childhood on. Presented, with the image of the literal or imagined photo album in the background, as a written chronicle with which the narrator is occupying his time during Rolando's growing absences, the narrative text foregrounds the conditions of its own telling in terms of the contract between a narrator and a reluctant addressee. Thus, allusions to the difficulty of writing, of finding the proper perspective, and of providing the appropriate framing of the story are correlated with repeated references to the probable reactions of the reader to the gist of what, because of lack of familiarity or sympathy, may appear alternately appalling and ridiculous:

> Ahora mismo, aunque de un modo atenuado, vuelvo a experimentar la agitación de entonces. Raro, después de tantos años. Quisiera registrar los hechos tal como ocurrieron. Pero me reprimo porque debo someter el relato a cierto rigor literario, aunque se modifiquen los acontecimientos en determinado aspecto, y sobre todo, se resientan de espontaneidad. Por otro lado es menester callar muchas cosas; porque si las revelara estoy cierto de que todo el mundo pondría el grito en el cielo, escandalizado.[4] (191)

This is a curious element of coyness in a narrative that is otherwise notably unabashed in covering what many readers might call the amoral nature of its chronicle of seduction, including specific (although not graphic) allusions to sexual acts between male lovers. Precisely, such a framing device recognizes that the narrative diverges from the criterion of moralism that customarily underlies Western sexual fiction, homoerotic or otherwise. Ceballos Maldonado's novel, through the metanovelistic nature of Javier Lavalle's story, demands the suspension of the moral stance that would either condemn the latter for his sexual deviance or couch it in terms of the ethical nobility of the protagonist's struggle.

Lavalle is proud to have lived his own life, but he does not utilize the vehicle of his chronicle to attach to it any significance other than being the narrative of how he sought to satisfy his sexual needs within the context of opportunities his society provided to him. Perhaps, from a sociological point of view, what might be most disturbing to the reader conditioned by a sense of moral propriety is that, like Oscar Lewis's anthropological narratives in which the attempt was made to let people speak in their own voices, no matter how much what they had to say might deviate from official social pieties, *Después de todo* reveals a market of sexual opportunity for Javier Lavalle very much at variance with the assumption of circumscribed sexuality for the middle-class boys he seduces. Whether because they require his emotional attentions, because they are happy to accept his gifts and payments of money, or simply because they too require a form of sexual experience they will abandon (but often not entirely) when they begin dating women, Lavalle's partners are as much seekers as they are sought, at least if we are to read his narrative as candid and free from self-justifying distortions.

> En este momento no hay nada más agradable para mí que estar circundado de recuerdos. Todo lo veo en orden, día por día, episodio tras episodio. Aunque ustedes no tengan el mismo juicio, creo que mi capacidad de evocación colinda con lo maravilloso.[5] (130)

As a variety of the self-reflective text that considers the difficulties and the risks of establishing the conditions of its own telling, difficulties compounded in the case of narratives on homosexuality by the gaps in the code of referentiality about the taboo, *Después de todo* makes use of its metanarrative postulates as a way of validating the amorality of its chronicle (as one individual's guilt-free sexual autobiography) and of guaranteeing the coherence of its scandalous story, whose details are measured over and over again against the reader's presumed unfamiliarity with and possible rejection of what is being narrated. Lavalle's leitmotif of the epiphany of self-reflection—what he has discovered about himself in the course of his experiences and what he continues to discover about himself in the process of reconstructing the past in a narrative exposition—underscores the importance of the self-reflexive framing of the narrative as part of the search for coherent explanations about one's life:

> Para mí ya es un hecho habitual permanecer inclinado sobre la mesa escribiendo estas notas. La familiaridad con el papel y la pluma, las evocaciones del tiempo de Guanajuato (gratas), la relación de los desacuerdos con Rolando, la referencia a mis apuros económicos, las llamadas por

teléfono y los toquidos en la ventana, en fin, todos los elementos que van integrando la historia, han desarrollado inopinadamente una especie de amor por este libro. Mi mundo se concreta, se materializa en estas páginas. Y como si se tratara de un espejo, aquí me contemplo a mi sabor.[6] (47)

2

Y ahora yo escribo esto, date cuenta, sólo porque me da mucha rabia callarme.[7] (Arcidiácono 119)

The Argentine Carlos Arcidiácono's unnamed narrator in *Ay de mí, Jonathan* (Woe Is Me, Jonathan, 1976) closes his quasi-epistolary narrative with the statement, "quise ver qué pasaba si cometía la cursilería de escribir unas lágrimas"[8] (199). Yet this trope provides a summary image for the narrative that is only partially accurate. While *Ay de mí, Jonathan* is a lament for an abruptly truncated relationship that the narrator's letter cannot really hope to revive, it is also a very funny review of some of the Chaplinesque aspects of pursuing a variety of sex that, because it is first forbidden and then problematized, ends up being a ridiculous distortion of human endeavor. The pratfalls of all human relations are exacerbated by the sociocultural framing of homosexual passion, and from the attempts to deal with what dominant society has come to view as a quintessential crisis of the psyche through psychiatry (*Ay de mí, Jonathan* joins a long line of Argentine novels burlesquing the obsession of the Buenos Aires intelligentsia with psychoanalysis) to the ethos of Turkish baths where "no one goes because he feels good" (*sic* in English, 127), Arcidiácono articulates a diversified fugue about lost objects of desire that overlays soap opera despair with a keen sense of self-reflection.

Ay de mí, Jonathan's narrator undertakes to compose his letter during carnival season, that pre-Christian remnant of the realm of Bacchus and Eros that is meant to give morality the value of a cleansing antidote to the excesses of fleshly delights, and the most elemental level of his despair is being left alone in the city for four days without someone with whom to share the virtually forced rites of homage to Bacchus and Eros. Like those love lyrics that involve a first-person speaker addressing an absent lover, Arcidiácono's novel is structured around the absent second person, Miguel, who can never be evoked, never constructed as present because his very disappearance from the narrator's world is the generating principle of the text. Were Miguel to answer the appeals to him (in this novel the actual manifestation of these appeals takes the form of waiting for him to call on the telephone, as he has deceitfully promised to do; all the narrator receives is wrong numbers and calls from friends whose solicitous attentions only tie up the phone so that Miguel, the narrator believes, cannot get through), the text we read would have no reason to exist.

Thus, *Ay de mí, Jonathan* is a text of supplement and deferment. It supplements the real conversation in which the narrator is unable to engage with Miguel, and the latter is addressed through the medium of the text as though he were actually present, while the fact that he is not is repeatedly underscored both by the narrator's overt declarations and by the foregrounded presence of the text as displaced conversation: "Se descubrirá, entre otras cosas, que la rosa vive en el tiempo y en el espacio, como vos, y mi amor por vos. Que por eso yo estoy escribiendo esto, solamente para que dure un poquitito más"[9] (23). Writing functions here as a form of deferment in the sense that it forestalls the definitive loss of Miguel, who can at least be "retained" through the medium of the text. The narrator conjures him up not only by recalling for himself physical and emotional details, but by making him exist as part of his narrative scheme.

That scheme is a form of dialogic address that obliges a second person to be present, even if completely mute. This address involves, with its attendant syntax, the correlation of a speaking *I* and a listening, but silent, *you*. As a consequence the Miguel who has refused to remain physically at the side of the narrator is retained through the fictional construct of the text. The text is equally a form of displacement because it displaces a real dialogue with a pretended dialogue in the form of a long and digressive letter; this letter in turn is displaced in the form of the novel *Ay de mí, Jonathan* that we read, with the reader in a certain sense replacing Miguel as the addressee. This network of supplements, deferrals, and displacements is evoked by one of the interior dialogues of the novel, one of the unwelcome telephone conversations that the narrator has with Soledad(!), a would-be lover who is confident that the narrator's conflicts can be resolved by some earnest heterosexual attentions:

> —Está bien, Soledad. Nos encontraremos a tomar una copa. Yo te llamo. A esta altura tenía miedo de que estuvieras llamando y te diera ocupado. Estaba dispuesto a prometer cualquier cosa. Pero ella quería hablar. El tipo nunca alcanzó a Julio. La maratón se dispersó, y los vecinos no entendieron nada.
>
> —¿Te seguís psicoanalizando?
>
> —No. Lo dejé.
>
> —Has hecho bien. Con más razón todavía yo quiero hablar con vos.

—Te llamo el lunes. (De acá hasta el lunes puede que vea a Miguel. Aunque el fin de semana está tan ocupado. Y hoy ya es jueves.)
—No me vas a llamar. Ya lo sé. Pero esto es el final.
Ya me había dado cuenta de que éste era un diálogo con vos. Y miré el tubo, como si del otro lado estuviera el destino, hijo de puta, haciendo otra maldad. Y el tubo dijo:
—No te lo digo por orgullo . . .
Evidentemente estaba hablando yo. Y vos te habías transformado en mí. Es decir, yo era un Miguel que escuchaba la queja, impasible, y absolutamente seguro de que aunque ella lo resolviera, los sentimientos no se decretan. Lo más que podía hacer era no llamar más.
—¿ . . . estás ahí?
—Sí. Estoy.
—No. Como estás tan callado.
—Estoy escuchando.[10] (48–49)

The configuration of the text of *Ay de mí, Jonathan*'s narrator is fugue-like in its pursuit of a number of interrelated themes having to do with the vagueries of human encounters and the particular fragility of liaisons, especially male gay ones, that are circumscribed by repressive and oppressive social or moral codes (Arcidiácono's novel was published just after the return to power of the Argentine military in 1976, an aspect of whose political program was the purging from the body politic of all vestiges of sexual immorality (Puig; Jáuregui; Avellaneda, passim; the large Buenos Aires gay community was particularly vulnerable during this period). This configuration involves a series of disjunctive circumstances that are based primarily on the presence/absence of the fundamental pretext of the novel, Miguel. By speaking around the problems of expression and description versus the inability to capture the essence of human experience and sexual relations, by juxtaposing the will to know with the perennial misunderstandings of personal relations, by producing a text that self-reflectively recognizes its limitations and its failures at achieving an adequate gesture of communication with its addressee, *Ay de mí, Jonathan* speaks both eloquently and humorously of the frustrations of dialogue as a basis of human interaction and as an integral element in sexual attraction. Thus, the text is as much a substitute for an erotic involvement that no longer exists (never existed?) as it is a part of an interpersonal relationship that it serves to characterize and to reinforce, if only as a figment of the narrator's imagination. The idea of writing because it allows desire, no matter how tenuous by now, to be sustained is complemented by the need to alleviate the rage of remaining silent. Like all writing about the human condition (and the narrator asserts throughout the first segment of his text that culture never exists because people are happy—if they were, they would have no need to occupy themselves with writing), *Ay de mí, Jonathan* discovers in the possibilities of textual configuration both a way to account for the narrator's despair and a way to enhance the presence of the object of his sexual desire, if only through the fiction of his text:

> Realmente me equivoqué. Me he equivocado siempre: de agujeros (como decía mi psicoanalista), de vida, de ilusiones, de profesión, sensaciones y presentimientos. Lo que amé fue mentira; lo que quise, ficción.[11] (195)

Yet, this rather self-pitying declaration is complemented by the status of the epistolary text as a concerted effort to reinforce the *mentira/ficción* with the creative act of self-expression. In the process, the narrator makes sure that Miguel stays on the line for good.

3

> Escribe hoy lo que hizo, lo que no hizo, para verificar fragmentos de un todo que se le escapa. Cree recuperarlos, con ellos—intenta—o—inventa—una constelación suya. Ya sabe que son restos, añicos ante los que se siente sorda, ciega, sin memoria: sin embargo se está diciendo que hubo una visión, una cara que ya no encuentra. Encerrada en este cuarto todo parece más fácil porque recompone. Querría escribir para saber qué hay más allá de estas cuatro paredes; o para saber qué hay dentro de estas cuatro paredes que elige, como recinto, para escribir.[12] (Molloy 13)

One of the amorous motifs of Western culture (indeed, it is probably universal) is that of the prison-house of love. Erotic attachment is seen as affording a bittersweet experience, the mixed blessing of being drawn to another human being, with all of the opportunity for tragic destruction or comic ridiculousness, and at the same time being tyrannically enchained in a relationship that appears to offer more opportunity for suffering than spiritual satisfaction. When language is also viewed as a form of imprisonment, the enforced circumscription of meaning is a consequence of the inherently determinate nature of semiotic structures. These structures depend on their users to sustain their validity more than the latter make use of such structures for an illusory "self-expression" or "self-affirmation." Furthermore, love as a language of human experience and language as a dominant vehicle for knowing that love become inextricably intertwined. The result is an elaborate conceit whereby there is a shifting relationship between the notions of language as creating a sense of experience and of experience demonstrating its quality through language. Finally, when language is conferred a special status as "literary" or "poetic" expression, with all of the attendant monumentalizations such a privileged category implies, and even more so when the nucleus of meaning refers to romantic love, one of our cultural monuments par excellence, surrounded by multiple intertextual echoes of a venerable tradition of amorous topoi, the elements are present for a dense narrative text juxtaposing the elaboration of a recreative expression and the recovery of primal human emotions. Sylvia Molloy's *En breve cárcel* (Brief Imprisonment, 1981; translated as *Certificate of Absence*), written by one of the deans of Latin American literary scholarship, has attracted considerable scholarly interest emphasizing Molloy's interest in exploring the various facets of the topos of the prison-house of love. The recollection of experience and the validity of the narrative recreation of the past are part of a shifting personal project to recover it, to exorcise it, and to understand and come to terms with it (García Pinto, "La escritura de la pasión" and "Sylvia Molloy"; Kaminsky; Montero). Organized around the circumstance of an Argentine woman who returns to take up residence in a rented New England room where she had once pursued a love affair with another woman, but this time to repursue that affair in the form of a written memoir about it, *En breve cárcel* extends the prison metaphor by concretizing it to mean not just a complex of constrictive sentiments, but specifically an actual physical setting in which the two stages of the *amor tirano* (tyrant love) are played out: its original enactment and the scriptive effort to recreate it. Moreover, such a recreation is real in that the text reinstalls many of the feelings of the original affair. At the same time it is an act of conjuration, inasmuch as the unnamed protagonist awaits the return to this nest of her now absent lover, a return that her memoir seeks in some displaced way to promote.

The movement back and forth of a crucial human experience between an interior reality (the enclosure of the room and its textual representation) and an exterior enactment (the establishment of contacts with places and people who figured in an erotic past time) lends the novel a haunting quality as the protagonist clings, with scant melodrama but a profound sense of severed emotions, to the images of a crucial personal experience (see Francine R. Masiello on the novel as subjective construction). By contrast to the breathless rhetoric of soap operas or romance novels, Molloy's narrator is content to record, with almost the neutral tone of the *nouveau roman*, the features of such an experience in order that one may sense the impingements on human lives of profound erotic encounters. Despite all of the pain and sense of loss, it is obvious that her relationship with Vera has given the protagonist a compelling point of reference for her life, one that is magnified through the complex undertaking of (con)textualizing it in life and in writing.

The process of (con)textualization that represents the narrative substance of *En breve cárcel* is striking for the handling of the specifics of lesbianism. The fact that the two lovers, whose affair is described with allusions derived from the naturalized heterosexual pair of Western culture, were engaged in a homosexual relationship is stated so neutrally that critics have chosen to make little of how *En breve cárcel* might be called the most notable lesbian novel to date in Latin American literature. Indeed, from one point of view, the off-handed treatment of the lesbian nature of the love affair described in Molloy's novel becomes one of its most salient textual features. Within the context of the exclusionary social and cultural codes against which homosexual relationships must be played out, whether in Argentina or New England, the sexual preference of lovers cannot be assumed to be immaterial or merely circumstantial. Since it is impossible to contemplate an "ideal" reader against the backdrop of these codes willing to read the story of Ramona and Juliet the same way she would read (in all senses) the story of Romeo and Juliet, homosexual plots cannot be assumed to be happenstance variants of heterosexual ones, as though the fact that the lovers are lesbians is no more than a minimal gesture toward necessary realistic detail like saying they are Argentine or American.

To the extent that the possible narrative universes naturalized within Western culture preclude homosexual love being preceived as a natural circumstance (just as they preclude other sorts of relationships as figuring as natural—i.e., the incestuous, the bestial, the extraterrestial, and so on), we can only approach as slyly ironic a novel that refuses to treat homosexuality as any more socioculturally marked than heterosexuality (Hokenson). By doing precisely this, Molloy defies that tradition whereby writing about a marked situation like homosexuality must treat it with a particular rhetoric that highlights its specific marginality. If the practice in fiction from the late nineteenth century on has been to treat homosexuality as a tragic affliction (of which individuals are either monstrous agents or tortured victims), the countermeasure has been the almost glib glorification of differences, as in Rita Mae Brown's joyously assertive *Rubyfruit Jungle* (1973), "about being different and loving it" as one of the paperback blurbs reads.

Without necessarily privileging homosexuality (which Foucault notes has been done as a defiant counterthrust to the superstructure of oppression that developed in modern society), the posture assumed by a writer like Brown can be viewed as a programmatic strategy for urging readers' consciousnesses toward the naturalization of homosexual relationships (at least in fiction and other cultural manifestations, if not in real life). Molloy creates a fictional world in which there can be no question about the gender of her characters and the erotic combinations in which they engage: except for her father, the novel focuses exclusively on women characters. The greater gender marking of Spanish only serves to underscore that *En breve cárcel* is a novel about women (critics have dwelt in detail on the relevant women's-issue details of this narrative, which are handled with exceptional insight). It must be stated, however, that *En breve cárcel*, while narrowing the nature of its characters, is not a utopian novel—not at least in the way in which Monique Wittig's *Les Guérrillères* (1969) is, with its emphasis on the portrayal of a potential ethos of a society created under the aegis of female domination and what that society might be like for both women and men. Rather, Molloy affirms the homosexual quality of the erotic relationship her novel describes by the particularly eloquent procedure of simply assuming that the lesbian matrix, surrounded by a realm of virtually completely female experience, can seem natural to her readers. Since it cannot, the result is a subtle affirmation of Hélène Cixous's laugh of the Medusa, because there is no way to read the novel except in terms of the complete and insouciant legitimation of its explicit erotic commitments.

The complex narrative structure of Molloy's novel employs prison-house conceits of language in the form of references to the literary motifs of the *cárcel de amor*. Thus, experience acquires, in the process of imposing a legitimized reading, a complementary dimension that rests on how such a narrative text can be read. The protagonist's struggle with expression refers to her own self-reading and, by extension, to her implicit appeal to the absent Vera to reappear as the anchor of the now strictly written references to her existence (i.e., the appeal to her is to become a "real" rather than a "literary" sign in the text). From this point of view, the Quevedian echoes of the prison-house of love and the Jameson-like analysis (*The Prison-House of Language*) of the circumscriptions of language characterize the nature of the protagonist's personal experience in its two stages, past event and present memoir, set in her two periods of residence in the New England rented room.

But when the reader attempts to read the protagonist's reading of her affair, the problematics of sexual codes and the language that both confirms and embodies them are interposed as a challenge to accept as legitimate the erotic experience being described. If the language of naturalized experiences (and romantic love is one of the conventionally celebrated forms of personal experience in our culture) may be viewed as problematical within the frame of reference of barriers to adequate expression, then at issue are dimensions of human affairs that are either unaccounted for or "written out" of sociocultural codes. Homosexuality is one such dimension. Language either pretends it does not exist (the lack of a vocabulary and a morphosyntax for describing it) or treats it as so unnatural or illegitimate that it can only be evoked with a rhetoric of quotation marks that imply it is being forced into the realm of discourse as an alien semantics that demands highlighting. To be able to read, to decode, a language of homosexual experience—in the case of Molloy's novel, as a lesbian subset of an equally problematical women's experience—is to call to the fore the *breve cárcel* of sociolinguistic codes that write out entire sectors of human experience (see Shari Benstock's valuable comments on the founding feminist challenges to the naturalized, male-dominated linguistic code by Gertrude Stein).

Seen from this perspective, Molloy's novel does not simply engage in the strategy of assuming that one can talk about lesbian love as naturally as one talks about heterosexual affairs; to do so would be an act of bad faith, since it would imply that the long tradition of the suppression of homosexual erotics and its expression is an irrelevant detail of our cultural history. Rather, the seeming naturalization of lesbianism in *En breve cárcel* is an act of engagement with the prison-house of an unreflective heterosexual discourse, first through concerns identified with women's issues and then through lesbianism, and a challenge to the "real" reader to pursue the details of the protagonist's specific love story as one legitimate variety of human experience.

4

—¡No te lo puedo creer![13] (Roffiel, *Amora* 30)
—Porque no quiero que se me acabe la rabia.[14] (81)

At one point in Rosamaría Roffiel's *Amora* (1989), the autobiographical narrator is asked to prepare a colloquium presentation on the subject of "bordando sobre la escritura y la cocina"[15] (invited by one Tununa; presumably the reference is to Tununa Mercado, the Argentine writer who worked for many years as a journalist in Mexico). Her essay is basically reproduced as part of her description of how she went about elaborating it, thereby nicely combining discourse and text while at the same time embedding the essay as a mosaic fragment in a narrative that, like the various domestic activities joined by the image of the embroidery thread, constitutes a textured whole about the experience of being a lesbian in contemporary Mexico City (curiously, Ana Lau Jaiven's much touted examination of Mexican feminism does not mention lesbian identities). Feminist theory has repeatedly evoked domestic activities, both as the literal metonymic routines of women's lives (e.g., the fabled kitchen anecdotes in Sor Juana Inés de la Cruz's *Respuesta a Sor Filotea* that serve her as points of departure for the more "masculine" business of philosophical speculation) and as metaphors of the way in which women's bodies and women's daily experiences are bound to the concrete reality masculinism evades with its abstractions. Using an image founded on one of the primordial tasks of women from the earliest periods of American history, Mary Daly speaks of women's discourse (written, to be sure, but more basically lived experientially) as an act of spinning, but the homology with Roffiel's embroidery (a delicate feminine occupation that is especially marked socioculturally in Latin America) is obvious. Roffiel pauses in her inventory to remark:

> De pronto, me surge una duda: ¿será la aguja como la esposa del hilo, que se ocupa de la ardua tarea de traspasar la tela para desaparecer después, dejando a su cónyuge plasmado en formas y colores espectaculares, como único objeto de admiraciones y de halagos? Duda que permanece.
>
> Hay hilos que resultan difíciles de seguir. [. . .]
>
> Y es que esto del hilo es muy relativo, digo yo, que llevo horas preguntándome: ¿y qué tengo yo que decir sobre el hilo si a lo más que llego es a pegar un botón o mal levantar un dobladillo?, ¿si apenas puedo seguir con cierta coherencia este enredo desmadejado que es mi vida en esos momentos?[16] (88–89)

Amora is, to the best of my knowledge, the first lesbian novel published in Mexico, a country that has been producing for over twenty-five years a rich vein of male gay writing, at least one of whose authors, Luis Zapata, has attained continental recognition. Although there has been intense activity surrounding lesbian consciousness formation in Mexico, along with a host of feminist issues associated with the review *fem*, which figures prominently in the novel and with which the author has been associated for a number of years, *Amora* appears to be the first explicit lesbian novel (one has yet to explore the potentially more fertile area of poetry)—explicit in the sense of focusing on lesbian issues as they are lived through the experience of the narrator and her circle, rather than appearing as a secondary theme (a passing conjunction of female "friends" as in Ibargüengoitia's *Las muertas*) or as a densely symbolic code of human relations (the "troublesome" passages in Sor Juana's poetry that Octavio Paz cannot quite come to grips with).

Amora is both the narrator's nickname and a strategically important feminization of the masculine-defined concept of *amor*, the combined traditions of romantic love, soap-opera melodramatic anguish, flesh-denying chastity, and Judeo-Christian marital propriety that Guadalupe and her associates strive to overcome, even if they are still almost hopelessly bound by all of the complex traps of its interwoven codes. The novel describes the initiation, development, setbacks, and final triumph of a love relationship between Guadalupe/Amora and Claudia, an upper-bourgeois woman who has a lot of conventional deadweight to shed in the process of accepting the naturalness of the erotic relationship with the narrator to which she is so compellingly drawn: "Bajo las sábanas, amor que pertenece al Cosmos, dos mujeres se aman con un lenguaje secreto, alejadas del mundo. A pesar de todo"[17] (72).

Roffiel's novel is an unabashed mosaic, with the qualifier meant to underscore how the text eschews the full modernist conception of fiction often associated with the gay novel in which there is an elaborate orchestration of motifs that converge on the depths of sincere passion and the all-too-often profound tragic implications that accompany the violation of the Great Taboo. American gay writing (or British; e.g., the paradigmatic lesbian potboiler, Radclyffe Hall's 1928 *The Well of Loneliness*) is filled with such somber texts, and there are a goodly number of Hispanic equivalents. Manuel Puig's postmodernist writing (at least, after *La traición de Rita Hayworth*) was able to break with this tradition, and Luis Zapata can also be counted on to dedramatize critically the suffering of outcast sex, thereby opening up the conventions of both homophobia and gay identity to much needed deconstructive analysis.

Amora is mostly a text of analysis. There are numerous occasions in which it reads like a self-help pamphlet, complete with an orderly procession of questions and answers that neatly cover the ground—the disquisition on the pejorative vocabulary for lesbians, the lecture by the narrator to her niece and naively bigoted girlfriend about how homosexuals are really no different from anyone else, the thinking through the problems of even attempting a relationship with the stridently self-proclaimed straight (*buga* is the key word to be learned here). But it would be inappropriate to dismiss *Amora* as a piece of gay-liberation propaganda thinly veiled as a novel by a writer unable properly to cope with the demands of full novelistic configurations. Rather, Roffiel has chosen an essentially testimonial mode ("*Casi todos los nombres fueron cambiados. Y casi todo ocurrió realmente*"[18] [5]) in which her dialogue, her interior monologue, and her overt declarations seemed designed to capture the flow of actual conversations and thoughts of individuals consumed by a series of life experiences that are of utmost importance to them.

Significantly, *Amora* provides a number of interlocking perspectives that correspond to a prominent late twentieth-century ethos in Latin America. The narrator and her associates work for the Grupo, a sort of Rape Crisis Clinic that represents women who have been sexually abused before the official male-dominated (and *macho*/masculinist-encoded) system. Although the cases with which they deal involve rape in its core legal definition, their concerns as articulated in their conversations explore wider feminist definitions of rape to include the free-floating and omnipresent harassment of women on a sustained and implacable basis. The result is that there are reasonable meditations on lesbianism as a way out of the no-win situation of masculinist ideology, although the narrator of *Amora* feels obliged to praise bisexuality and to give voice to women who still believe that a feminization of men is possible. Rather than a question of "playing it safe" in order not to appear to be unduly strident, Roffiel's sensitivity to these voices is certainly to be viewed as predicated on a feminist ethic of nonexclusionary discourse. By extension, the specifically feminist and lesbian dimensions of the activities of Guadalupe and friends extends to larger social and political issues (the economic deterioration of Mexico, skepticism about the political process, the situation in Central America), creative concerns (the practice of literature and journalism, including the discovery of authentic speaking voices for women who experience multiple marginalizations), and the generally social (the problems of leading a life of dignity in the decaying megalopolis). All of these dimensions interlock in the skillful juxtaposition of narrative fragments that make up this testimonial of voices.

As regards the more immediate issue of the feminization of narrative discourse, which is accomplished in great part through the implicit repudiation of the highly symbolic or poetic modernist narrative of tragic sexuality (as in the dramas of Tennessee Williams, which can now be read as parables of homosexuality, especially *A Streetcar Named Desire* and *Summer and Smoke*, but also *Orpheus Descending* and *Sweet Bird of*

Youth), *Amora* has some tentative explorations of feminine-marked discourse, as in the case of the title, the naturalization of solecisms like *personaja*, and the conversion into specifically feminine versions of popular sayings; one wishes that there were more explorations of the resexualization of Spanish, but perhaps this would have moved the novel away from the testimonial, conversational mode toward noncolloquial linguistic experimentation. Far more significant is the basic assumption of a plausible narrative pattern that, as it adopts an insouciant tone toward routinely euphemized bodily functions, includes a happy ending (albeit in an antiromantic world in which nothing is forever) for a passionate relationship based on sexual outlawry. The assumption that such a relationship is both legitimate and realizable constitutes, in a novel like *Amora*, the most outrageous deviation from the conventions of narrative language:

> Nos imagino tomando té, las dos muy juntas, contándonos cómo, a veces, la menstruación nos abre más los sentidos y nos conduce de los ovarios a la creación. O, al contrario, nos aleja de ella. Cómo, con la sangre, mujeres nuevas se posesionan de nosotras, algunas conmovedoramente cercanas; otras, ajenas y terribles. Porque nuestra sangre mensual encierra la ferocidad y el color de la vida, pero también el germen de la locura.[19] (148)

CHAPTER EIGHT

UTOPIAN DESIGNS

I

> Quem poderia explicar?[1] (Rios 106)

In Brazil, it is not unusual, of a list of ten bestsellers in fiction, for eight or nine to be foreign titles in translation: French, American, perhaps British. Maybe one might be a Brazilian author. Although there are many Brazilian novelists who have authored national bestsellers—Jorge Amado's fifty-year career has included an ample inventory of successes—few of them are women: in a country that produces considerable literature and where women enjoy a high degree of freedom from convention (Moraes), there are, nevertheless, few exceptionally prominent women writers. Cassandra Rios, however, is one notable exception, and her novels, in the sensationalist vein of a Harold Robbins, certainly count as bestsellers by any sales standard, with the result that she produces a steady flow of titles for mass consumption (Caldas).

There are two distinctive features about Rios's writing: the concentration on the details of Brazil's much vaunted freewheeling sexual freedom and experimentation, and the participation of women in upper-middle-class high jinks. The findings of social scientists might or might not support Brazil's reputation as a country—at least, in its major urban centers—on the farthest reaches of sexual freedom. Popular belief would have us understand that, at least among those with a certain economic independence, all sorts of combinations of sexual alliance are permissible; whether or not this belief is an upward extension of the racist and classist belief that those at the bottom of the power structure are essentially licentious, polymorphously perverse, and sexually indiscriminate is an open question. Concomitantly, the issue of sexual latitude normally available to women in Brazil is not amenable to facile characterizations, despite the popular belief that Brazilian women of all social classes, particularly also those with a high degree of economic independence, enjoy a wide range of freedoms, including unconventionally sexual ones (Mott, *O lesbianismo no Brasil*; see for example Sérgio Santa'Anna, *Amazona* [1986], where a lesbian relationship is a metonym for an ideal of personal, including feminist, liberation from the repressively conventional).

It may well be that Rios's fiction exploits a Brazilian fantasy of sexual liberation, that in the best tradition of considering culture as a form of utopian writing, her novels allude to a circumstance of individual realization that is, at least in the fictional realm, a definitive transcendence of what, for her readers, is an oppressive social reality. Writing principally for economically well-situated women (as in the best of the soap-opera genre, Rios's women are all economically secure and materially free to pursue their personal psychological needs), Rios presents heroines who supplement the real urban situations of her readers by offering an image of personal sexual realization that, because it is the stuff of her novels, is not likely to be actual sociocultural fact. As wish-fulfillment, and quite trashy writing at that, her novels provide an image of what sex, as a/the central experience of life for her readers, might be beyond the real-life confines of their actual sociohistorical circumstances. And with only some measure of exaggeration, the blurb on the back of her 1980 *Copacabana, posto 6 (a madrasta)* (Copacabana, Station 6 [The Stepmother]) can claim that Rios is "A autora mais proibida do Brasil,"[2] to the extent that many of her novels were in direct defiance of the futile attempts of tyrannical agents to clean up Brazilian morals after the 1964 military coup.

In a novel like *A borboleta branca* (The White Butterfly, 5th ed., 1980), one of the recurring dimensions of Rios's fiction, enriching lesbian relationships between women, is explored within the context of a flight from an intolerable, while yet socially conventional, life. Paula returns to Brazil from the United States after more than a decade of absence. She finds that her sister's daughter has become a very difficult teenager living with her father, who threw her mother out of the house for having an affair with his male secretary and confidant. Although the whereabouts of her sister are unknown, Paula establishes herself in her brother-in-law's house. Her reentry into the Brazilian society from which she fled to marry an American, who has since died, involves the discovery of the devastating relationship between her niece and the latter's father, a relationship that undoubtedly involves sexual exploitation by him and his associates in his luxurious but sinister São Paulo mansion. All of the elements of melodramatic soap opera are present in *A borboleta branca*: mysterious comings and goings, the possible influence of the dead beyond the grave, high-intensity emotion, rapes, drunken orgies, acts of random violence—in short, an entire array of stock narrative ploys to keep the novel going and to submerge the reader in revelations of the gothically grotesque and the scandalous.

What Paula discovers is that her niece has been psychologically marred by her father's abnormal appetites involving other women as well as her, and that she, Paula, is viewed by her niece as the one refuge from the degradation imposed on her by her father and the life she is forced to live in his house. Although a young woman of apparent cynicism, Fernanda reveals to Paula, chiefly through her poetry and through small acts of touching courtesy, a depth of human suffering that vindicates her overt aggressions. When Paula, who ends up being raped by her brother-in-law as part of her gruesome reacquaintance with the Brazil she abandoned for her American idyll, attempts to flee his house, she finds she cannot escape Fernanda's piteous demands for affection and salvation. The novel closes with Paula's promise to establish a space on the margins of Brazilian society where she can redeem Fernanda and possibly rehabilitate her for a "normal," heterosexual life.

Clearly, Rios's novel cannot decide whether female homosexuality is a good thing or not. Paula experiences all of the horrors of purple prose on the subject when she discovers that Fernanda's dependency on her includes in its complex of emotions the need to love her physically:

> Então, foi uma estranha luta. Fernanda segurava Paula pelas costas e Paula empurrando-a delicadamente para não magoá-la procurava desprender-se. Não falavam, mas ela ouvia o tique-taque do coração em tumulto, enquanto a respiração ofegante batia-lhe na nuca. Os movimentos de Fernanda eram calculados, maliciosos e todos os seus gestos estavam abrindo-lhe os olhos sobre coisas de que até então não suspeitava: Que o sexo, o amor, o desejo, ou seja o que for capaz de provocar aquela ânsia, era um mistério capaz de conduzir às piores coisas como àquela sensação que a percorria, que a fazia vacilar e chegar a ter medo que Fernanda recuasse vencida em seu empenho.[3] (88)

And Fernanda, who is the essence of go-to-hell rebelliousness, is also startled by the sexual desire that has, almost spontaneously, defined itself between her and her aunt, between one woman despairing of obtaining any sympathy and another woman whose greatest virtue is her capacity to provide understanding and solace:

> feliz, ser o que se deseja e ter o que nos faz bem . . . você me faz bem, não tenho vontade de fazer-lhe mal . . . eu não entendo porque gosto de você como deveria gostar de um homem . . . não entendo, sinto apenas e isso

> me basta . . . não vou perguntar a ninguém se está certo ou errado. Certo? Errado? Por que você gosta tanto de vestidos brancos? Por que eu gosto de lhe trazer rosas vermelhas? . . . Por que Filipe [her father] prefere cachimbo ao cigarro? Por que Ariette [her absent mother] gosta tanto de tomar Manhatan?[4] (99)

Yet, despite Fernanda's justification of sex both as an unexplainable personal preference whose legitimacy comes from the fact that it answers deep personal needs, her rhetorical questions and the vocabulary of a terrible forbidden fruit that has flowered before anyone could suppress it return Rios's novel to the very sociocultural conventions that it appears to be denying: by no means could the reader confuse this portrait of lesbianism with the attitude of "being different and loving it" to be found in Rita Mae Brown's pioneering *Rubyfruit Jungle* (1973) or even in the more traditionally "psychological" analyses of a Jane Rule.

That is, when Paula and Fernanda question the validity of the emotion that brings them together, resolving for each the alienation—nostalgic in the case of the young widow, psychotic in the case of the abused adolescent—that she experiences in her social setting, they are echoing the language of immorality and abnormality that has traditionally circumscribed the treatment of lesbianism, with all of the morbid fascination it holds for the self-allegedly sexually normal.

One of the interesting ideological problems that accompany Rios's writing is the fact that, while it makes ample use of a vocabulary of moral indignation (in the case of *A borboleta branca*, first to denounce Filipe's decadent soirées that shock the sensitive woman recently returned to Brazil from a tranquil life in the United States and then to question, if not to decry, the lesbian relationship between her and her niece—their blood relationship is a conventionally Gothic twist of morbidity in the novel), it is addressed to a presumed reader who shares—or, more likely, aspires to share—in the glamorous style of life that it is denouncing: an upper middle-class woman with the economic resources to imprint on her existence a significant degree of personal, including sexual, freedom.

Of considerable interest is the metanarrative presence of Paula. In addition to the recurrent use of variations on the verb *espiar* (to spy), Paula is the discoverer and the decipherer of Fernanda's ugly exploitation and of her deep need for understanding and restorative love. The novel is written from the perspective of Paula's consciousness, and it is based on the need to speak *o segredo* (the secret) (p. 5), the terrible epigraphic secret of Fernanda's sexual abuse that, once brought to light, can then be corrected by Paula's redemptive kindness. And by penetrating the world of this secret and laying it bare, Paula reestablishes herself in Brazilian life at the same time as her horrible brother-in-law is brought down by the discovery of his incestous relationship with Fernanda (who may or may not be his real daughter, a biological detail that does not affect their social arrangement). Paula's status as a Brazilian who has become an outsider, but one who undergoes throughout the novel a process of becoming once again an insider, is the mainspring of the plot revelations in *A borboleta branca.* Her reinstallation in Brazilian life involves seeing the demise of her odious brother-in-law. In the development of the novel he first attempts to co-opt her and then rapes her under the portrait of his missing wife and her sister. Subsequently, this reinstallation involves the initiation of a lesbian relationship with her niece in the interests of offering her a redemptive love (cf. Lillian Faderman and the motif "surpassing the love of man"). This love must also be a secret, since Paula cannot confess to the male psychiatrist who entrusts Fernanda to her that she will save Fernanda by loving her in a way that psychiatry has traditionally considered to be destructive (see the concluding chapter of the novel [pp. 129–135], which is based on Paula's interview with Fernanda's doctor, who has no idea whatever of why Fernanda responds so positively to Paula's presence).

What is fascinating about Rios's novel is that, in addition to the simple fact that it treats lesbian sexuality as the key to the psychological salvation of a much-trampled child of Brazilian high society, it structures the discovery of the need for that sexuality around the motif of Paula's reentry into contemporary Brazilian life and her disdainful and repulsed contemplation of an existence totally disconsonant with the placid routine of daily life that she had enjoyed with her American husband. (For this reason, I cannot agree with Caldas [9] that homosexuality is only a pretext in Rios's novels.) Although Paula emerges, via her conversion into her niece's lover, as the source of psychological healing in the novel, this healing requires also the reinstitution of her contacts with a culture that she had abandoned for other social norms. Paula both (re)discovers and acts decisively on what the novel considers an important sociocultural reality—the decadent mores of the São Paulo plutocracy—and in the process her consciousness offers Rios's readers both their own self-image and a horrified rejection of it:

> Paula não evitou o gesto de Fernanda, que ergueu as cobertas e admirou-a com atenção.
>
> —Eu já sabia que o seu corpo é lindo . . . já o tinha visto . . . mas não aqui . . . na minha cama . . . mulher-fêmea . . . dorme . . . como vou des-

> cobrir o que sinto? . . . Tudo é pecado . . . pecado não . . . crime . . . imundície . . . *mas aqui não* . . . aqui é sonho e fantasia . . . uma mistura de champanha e água límpida . . . Paula, você é água e eu tenho sede . . .[5] (69; emphasis added)

The horror over so-called deviant sexuality, even in nominally liberated Brazil, allows Rios's novel both to be titillating to its readers and, within the world of the fictional narrative, to provide a secret space in which the two women can undertake a process of regeneration of one of them by the other. This conflict between the superficial rhetoric of the novel, whereby both the narrator and the self-reflecting interior monologue of the characters that the former cites in indirect discourse engage in exclamation-point-studded lucubrations about the sin and pathology of homosexual attraction, and the way in which it is yet at the same time a disruptive strategy for questioning social and moral and, ultimately, political values is both the fascination and the problematics of this sort of bestsellerism. It is fascinating because the need to provide the audience with readily seductive writing permits the entrance into the fictional discourse of thematic elements that "serious" fiction might deplore as sensationalistic. But it is problematical because the limited and mostly un-self-examined ideological pretensions of the text—a text that is, after all, most likely addressed to members of the very society that Rios is dissecting in her notorious and immensely popular fiction—can never find the opportunity to think through in any satisfying fashion the significant and substantial issues that do, in the process of writing bestsellers, if only by accident get raised.

2

> ¿Escribirán mis hermanos un libro tierno para recordarme? Ahora sé que no. El libro lo escribo yo o me tiran al bote del olvido.[6] (Vallejo 104)

> La otra noche soñé con Jesús Lopera. Un sueño nítido. Tanto como pueden ser confusas mis palabras para recobrarlo. El idioma es una red de trama tan burda, tan ancha que deja colar la realidad.[7] (165)

Cast as a personal memoir, the Colombian Fernando Vallejo's *El fuego secreto* (The Secret Fire, 1986) is a sort of Pilgrim's Progress through the secret spaces of Colombia's gay community in Medellín. The story corresponds to the first-person narrator's coming of age in his society, of his taking stock of the sexual and political hypocrisies of that world, and of his need to record an alternate vision which may not necessarily provide a great sense of human fulfillment but which at least has the virtue of being his own personal reality (Martínez; Gómez Ocampo). Thus, Vallejo's text, like so many examples of the Bildungsroman, moves through two conscious realms, that of public reality and its corresponding official morality and that of a world truer to the protagonist's actual perceptions of intense personal needs that are often distorted by their conflict with official morality.

This disjunction has traditionally led to a sense of despair and even cynicism on the part of the individual in view of the suffering that it may occasion in someone who cannot abide by its falseness, a suffering that is often given tragic dimensions in the case of proscribed sexual desires. But in the case of Vallejo's first-person protagonist, there is an insouciant acceptance of the ethical imperative to forge a private reality that will destroy the burden of official morality. Although such an effort may not yield optimal results, *El fuego secreto* details an inventory of reasonable strategies in striving toward it. The conclusion of the novel, after the protagonist has fulfilled the social rite of receiving his university diploma from the hands of his father, a national senator for the Conservative Party, is an apocalyptic vision in which the statue of Bolívar, the Liberator who is the symbol of Colombia's repressive macho society, is consumed in the secret fires of the protagonist's inner world: "Lo último que ví fue el parque, y en el parque, en llamas, el Libertador, la estatua. Ardía el mármol, ardía el bronce, ardía el caballo, ardía el héroe. ¡Adiós gran hijueputa!"[8] (188). This *adiós* cast after the burning Liberator cannot be other than a definitive rejection of the hypocritical values represented by public monuments.

El fuego secreto is the protagonist's attempt to chronicle his transit through his social world and to stake out for himself a realm of personal freedom beyond the confines of public morals. His voyage of discovery is centered on the low dives and bars of Medellín's Calle Junín (named after one of the decisive battles of the War of Liberation led by Bolívar). These haunts are frequented not only by individuals who are alternately ignored and oppressed by the denizens of official morality, but by the very individuals who in their guise of public men are the champions of its structures:

> Pero de esa turbamulta que pasaba por Junín, óigame usted, algunos después sonaron mucho: a mediodía, a las tres, a las seis, a las nueve en

> los noticieros cacaraquientes de la radio. De alcaldes ellos o inspectores, procuradores, directores, gobernadores, contralores, personeros, tesoreros, cada quien con su codiciado cargo público y su mujer, privada, un adefesio, sus hijos, el radio que ahora suena y el televisor, y esos dobles apellidos ramplones de Antioquia [. . .] y la soberbia infinita de la ignorancia.[9] (182)

The *usted* of this quote is the reader, who is asked both to be an accomplice of the narrator and to separate himself from values of sexual repression that the novel details with a considerable sense of humor. Defiantly, the narrator assumes the legitimacy of the demand "Pues que cambie [el mundo] porque yo no pienso cambiar"[10] (183), and in so doing he separates himself from the tradition of narratives detailing the annihilation of the protagonist by a dystopian social dynamic unable to accommodate his sexuality. Part of the narrator's assessment of the hypocrisy of his social world and the construction of a personal ethic of sexual conduct in conformance with his own identity is the plea to the reader to understand the limits on the narrator's chronicle, both as an interpretation of his own identity and the experiences related to it and as an assessment of the peculiar circumstances of other individuals, each concerned with his own intimate struggle. (I use masculine references here in order to underscore the clearly male-centered scope of the novel.) As a consequence, the narrator is able to adopt an ironic stance toward his process of narration and to challenge the reader's expectations of what he is able to depict and interpret:

> los eternos interrogantes del hombre que no tienen respuesta. ¿Fluyendo? Esa es la palabra, la gran palabra de Heráclito: panta rhei, todo fluye. Fluye este libro que es remedo de la vida como fluye el río, potamos, donde me baño yo y se baña el hipopótamo, y juntos vamos pasando con las aguas cambiantes.[11] (142)

By contrast to those texts that propose a consolidated interpretation of social reality, an interpretation whose possibilities the narrator attacks and even links on several occasions to the official moral code he is rejecting ("¡Al diablo con el gobierno y con la novela!"[12] [135; see also 165 and 179), the narrator employs an uninterrupted flow of details (the novel has no internal divisions beyond the paragraphic) that provide a cumulative image of the ethics he has discovered for himself. In the place of a novelistic structure that is marked by the assimilation of a coherent and rigidified social code whose omnipresent force is the source of the annihilation of gay antiheroes, Vallejo's narrator set out to transcend this dynamic by substituting a free-form narrative that can move between the repressed and the repressive levels of the social text in a process of analysis, revision, and debunking of public morality. For an individual like Vallejo's narrator, the process involves stepping back from or out of that world (to whatever extent self-distancing is possible) in order to describe the machinations of its repressive hypocrisy, while understanding at the same time that description can never be more than a feeble attempt to go beyond its compact dynamics; such a limitation is the coefficient of the extent to which the individual's identity, whether acquiescent or rebellious, is determined by society. Thus, his narrative moves between two ironic poles of frustration:

> Yo soy muy dado a presumir que al abrir por primera vez los ojos el mundo lo descubrí yo.[13] (13)

> La vida está llena de condicionales. He dado cuenta, si acaso, de lo que dijo el doctor: un mísero uno por ciento. El resto, por una razón o por otra, se me escapa. La literatura es así, e igual la vida: uno no es, ni vive, ni escribe lo que quiere, sino lo que puede.[14] (187)

Yet it is this ethics of "lo que puede" that marks the protagonist's dual project, his personal identity based on the circumstance of his homosexuality and his personal narrative based on the need to describe his social world, which must be legitimated against prevailing hypocrisies.

In order to pursue this plan, it is obvious that the narrator must assume an ethical pose of personal superiority toward this world, including the ability (and the privilege) to point out what he considers to be its hypocrisies. He must also assume an interpretive stance that allows him the sense of transcending the horizons of the social code within which he was formed. Either assumption is not without considerable problems with reference to the right and the possibility of the individual of adopting such postures, and even if one concedes the legitimacy of the individual's defying the moral code of his society on the basis of higher personal commitments, the metaphysical question remains as regards the degree to which the structures of meaning, linguistic or social, can be set aside in favor of an interpretive gesture that dismisses their established prevalence.

It is for this reason that the ironic stance of the narrator is important, for it is his ability to gauge the difficulties and setbacks of constructing a personal identity within the confines of official morality and to gauge the problems of construction to limitations of narrative representation that gives *El fuego secreto* interest as an account of the discovery of an alternate social reality beneath the façade of public life. Although the novel proposes that the Bar Miami, a typical establishment on Calle Junín, is the "centro del centro, corazón de la tierra"[15] (13), the narrator's preoccupation with the strategies of narrative representation underscores the inherent complications of such a proposal.

El fuego secreto works, therefore, as an example of one related series of narrative conventions for the task of establishing an analytical coordination between social hypocrisy and personal sexuality. It is especially effective in proposing a working through of the necessary conflicts of such a project in order to define the problematical legitimacy of the protagonist's view of himself and his world: "no buscando la distorsión de la realidad. ¿Para qúe iba a buscarla? Siempre la he encontrado de sobra distorsionada"[16] (169).

3

Another version of the possibility of a release from the constraints conventional sexual morality imposes on homosexuality is offered by the Brazilian Aguinaldo Silva in his *Primeira carta aos andróginos* (First Letter to the Androgynes, 1975). After confronting four primary realms of social persecution represented by the family home, the neighborhood, the bar, and one individually established abode (represented by the rooming house where he lives), the first-person protagonist Davi/Salomão finds himself whisked off in a space capsule to Phaeton, the lost planet between Mars and Jupiter, where an androgynous Garden of Eden restores his sense of human dignity and wholeness (the latter in the sense of the recovery of a shattered organic human identity) and where he is able to propose a new Adamic lineage that challenges the destructive cowardliness of the old Earth.

Although *andrógino* in Portuguese is often used as a vague synonym of homosexual, in Silva's novel it is used with exactitude to describe an Edenic androgyny whereby all of the members of an entire human community can interact erotically beyond the boundaries of the rigid and, therefore, debasing sexuality of the capitalistic and bourgeois society the narrator leaves behind in his journey of access to a utopia of pansexuality:

> E finalmente ela gritou, goza, Salomão, goza porque é preciso, e num rugido a meio tom precipitei-me por ela adentro e lá no fundo, entre grandes barris onde o vinho cheio de tradições fermentava, fazendo funcionar as máquinas de fabricar tantos mistérios, depositei minha semente—a primeira nessa terra gloriosamente jovem plantada pela mão do homem—e o fiz enquanto ouvia—meio distante, quase próximo—o coro selvagem e violento dos animaes de Faeton, sua concórdia mesmo quando tinham de matar para viver obedecendo, apenas, às leis da natureza.[17] (Silva, *Primeira carta* 124–125)

Silva offers, in the place of one more pathetic autobiography of the humiliation of a man who seeks sexual fulfillment with other men, the possibility of an inner transcendence that, within the novel's fictional world, literarily casts him into another universe of meaning. While Davi/Salomão experiences his share of scorn and persecution (the novel's composition is specified by the author as 1967–71, the height of recent moralizing military regimes in Brazil), and, indeed, his final humiliation at the hands of the police is described in Christological images (93ff.), Phaeton, whether as an alternate physical reality or as an emotional escapist fantasy, offers him the vision of a realm where the monsters of hatred, exploitation, and oppression can be conquered in order to (re)attain a Marcusian Eden of integral human sexuality.

Like Phaeton, Silva's utopian discourse, which is marked by the emergence of the noncolloquial (i.e., ceremonial) *tu* as the form of Edenic address, posits for the reader an otherworldly realm that postulates the possibility of a sexual (re)integration in the place of the real-world, identity-fragmenting homophobia that is the shared experience of both the reader and the character on Earth. This is why, although the reader is never directly evoked by Silva's narrator, the novel is presented as a letter to *andróginos*. Actual readers may not share Davi/Salomão's sexual history. Yet the text as narrative discourse is itself a utopian realm that can, against the ample dystopian evidence presented by real-world human experience, serve itself as an alternate realm. In this realm, the seemingly irresolvable conflicts of an adequate human sexual integration can be solved through the agency of the narrator's emigration from Earth to Phaeton. That is, fantastic though it may seem to readers firmly anchored in the morass of oppressive sexuality typified by the Brazil of the narrator, the novel offers the image of a potential release from dystopia and the attainment of the utopian Phaeton. The closing words of the text, "OS HOMENS QUE SE CUIDEM"[18] (134), is as much a promise of the Tlön-like infiltration of the real-world Earth by the principles of the Edenic Phaeton as it is a warning to the homophobic legions that drive Davi/Salomão to escape to the "lost" realm of Phaeton.

The concept of a lost planet implies one that was once present and that can be recovered, a dominant axiom of several varieties of utopian thinking. The narrator's Adamic experiences on Phaeton speak, much in the terms of traditional Marxian reintegration, of the recovery of a spiritual—and, therefore, erotic—wholeness that humanity once had and that was lost or repressed by the modern world of destructive exploitation and its concomitant hatred of the body in its erotic plenitude, in the denial both of the whole body and of various activities not generally considered sexual. Significantly, Silva's Adam addresses the repressed aspects of the official Christian account of the originary Eden by describing the sexual union of Eve (Sibila in the novel) with her own sons, clearly necessary in order to provide successive generations (unless the sons were mated with a sister unnamed in the Biblical account—in either case an incestuous relationship). And, in keeping with the polymorphous sexuality of this renewed realm forged by human beings for their own needs (124), the narrator describes his own union with his sons in the exploration of the full range of sexuality permitted in Phaeton (128; the missing or suppressed "combinatory" variants are Sibila's and Adam's unions with their daughters). While on Earth, the narrator experiences an unfulfilled sexual desire toward his father; Phaeton allows him to make love to his son as he would have wanted his father to make love to him rather than cast him out of the house as an abomination of nature.

Silva's novel, like much utopian writing, is necessarily schematic, with Phaeton providing a counterimage to Earth, just as the novel as fictional narrative provides a counterimage to documentary accounts of the repression of eroticism, homosexual or otherwise, in the real-world society of the reader. Phaeton may be understood as a sort of science-fiction metaphor or as a compensatory escapist fantasy induced by the everyday woes of an omnipresent homophobia, although it is important to distinguish between viewing utopian visions as mere fantasy and seeing them as logical extensions of nascent, yet repressed, potentialities in the currently existing society. Phaeton functions in Silva's novel primarily as a sign for a utopian social world that can free individuals from an oppressive moral code, just as the narrative text—a real cultural document in a real social world—can be an alternate realm of experience wherein lies the possibility for transformation.

4

Originally published in 1983, the Argentine Susana Torres Molina's *Dueña y señora* (Lady and Mistress) is notable for being the first collection by any Latin American writer of explicitly lesbian stories. The paucity in Latin America of lesbian writing (whether identifiable because of unequivocal references to female homoeroticism or by virtue of a critical hermeneutics applied to a text not generally viewed as dealing with lesbianism) created immediate interest in Torres Molina's book, explaining in part the three printings in five months. Moreover, the nature of the author's stories represents a significant departure from the canon of homosexual writing that underscores the tragic consequences of homoerotic feelings and experiences. While the exposition of homosexuality within a setting where homoeroticism is not treated as deviant continues to verge on the utopian, the repudiation of the consequences of sustaining the image of the homosexual as the pitiful victim of tragedy and the insistence on openly assuming an aggressive stance of gay dignity, the most radical variant of which is the defense of the radical naturalization of homosexuality by society, contribute to the attraction of writing in which participants in homosexuality assume a defiant posture.

Whether in the form of outrageous behavior on the part of characters in a story who behave as though there were no untoward consequences deriving from their open homoeroticism or a narrator's challenge to the prejudices of a presumed unreconstructed reader, writing that projects a naturalized image of homosexuality continues to be in the minority and, therefore, that much more compelling. Like ethnic writers who discovered that there was a necessary transition to be made from the portrayal of the human suffering of racial discrimination to the benefit to be derived from the (defiant) depiction of a (defiant) naturalization of personal and collective aspirations, authors on homoerotic topics (who rarely now include those unsympathetic to gay rights) have begun to explore contexts where homosexual experiences are affirmed despite the continued hostility of wider social structures. In the case of José Rafael Calva's novel discussed below, the postulation is essentially fantastic, and therefore exceptionally brash as a flouting of the real-world limits of biology in addition to the contravening of social codes (concerning feminist plots that, by the conventions of masculinist literature, may appear to be outrageous, see Miller). In Torres Molina's stories, the stance assumed is the insouciant pursuit of a personal ethic as though it were completely legitimatized within those social codes.

Torres Molina has established herself as a dramatist, particularly with *Extraño juguete* (Strange Toy, 1978), which is notable for its exploration of role playing as part of a questioning of social codes (D. W. Foster, "Identidades polimórficas"); *Dueña y señora* is her first published fiction. Enrique Medina's commentary on the stories, which appears on the back cover, underscores the iconoclastic nature of her writing: "Este libro nos habla de lugares comunes, trivialidades, falsa concepción de la vida por parte de los que integran rebaños. Desfilan personajes y comportamientos que Susana Torres Molina derriba sin piedad; escribe multiplicándose narrativamente, desmitificando tabúes machistas incrustados como esquirlas innatas en nuestro lastimado cuerpo social." [19]

Undoubtedly, the most immediately notable characteristic of *Dueña y señora*—the title is a troping, via a gender change, on the master metaphor of the patriarchy, "dueño y señor" (lord and master)—is its participation in the new democratic climate in Argentina and the possibility of a cultural production that openly counters established social codes defended both implacably and violently by recent military tyrannies. Therefore, the first reading of Torres Molina's book is the general one suggested by Medina's comments: as an open challenge to a particular set of repressive social values broader than the issues of homosexuality or, more specifically, lesbianism. Yet homosexuality and the demand that it be naturalized within the "cuerpo social" must surely be considered one of the most pointed tests for a democratic pluralistic culture in Argentina or anywhere because of the wealth of taboos it involves. As a consequence, it is not surprising that texts like *Dueña y señora* have surfaced since the return to democracy in Argentina (actually, the book was published before the official cancellation of censorship, but with little apprehension of the already-disabled military government) and that writing on the limits of the social code of the respectable society that considered itself the main support of the authoritarian culture of the military assumes particular prominence (D. W. Foster, "Los parámetros").

The essentially utopian stance that it is possible to assume the naturalization of phenomena like homosexuality (utopian because the social code demanding the censorship of certain forms of cultural production has not been simply wiped away by the cancellation of formal censorship) is all the more defiant for refusing to accept the long since conventionalized tragic interpretation of the homosexual protagonist. Within the latter's world, narrative schemata trace the inevitable suffering and emotional, psychological derangement, often attended by suicide, of the sexual deviant; in the former, the ability to pursue affirmatively one's sexual needs within either a hostile world or—should the text be truly utopian—a tolerant one provides the point of reference for an image of the acceptance of the complexities of life (see Schaefer-Rodríguez).

Where the insouciant textual represention of homosexuality is of interest is in the challenge to the reader's normalized social and cultural codes. The tragic representation of homosexuality quite often involves, as many of the works examined in this study exemplify, a concern for the adequate representation of sexual preferences that are either excluded or denigrated by the dominant social language. By contrast, the representation of a utopian or quasiutopian nature—such as the lesbian writing of the American Rita Mae Brown or the Canadian Jane Rule—involves a problematic textuality because of the possibility readers may not accept the naturalized parameters of sexuality promoted by the narrative. By flagrantly disregarding established social norms, or, especially, by confronting the hypocrisy of norms that are shown to be disconsonant with official, perhaps even constitutional, myths, such comic writing exchanges the risk of a dismissive marginalization (because it has "nothing to do with an appropriately ordered society") for a radically deconstructive view of what may constitute satisfying interpersonal relations.

Torres Molina's concluding story, of the nine that make up *Dueña y señora*, is illustrative of this comic mode. "Impresiones de una futura mamá" (Impressions of a Mother-to-Be), which plays on the instantly evoked images of a zero-degree heterosexual motherhood (and, in Argentina, on the evocation of a chain of middle-class maternity shops called La Futura Mamá), is a series of fragments that propose the possibility of a lesbian lover ending up pregnant as a consequence of her erotic idyll with the feminine narrator.

Torres Molina's narrator avails herself of the structure of the venerable narrative commonplace of lover-meets-lover (wherein boy-meets-girl is converted into the scandalous dyke-meets-femme, where the very implied terminology continues to be terrifying for the homophobic) in order, point by point, to transform the expected or neutral relationship of assertive male and passive female (with the various attendant antonymic clichés like imposing versus swooning, expressive versus silent, and so on) into a paradigm of a lesbian relationship that results in the socially valuable pregnancy of María. Understandably, it is the active partner who narrates, with laconic masculinity, of course, how she meets, courts, seduces, and impregnates María, who, in the tradition of her namesake, is a shadowy and passive witness to her maternal role.

Torres Molina takes the risk of converting her lesbian lovers into parodying caricatures in order to superimpose their legitimate erotic relationship (per the extrapolation the reader performs on the basis of the other stories in the text) on the dominant heterosexual matrix. From the opening sentence-paragraph, "Conozco a María"[20] (83), "Impresiones" is essentially a schematic rewriting of a soap opera script of idyllic love. The result of this choice of narrative mode is the inevitable use of the fossilized language of amorous description, coupled with the unavoidable presence of an aggressively phallocentric perspective of the erotic union, so much so that the cluster of sequential images assumes an immediately masculine connotation:

> Ese es el momento en que todos mis sentidos están concentrados en mis dedos sobre su textura clitoriana, como un experto delincuente que intentara abrir una cerradura.
>
> Hay que contentarse con pequeñas acciones, sutiles y precisas y al mismo tiempo estar atenta a cualquier gesto revelador. Alerta al menor signo. Sin perder el ritmo. Intentándolo una vez y una vez más.
>
> Mis labios dentro de los suyos y su lengua penetrándome sin piedad.
>
> Siento en la exigencia y agitación de nuestros cuerpos en el contacto cada vez más vertiginoso y convulsionado de nuestras caricias y abrazos, que el gran momento se avecina. Y tan en lo cierto estoy, que ella se abre a mí como la más maravillosa y exótica de las flores salvajes. Y es ahí, cuando yo disparo hacia sus entrañas vírgenes y deseosas, el líquido vital.[21] (92)

The language of this passage is a broad burlesque of the worst clichés of heterosexual male pornography: the mixture of sexual hydraulics with images of heavy-breathing emotional response, the alternation of directly descriptive vocabulary with pretentious metaphors (e.g., "textura clitoriana"), the disjunction between the sensual crescendo of the action described and the clinical detachment of the measured periods of the narrative voice. Whatever else we may claim male-oriented pornography to be, one of the distinctive stylistic features of those texts generally agreed to merit such classification is this kind of trite, because endlessly repeated, discourse. Torres Molina's accommodation of the narrative pattern of heterosexual romance to insouciant lesbian lovemaking is especially outrageous because, unlike the private worlds of a conventionalized forbidden and tragic homosexual lust, it does not posit a separate symbolic realm for the elaboration of the form of sexual coupling. Rather, it naturalizes that coupling by conveniently fitting it into a preexisting erotic structure, thereby seeking to demonstrate that it is not substantively deviant from the sexual ethics of that structure.

But of course it is. Where the outrageousness of Torres Molina's heavy-handed accommodation becomes strikingly evident is in the clash between the unstoppable orgasmic culmination in penetration and ejaculation and the subversion of the role of male aggressiveness in this culmination by the linguistic markers that betray the unconventional gender of the narrator. This occurs when the otherwise conventional maleness of the narrator (cf. "como *un* expert*o* delincuente") is qualified by the statement "al mismo tiempo estar atent*a*." (The adjective "Alerta" that occurs in the following sentence is actually common, although it is curious that Spanish has normalized the feminine form, which is also both singular and plural, over the archaic *alerto*.) This sly deviation from the presumed masculine gender of the passage, confirmed by both the conventional texture of the linguistic expression and the actions it represents, is the breaking of the symbolic code of sexual stereotyping necessary to separate "Impresiones" from the schematic narrative pattern it employs and to place it within the alternate deconstructive mode of lesbian writing. This rupture is confirmed by the subsequent concluding segment, which closes off the display of traditional pride of the masculine progenitor with a defiantly contradictory exclamation:

> Más que intuir tengo la certeza de que de aquí en más, mi vida no tendrá un momento de tregua.
> Pero eso es justamente lo que he elegido. No dar ni pedir tregua.
> ¡Las mujeres somos así![22] (93)

This coda, which is also the final sentence in "Impresiones," is actually anticipated by a slightly deviant assertion earlier in this segment: "Y yo haré las cortinas, porque María odia coser."[23] Taken as a whole, Torres Molina's stories in *Dueña y señora* are not particularly innovative in their treatment of lesbianism; certainly, they lack the elaborate verbal synthesis of Pizarnik's *La condesa sangrienta*. Moreover, the use of stereotyped narrative models—what I have called soap opera formulas—leads to an inescapable triteness of expression. However, it is the transformations Torres Molina introduces into these formulas that make her stories of interest within the context of the production of a deconstructive lesbian writing, particularly as it relates to the textual features of a comic or utopian mode that presumes the naturalization of homosexuality within prevailing social codes. That such a revindication has yet to take place is what confirms and sustains the outrageousness of this mode of writing, while at the same time the textual strategies of naturalization can make sense only within the context of a potential revindication and the accompanying adjustment of the social code and its definition of what is natural sexuality.

5

In a parenthesis within a parenthesis, in his "Prólogo" which comes as a parenthesis within the text of his novel in the form of a penultimate chapter, José Rafael Calva states that one of the goals of *Utopía gay* (Gay Utopia, 1983) is to show that a homosexual relationship need not conform to the Wilde-Bosie model. This model, whereby Oscar Wilde was cruelly victimized both by his lover and by a vengeful, self-righteous society, has served too often as a paradigm for an inevitably tragic or at least pathetic homoerotic relationship: there is frequently a high price to be paid for a gay presentation of self which involves the gay person's relation with straight society and not just the cost of passion with a gay lover. It may be utopian to believe that a gay relationship can just be lasting, satisfying, and free from melodramatic suffering, but Calva—certainly echoing numerous American writers—wishes to entertain in his novel such a possibility (see also the protagonist of Walmir Ayala's 1965 play, *Nosso filho vai ser mãe* [Our Son Is Going to Be a Mother]).

Beginning with the simple fact that Adrián finds himself pregnant by Carlos, the novel explores the consequences of such a logical impossibility (yet see Delpech concerning the recurrent motif of "el hombre preñado" in Hispanic literature). Calva builds the novel around variations on the formula "As impossible as it may seem, the fact is that . . . ," and the novel juxtaposes the unreality of such an event and the characters' reactions to it and what the consequences of it might be for a new model of human relations beyond the repressive structures that inhibit—and usually destroy—the chances for satisfactory (typically, male) gay relationships of marriage-like commitment. Obviously, Calva's characters are committed to one version of a homosexual relationship, one that contemplates the naturalness of a male-male (or female-female) marriage within the confines of conventional heterosexual unions sanctified by law and custom.

Adrián and Carlos have ample space in the novel to talk, but mostly to meditate in large chunks of stream-of-consciousness, about the implications of their version of marriage and the "miracle" of Adrián's pregnancy. While the characters speak out against repressive moral principles, typically embodied in their Latin American society by the Church, it is not difficult to miss the implication that the narrative nucleus of *Utopía gay* is a transformation of the story of the Divine Conception. As an Illogical Conception, it propels the dialogues and interior monologues of the various characters in their exploration of the radical reshuffling of semantic, biological, and social categories that has been made possible by Adrián's pregnancy:

> No puede ser. Simplemente no puede ser y sin embargo he visto las radiografías y no cabe la menor duda que dentro de Adrián se desarrolla un feto vivo. Ya ni cabe la noción de que el sistema no lo permite. Esto es nuestra salida de la humanidad, seremos un grupo aparte de entes extraños. Lo mismo da vivir como Adrián quiere o no. De todos modos ya no seremos como los demás, ni siquiera como los demás homosexuales. Yo que jamás creí que como homosexuales éramos como los demás y que por eso vivimos en sociedad castrados pero en la sociedad, ocultos y perseguidos pero en la sociedad. No cabe duda que la vida nos revela algo cada día pero este hijo mío nos está sacando del mundo.[24] (Calva 84)

This "moving outside the world" is the utopian basis for Adrián's extensive meditations. Adrián is the miraculous figure of this narrative of annunciation, and it is appropriate that he be mostly involved in attempting to define what the consequences of his pregnancy are. He is not free from internal contradiction in his exposition—in fact, he alternates very rational thinking of an acceptedly conventional sort with campy rhetorical extravagances that challenge the value of such thinking—but Adrián has no reservations about the choices he has made. What at first seems to be emotional nonsense comes to sound convincing to his lover Carlos, who, as a professor of philosophy, is tied both to conventional modes of thought and to primmer traditional Marxist schematics (which come in for some hard knocks in the novel for their legendary homophobic posture): "Si antes me sentía un desmadre ahora sé que lo soy y todo desde que Adrián comenzó a decir cosas interesantes cuando se embarazó y se puso a hablar de la vida que me puse a releer a los existencialistas para darme cuenta que cuando le decía o asentía mentalmente no era asimilándolos a ellos sino la peculiar visión de Adrián"[25] (167).

Adrián's "peculiar visión" is the belief in the utopian possibility of a relationship that will radically alter social and sexual schemes in favor of healthier human beings. Some readers (leaving aside those who will find the subject too painful to confront) will approach *Utopía gay* as an example of science fiction. Since science fiction functions on the basis of narrative schemata that do not necessarily obey those that we associate with the "real" world, it permits the exploration of unheard of possibilities in, among other things, human relations and social arrangements, what Robert E. Scholes has called "structuralist fabulation." In the more traditional realm of utopian literature, Calva's novel may be taken as an extended metaphor that functions less because Adrián is really pregnant in this or other narrative worlds, than because he and others are convinced that he is willing to entertain the implications of such a state. But, while Calva's narrative does not cover Adrián's accouchement, some readers will be able to read it as no more or less fantastic than the traditional story of the Divine Conception. If the latter, as a major event of Christian mythology, involves the acceptance of a radical shift in the signs of what is really possible, Adrián's proposals demand no less. Calva, to judge by his prologue and by the discourse of his characters, is earnest in the proposal of such a utopian possibility, and it would be difficult to see *Utopía gay* as the campy narrative a plot summary of it might imply.

What *Utopía gay* proposes is a world of redefined semantic dimensions that would allow for the realization of the amorous idyll Adrián proposes. His discourse, as well as that of his lover Carlos, who comes to accept the naturalness of its irrationality, is abetted by a process of verbalizing that strives to go beyond the confines of the conventional, repressive, and homophobic Western-Mexican society the couple is faced with. Throughout, language is an instrument to transcend the limitations of this society. Transcendence is achieved first in the grammatical realignments necessitated by the acceptance of Adrián's condition and subsequently by the extensive processes of dreaming, imagining, and fantasizing in order to confirm and legitimate this vision of an erotic utopia. Because the novel is based primarily on the characters' stream-of-consciousness interior monologues, the intrusions of conventional reality, including the denial that Adrián is pregnant, can be glossed over by the power of verbalizing a more fulfilling, more natural utopian world. Thus, there is a homology between Calva's novel and Adrián's inner narrative as verbal spaces that strive to postulate and then impose on the reader a sign system of the homosexual experience radically different from the one codified by conventional accounts. What is utopian about Calva's novel is less the possibility of Adrián's pregnancy than the legitimacy of his relationship with his lover as decent, satisfying, and, ultimately, natural—precisely the sort of projection of the inherent potentialities in the present social world referred to above, rather than a fantasy that may be dismissed as merely escapist. Undoubtedly, the latter is the "natural" reaction to Calva's narrative proposal, although one may also insist that the degree to which the reader is able to accept as coherent the proposal of *Utopía gay* becomes a reliable metric of the ability to contemplate radical realignments in a world customarily viewed as completely natural.

CHAPTER NINE

CONCLUSIONS

Michel Foucault has maintained that, far from being the victim of repression in our modern bourgeois society, sexuality in fact constitutes the fundamental discourse of modern Western culture (Foucault; Cohen, "Foucauldian Necrologies"); rather than repression, what is at issue is the definition, within always more circumscribed parameters, of a permissible, socially redeeming sexuality. Moreover, the very notion of sexuality is an ideological construct of that discourse, both in what forms of sexuality are contemplated and in what is allowed or proscribed. By extension, the whole thematics of sexuality, including homosexuality, is an integral element of such a constructed ideology: "[There occurred] the formation of a 'reverse' discourse: homosexuality began to speak in its own behalf, to demand that its legitimacy of 'naturality' be acknowledged, often in the same vocabulary, using the same categories by which it was medically disqualified" (Foucault 101). From the point of view of Foucault's "deconstruction" of the hypothesis of the repression of a discourse of sexuality, it becomes possible to survey a body of cultural and social texts for the presence, implicit or otherwise, of this complex semiotics of obsessive sexuality.

Yet it continues to be the accepted view that Latin American literature is especially silent about sexual themes, and even more so when it comes to lesbianism and gayness and the belief maintained by the spokespersons of certain societies or social classes that homosexuality simply does not exist or exists only within clearly marginal enclaves. As a consequence, not even the bourgeoning feminist criticism of Latin American literature deals much with sexuality, despite the ways in which it is a central issue for Anglo-American criticism. Nevertheless, it is now becoming possible to establish an inventory of homosexual writing for Latin America.

What I have attempted to do, rather than survey all of the growing list of those works in which female and male homosexuality is the central narrative issue, is to identify those texts in which one dominant concern is a grappling with the discourse of sexuality—first by overcoming the much-touted silence about this variety of human sexuality (cf. Norton iii) and then by textualizing (whether consciously or unconsciously cannot be adequately determined) the problems of writing about a subject that cannot be satisfactorily accommodated within the dominant discourse. Undoubtedly, much of the writing one could identify echoes the themes and strategies of representation to be found in major U.S. and European texts, which would attest to the multinational nature of contemporary fiction. However, we also know that Latin American writing as a whole is marked by a manifest interest in exploring varieties of social and historical consciousness, as befits texts produced under the difficult circumstances of life in countries where censorship and repressive public morality may inhibit cultural expression.

The point to be made about these works, what justifies bringing them together both as a representative sample of contemporary Latin American narrative and as an important subcategory of Latin American gay writing, is that they show a concern for a legitimate discourse about homosexuality, especially one that calls into question the "reverse" as well as the "obverse" discourse about which Foucault speaks. A metafictional interest on the part of the writer is only in part a reflex of how to write under the specific circumstances of Latin America and how to make the act of text production meaningful in a society the writer recognizes as particularly repressive. It bespeaks also the preoccupation with the status of a discourse about homosexuality, the very notion itself, in contemporary Western culture. Therefore, the attempts on the part of the approximately two dozen writers examined in this study to correlate the personal experiences associated with homosexuality and social dynamics, on the one hand, and the nature of such experiences and how to go about reporting on them in works of fiction, on the other, makes these texts germane to the issues of both contemporary Latin American narrative and a larger Western social text.

There are, it seems to me, three ways to justify a study on homosexual writing, especially if one maintains in perspective a doubt as to whether homosexuality should be a bracketed conduct in the first place.

The first argument is the sociocultural one: to the extent that homosexuality continues to be defined by our culture as a "problem," then it is legitimate to seek out those works that accept such a definition. The ideological focus they marshal may serve either to sustain the treatment of homosexuality as a social or psychological problem (as in the novels by the Chileans D'Halmar and Wácquez or the play by González Castillo, for example) or to explore the oppression such definitions create, which is one facet of Caminha's pioneering narrative. However, it is the decision to include only content analysis of these dimensions that makes James Levin's study of the gay novel in the United States of such limited critical usefulness.

The second approach involves the attempt to identify specific lesbian and gay concerns in cultural texts, whether those issues are to be discovered as being overtly present (usually the case) or ciphered (the probable strategy of Rafael Arévalo Martínez's story "El hombre que parecía un caballo"). Such a dimension may be relatively superficial, as in the focus on denouncing generalized homophobia (the Mexicans Zapata, Calva, and Ceballos Maldonado), or it may be richly complex, as in the view of homosexuality as a subset of the code of power in Donoso or in a dominant structure of social oppression (the bulk of Argentine novels dealt with, beginning with Manuel Puig, whose fiction has been excluded from this study since it has been so extensively analyzed by other critics [Kerr; Muñoz]).

As appropriate as these matrixes might be, however, they do not sufficently capture the originality of Latin American gay and lesbian writing as announced in the introduction to this study. I refer to the sustained emphasis on metatextual matters, whether in the form of discontinuities and ruptures in the text the critic might identify or in the specifically self-reflective nature of the narrative act. The models that have been discussed that involve a reduplication of narrative (e.g., Chocrón, Zapata, Ceballos Maldonado, Silva, Molloy, Arenas), intertextuality with established cultural codes (e.g., Villordo, Torres Molina, Penteado), a preoccupation with the complex interrelationships between viewing and naming (e.g., Denser, Pizarnik, Correas, Vallejo), and the imperative to develop a sexual discourse that naturalizes the proscribed and the taboo (e.g., Molloy, Villordo, Arenas, Rios, Arcidiácono) are all texts that impose a discussion of cultural manifestations of homosexuality on the basis of the problematics of emplotment, narrativity, and semantic configurations. From this point of view, the works examined in this study, works that are representative of a far larger (and in some cases, as yet ill-mapped) corpus, are compelling less because of their specific thematics than for the ways in which they undertake to construct an ideologically coherent discourse about sexual matters.

If an attention to literary texts solely on the basis of the fact that they deal with this or that theme of sexuality can, regrettably, serve to sustain the prejudicial and repressive bracketing of many dimensions of human eroticism, the analysis of the discourse processes they deploy in the search for adequate forms of cultural textualization can, quite to the contrary, contribute to revealing the ways (successful and foreshortened) they undertake to interact with the social text in the interests of historical revaluation.

It should be obvious to the reader by this point that this study has been the record of a necessary, intrinsically predictable failure. I am not referring to the localized errors in facts, interpretations, and assessments that may beleaguer the individual fragments, but to the attempt to propose a reading of homosexuality in Latin American narrative. Such a failure cannot help but echo the radical impossibility of configuring a discourse of sexuality that lies outside the received Judeo-Christian tradition whose compactness is readily apparent to the most jejune of observers. To the extent that it may be impossible to configure a life outside that tradition and to propose a narrative (re)reading of the ideologies that sustain it, along with the frustrations of a critical enterprise that charts skirmishes of counterhegemonic consciousness, the very underlying assumptions of the present critical enterprise are called into question.

The necessity of failure, in the sense that Jameson outlines in "Architecture and the Critique of Ideology"—that is, an understanding of the futility of proposing ideologically contestatory positions within a system of aggressive closure and exclusion—must lead one to the realization that the narrative project described cannot transcend either the systematic de-existence of homosexuality as a legitimate sociocultural discourse (or even as an ontological state of being) or the incontrovertible ridiculousness of its Utopian proposals (ridiculous because they fail to correspond to anything taken consensually to be a viable social praxis). The possibility of specific, bracketed challenges to sociocultural hegemony, in their isolation from the canonized cultural text, does no more than bear unintentionally eloquent testimony to that very hegemony, which is why the forms of opposition inscribe themselves as fundamentally extravagant and fantastic, categories that mark the distance from a ground zero of dominant meanings.

The critical discourse that accompanies an artistic project of such radical foreclosure—which, as I announced in my preface, is nothing more nor less than the denial that such a project can exist in the first place, either because homosexuality continues to have no valid existence for so many or because, when it does exist, it is meaningless in any of its facets as an activity that is understood as purely antisocial and illegal—has no point at which it can make an appeal, contrapuntal or otherwise, to the prevailing sexual ideology: at best it is an exercise in cultural curiosities (the indulgence of alterity in the name of broadmindedness), while at worst it is the consecration of a demonic anticulturalism.

Yet herein must lie the validation of any critical project that would insist on echoing that which is barely tolerable if not directly unspeakable: not so much the challenge to a cultural system (in this case academic criticism) to accept a radical Other, as it is the demarcation, whether at the level of the literary texts that are the objects of analysis or at the level of the interpretive discourse that is predicated on the recognition of the former texts, of a sociocultural discourse that cannot be subverted with impunity. To believe otherwise is merely to collaborate, in a strangely perverse fashion, with the hegemony of those circumscriptions.

NOTES: TRANSLATIONS OF QUOTATIONS

Translations are my own unless otherwise indicated.

Epigraph

1. "What are you doing?" I asked him once we were alone in the hall.
"What do you think? It's a long story."
I don't understand a thing.
If I told you, would you understand?
I would try to at least.

2. *Adolfo Caminha's* Bom-Crioulo: *A Founding Text of Brazilian Gay Literature*

Translations in notes 1 and 3–10 are from Adolfo Caminha, *Bom-Crioulo: The Black Man and the Cabin Boy,* translated from the Portuguese by E. A. Lacey (San Francisco: Gay Sunshine Press, 1982).

1. Bom-Crioulo forgot about all his fellow-seamen, forgot everything around him and thought only [. . .] about the future of that inexplicable friendship. (56)

2. It is obvious that *Bom-Crioulo* would not win any school-contest prizes. Writing for coeds is one thing, and writing for emancipated spirits is something else. (My translation from flap.)

3. At the thought of this, Bom-Crioulo felt an extraordinary fever of eroticism, an uncontrollable ecstasy of homosexual pleasure. Now he understood clearly that only with a man, with a man like himself, could he find what in vain he had looked for among women.

He had never been aware of this anomaly in himself; never in his life did he recall having had to examine his sexual tendencies. Women left him impotent for the act of love, it's true, but it was also impossible for him to imagine, in any way, that sort of vulgar intercourse between individuals of the same sex. And yet—who could have imagined it!—it was happening to him himself now, unexpectedly, with no premeditation on his part. And what was strangest was that "things" threatened to continue this way, as a punishment for his sins, no doubt. Well, there was nothing he could do except be patient, seeing that it was "nature" herself who was imposing this punishment on him. (63–64)

4. Everybody has his own peculiarities. (30)

5. The reason for his present imprisonment, however, on the high seas, on board the corvette, was different, completely different. Bom-Crioulo had barbarously beaten up one of the second-class sailors because the fellow had dared, "without his permission," to mistreat Aleixo the cabin-boy, a handsome little blue-eyed sailor-boy, who was everybody's favourite and about whom certain "things" were rumoured.

Shackled and chained in the hold, Bom-Crioulo didn't utter a word of protest. He was admirably meek when he was in his normal state of mind and not under the influence of alcohol, and he bowed to the will of authority and resignedly awaited his punishment. He realized he had done wrong and that he should be punished, that he was no better than any other sailor, but—what the hell!—he was satisfied. He'd shown them once again that he was a man. And besides that, he was very fond of the cabin-boy, and he was sure that now he could win him over completely, the way one conquers a beautiful woman, a virgin wilderness, a land of gold. He was damn well satisfied! (35)

6. And he thought of the boy, with his blue eyes, with his blond hair, his soft, plump curves, his whole tempting being.

In his leisure hours, when he was on the job, whether it rained or whether fire fell from heaven, nothing and no one could get the boy off his mind. It was a constant obsession, a fixed, stubborn idea, a weakness of his will, which was irresistibly dominated by the desire to unite himself to the sailor-boy as though he were of the opposite sex, to possess him, to have him by his side, to love him, to enjoy him! (49)

7. As for when he was ashore, in the room on Misericórdia Street, why even mention that? There he led the life of a prince! He and the black man would sit around in their undershorts and tumble about as they pleased on the old canvas bed (which was very cool in hot weather), with the bottle of white rum standing by, by themselves there, absolutely free and independent, laughing and chatting at ease, without anyone ever coming to disturb them, with the door locked just as an extra precaution.

Only one thing vexed the cabin-boy—the black man's sexual whims. Because Bom-Crioulo was not satisfied merely with possessing him sexually at any hour of the day or night. He wanted much more; he obliged the boy to go to extremes, he made a slave, a whore of him, suggesting to him that they perform every extravagant act that came into his mind! [. . .]

And the boy, obedient and afraid, slowly unbuttoned his flannel shirt and then his trousers. He was standing, and he placed his clothes on the bed, item by item.

Bom-Crioulo's desire was satisfied. (74–75)

8. Disobedience, drunkenness and pederasty are very serious crimes. (102)

9. Aleixo hung up his blue-flannel sailor-shirt and sat in his knit undershirt, listening to the song of the water, while Miz Carolina rinsed her clothes.

They talked about Bom-Crioulo and laughed hypocritically at the black man, in low tones.

"A good fellow," pontificated the landlady, with just a touch of irony in her voice.

"Good to make a bonfire of!" added Aleixo. (104)

10. The big fag! She had never imagined that a love affair between two men could last so long and be so persistent! And a Negro at that, good Lord, an immoral, loathsome nigger like that. (119)

3. Vampire Versions of Homosexuality: Seduction and Ruin

1. This is my home, Clara . . . My garçonnière, as the French call it . . . I am the only one who comes here, and all these things that strike you as so feminine are nothing more than the refinement with which I prefer to live, creating for myself the illusion that, even if I'm all alone and sad, this bachelor's home houses a feminine spirit, one delicate and cultured like your own, giving order to everything, arranging and directing it . . .

2. Stop! . . . I don't need your explanations. You are a cad! [. . .] What do you take me for? You degenerate! . . . I've heard enough . . . I've seen enough . . . You swine! [. . .] Let me go, I tell you! . . . You make me sick! . . . (*She strikes him on the face and runs out through the back, almost sobbing* [. . .]).

3. FLÓREZ: What are you doing?

PÉREZ: Forcing you to face up to the reality of your own misery, of the misery that is ours, hidden in the shadows . . . Forcing you to forget yourself and the manhood you'd like to project, even though it's nothing but an illusion . . . I want to keep you from seeing yourself . . . from seeing us . . .

FLÓREZ: No . . . Get out of here . . . Go . . .

PÉREZ: No, I tell you. I won't go . . . I want to see you docile, just like you've always been, submissive, feminine, which is your true nature . . . That's it . . . I want you to forget that you're a man and that there lies your own infamy, but also your true happiness, just as daylight is your executioner (*he caresses him*). That's it . . . That's it . . . Just like when you were a child . . . And just like you'll be for the rest of your life, without redemption, without change. (*He bends over him until his lips graze his neck. In the semidarkness next to the door, the figure of Clara appears. She is wearing a white peignoir. She anxiously leans closer in order to hear. As the conversation seems to reach its climax, her arm extended, she slowly opens the drawer of the desk and takes out the revolver.*) You are not acting like yourself . . . Be again who you've always been . . . (*A kiss is heard, long and slow. Clara, with a rapid gesture, turns the light on in the room. The two men, startled, attempt to stand up.*)

4. You wretched men! . . . You make me sick! . . .

5. FLÓREZ: Clara! What have you done! Woman!

CLARA: (With a grave and energetic gesture, as though giving an order). Shut up! . . . It's your fault! It's your fault! . . . Take it . . . (*She hands the gun to him.*) Now! . . . Now all you have left is what you call the last evolutionary step . . . Your good evolutionary step!

6. PETRONA: Ah! . . . A queer . . . Bah! . . . I've known so many . . . And what do you say these queers are called?

JULIÁN: Hermaphrodites . . . Inverts

PETRONA: Maphrodite . . . Bah! Doctors and prosecutors are always making up strange names for the simplest of things . . . In my day we called them fairies, which is really more to the point . . . Why so many terms . . . I've known more than a hundred! . . .

JULIÁN: You have? Where? . . .

PETRONA: Where do you think? Out in the world! . . . What do you think? There are more of those maphrodites than you have any idea. How does that strike you?

7. BENITO: And . . . False women, you know? Men of "both sexes," as they say . . .

CLARA: But . . . That means . . . No! That's impossible . . . You're lying!

BENITO: Madam . . . Allow me. I'm not lying at all . . .

CLARA: But, tell me! My husband . . . What's my husband doing there? . . . What's he doing? . . .

BENITO: Well, madam . . . That's the way life is . . . How can that surprise you! Every man has some vice, you know.

8. "Be quiet, Monica!" the priest ordered.

"Why, when there are others who would speak for me, and sooner or later you'll find out what only you seem not to know?"

9. Careful! If you sleep with babies, you'll wake up wet.

10. "My poor Deusto," he said, taking both of the priest's hands in his in an unexpected movement. "You have all my best wishes and my blessing [. . .]"

11. Excessively pious women who virtually live in church.

12. "What do you say to all of that, Sem Rubi?"

There was a silence. The boy, shrugging his shoulders, had lost himself again in his task. The artist and Monica, without Deusto taking notice, had exchanged looks over his head.

"Well, nothing, really," Sem Rubi said. "You must expect things like this to happen."

"I don't understand," the Basque said, using his favorite phrase. "It must be idleness that puts such senseless things into the head of these gossipy women."

13. With a burning glow in his eyes, his voice quavering and his whole being trembling, Pedro Miguel grabbed his right hand again and fitting the ring on his hand, as though in a dream, he bent over until he brushed his ear.

"Tell me," he asserted more than asking, "do you have any idea of how much I love you?"

Deusto put both hands on his chest as though shoving him away.

"Now I know and, out of pity, I beg you not to say it. I have also seen clearly into myself!"

14. My story (the story of my relationship with A., the only one that matters) is no longer marked by grandiloquent, operatic events. The time is now past for exalted manifestations, for the suffering over not being loved as much. I am comfortably installed in the folds of day-to-day life. The banner headlines have disappeared from the tabloid of my life. The headlines, just as in an election year, are ebullient, promising. There are few misprints. Now and then an unexpected argument with A., a certain malaise that passes like crushed ice coming into contact with the skin, always warm and moist.

15. If this story is lacking in climax (or, maybe, the climaxes are the moments of despair? Or maybe the fucking codes?), maybe all it can have is an ending? Maybe only A.'s death or my own would be the real ending? Or not even this: the story would go on and on, on and on?

16. I would like to invent new insults, new ways to drag you through the mud, to demean you . . . I cannot keep telling you that you're a son-of-a-bitch, even if that's all you are . . . I would like to be able to invent worse insults . . . to really wound you in thought, word, and deed.

17. A. comes by. We fuck.

18. The need to write in this notebook had not completely disappeared. It now serves for me as a placebo to trick my impatience: I substitute the presence of A. with words that attempt to bring him closer, to sketch him in barely, even though he is not susceptible to description and only a few traces of his conduct remain. He only emerges in a few anecdotes that are almost invisible, like the stain of semen on your chest the next day.

19. Shit, no. Why do I have to think about so many stupid things? Shouldn't I just feel satisfied, happy? Why should all my dumb acts have their corollary in words, which are as useless as they are worn? One should situate himself in what is immediate, in what is palpable and limit himself to saying, if that much: A. was here with me today; we fucked. Or not even that, but to mistrust anything that can be verbalized. Only what cannot be written, formulated in words, is valid, at least as far as desire and satisfaction are concerned. Everything else is crap.

20. The impression that I've already said all of this before (before? when? a long time ago?), *in the same words.*

4. *The Deconstruction of Personal Identity*

1. After a carefully observed ritual of preparation, like a knight initiated into a very ancient cult, and when our souls had become concave, he took out the folder of his verses with the same unctuous calmness with which a priest approaches the altar. He was so grave that he commanded respect. Any laughter would have been abruptly severed in its inception.

He produced his first necklace of topazes, or better, his first series of topaz necklaces, translucent and brilliant. He raised his hands with such cadence that the rhythm extended out to three worlds. Because of the power of the rhythm, the room we were in vibrated throughout the second floor, like a trapped sphere, until it shook loose its terrestrial bonds to bear us forth in a silent aerial journey. But I was unmoved by his verses, because they were inorganic verses. They were the translucent and radiant soul of minerals; they were the symmetrical and hard soul of minerals.

2. And then, in a sudden explosion of offended dignity, feeling himself deceived, the Officiant reclaimed from me his necklace of carbuncles in a movement so full of violence, but yet so just, that I was left more perplexed than pained. If he had been the Officiant of the Roses, he would not have proceeded in that manner.

And then, as though breaking a spell with that act of violence, the enchantment of the rhythm dissolved. And the little white ship in which we had sailed through the blue of the sky found itself suddenly moored to the lower floor of a house.

3. And then suddenly around the transparent angel of Sr. Aretal there began to form an irregular dark cloud. It was the shadow projected by the approaching horse.

Who could express my pain when around the angel of Sr. Aretal that dark thing, vague and irregular, appeared?

4. Gentleman of the topazes / horse man / with a human face and the body of an animal.

5. But you do love them as a man? No, friend, no. You sever in those delicate and divine beings a thousand fragile threads that constitute an entire life.

6. "I have never had a friend." And he bled all over as he said this. I explained to him that no man could give him his friendship because he was not a man and, thus, friendship would have been monstrous. Sr. Aretal had no familiarity with friendship and was indelicate in his relations with men, like an animal.

7. I separated from the lord of the topazes, and a few days later the final act of our relationship took place. Sr. Aretal sensed that all of a sudden my handshake was not very firm, that it was reluctant and cowardly, and the brute nobility in him protested. He suddenly hurled me away from him, and I felt his hooves upon my forehead, followed by a rhythmic and martial gallop raising the sands of the Desert. I directed my gaze to where the Sphynx reclined in her eternal mystery, and I could not see her. The Sphynx was Sr. Aretal, who had revealed his secret to me, the same secret as that of the Centaur!

8. Oh, the things that I saw in that pit! That pit was for me the very pit of mystery. Approaching a human soul, one as wide open as a pit, an eye of the earth, is the same as approaching God.

9. Besides, I was inflamed. [. . .]

I burned in flames and Sr. Aretal saw me burn. In a marvelous harmony, our two atoms of hydrogen and oxygen had come so close together that they almost became a single living thing with its own extended emanations.

10. Man is more than that: man is solidarity. You love your friends, but do you love them with human love? No. You offend a thousand intangible things in *us*.

11. Time has made me forget the question, or perhaps I have forgotten it thanks to the imperfect replies that helped me to cease thinking about this part of my life, that year and a half when I patiently, almost confidently, waited for happiness, my happiness, to begin, when instead I experienced the severity of the indifference of the person I loved. I think I was in love with Micky. Why did I love him? What made me love him? I believe that it was because I saw him as someone adrift, rather confused, floundering in his internal sea, feeling latent possibilities without knowing the nature of those possibilities. Nor did I know the nature of his possibilities, but I was certain that he had them, and my certainty was what provoked my interest, my affection, and my love toward him. The first two of these sentiments were returned, and for that I am grateful. Micky preferred to ignore my love. Perhaps it was cruel on his part to offer me interest and affection, knowing that what I wanted was love. It was cruelty on

his part or stupid insistence on mine, so much so that after he had returned to Caracas, I would telephone him now and then, write him letters, all the while stupidly hoping that some day he would return to New York or would ask me to go to Caracas and that, once together again, he would be fed up with refusing to face up to himself and recognize my loving loyalty, announcing his desire to be with me.

12. Bofors plunged into the water and surfaced, waving his bathing suit in the air as though it were a trophy, all the while shouting: "Come on, everybody strip! Everybody strip!" Sonia and Adolfo ran toward the beach away from Bofors, who then went over to Micky and yanked his suit down with one pull. Micky fell beneath the water and felt Bofors' hands taking the suit off of him. When Micky came to the surface, he saw Bofors yelling and showing Sonia and Adolfo the two suits, while the two laughed from the beach. There was an instant there in which Micky exchanged glances with Bofors and Elena. It was only an instant, a thousandth of a second, just the hair of a glance, because Bofors quickly threw Micky his suit and put his own on, while Elena covered herself with her halter.

13. Lying back in his bed with his eyes closed, Micky saw everything as a blank page and knew that soon, tomorrow, it would begin to fill up with incidents and chance events that like doodles or flyspecks would slowly cover its surface in a random disorder. The page for New York lay behind him. Here, before his closed eyes, he had the new page waiting for him. He wanted it to have an order and a design. He would make himself give it one, just the way he forced himself when he was designing a poster or a cover. This would be his first true poster, his first true cover. His alone.

14. Should I begin? I didn't notice when you pressed the record button. This is a lot of fun. I swear to you that this is the first time this sort of thing has happened to me, and in my profession you see all kinds . . . Don't get me wrong. I don't want to offend you, but it seems funny you should come looking for me here where I work and offer me a hundred dollars just for me to tell you whatever I want to about Micky. The business about the money doesn't surprise me because the most incredible propositions you can imagine have been made to me at this bar, almost always by American tourists, including women tourists. They fold a bill in my hands like bait, but never before has anyone suggesting paying me to recall prehistoric episodes of my life. I swear to you that if you hadn't been there to remind me all about it in such detail, I would never have remembered any of this.

15. Watch out for the queers!

16. That's the way Micky was: a complete enigma.

17. Aside from the above, the only thing left to remember Micky by are these pages. They make up a rather tenuous memoir, one that is decidedly imaginary, with no pretensions at constituting a homage. And maybe they have been written because the living person intrigued the author enough for him to invent a lie, a fiction with traces of truth and reality.

18. When you overheard them talking on the bus, you misjudged their behavior, the intimacy that bound them.

19. Sick to his soul.

20. Even though you were unsuccessful in expressing it in the diary, because of the impossibility of rationalizing your sensations, everything that morning seemed to you to have only recently taken shape, as though persons and objects existed for the first time.

21. It was that capacity to deceive myself that, in the end, constituted the only thing that could tie me to any special sort of dimension or order, an order linked to my simple projection toward things, to my possibility of controlling a world that in the end did not belong to me.

22. An order. The dimension that the world has rejected and that I cannot give to it. Because the world . . . the world is oblivious and has no desire for balance.

23. Certainly, order is to be found anywhere.

24. Over and over again, I tried to find out what was true in me, in Marcelo, in our lives. I was anxious to get our story over with, even if it was a book that at any time could come to an end and that, nevertheless, continues toward that end that has nothing in common with us.

25. The weight of this entire disjointed story leaves a wake behind it I didn't count on. That really upsets me. I thought reality was a lot simpler. But there it is. Burning.

26. That's all there is. Last night we finally came back from the country. In just another minute I have to get dressed and go out to eat with Paulina. I would, nevertheless, like to stay here writing, in order to reduce the impatience I feel.

5. The Sociopolitical Matrix

1. The only function of the past was to explain the present and help to modify it.

2. Both of them were trembling and, although I wanted them to, they never looked at each other. I comforted myself by thinking that perhaps they were already a long way from there, far off and away and together forever. It was that belief that allowed me to stand the execution (ah, the slow dance of the hangman, his black hood like the face of death itself), the certainty that even there, and despite everything that had happened to them, they still loved each other. That was what I thought about when suddenly the trapdoor fell open and the two struggled in space for a few brief seconds. And then, when everyone had left and I was left all alone and facing their two hanging bodies, it was then that I meditated on how, after all, they had done nothing more than heeded what that good and powerful nature had told them to do.

3. And in the conclusion of the documents he reproduced, "for future comparison," the confession of the prisoner himself, which he had helped to elaborate and which was the only one cited during the trial and on the basis of which the two soldiers had been sentenced to death: ". . . After our meetings and the many times our bodies were entwined together, we came to see that life was made for much more: it is man's lot to shout his beliefs and to defend them. With this in mind, we set out to observe what lay around us, and we thus took note of the cruelest of injustices. The colonies suffered from the consequences of the Crown's unchecked earnings. We were all dying here and that was the only

right people had, while the King was living over there in rich splendor. And even here, among the unfortunate, there were those who cruelly worked against them. That was the basis for the more and more precise conclusions we drew, and one day we realized that we had drawn a circle around our thoughts and concluded that we had to struggle against the forces that were consuming us. Antonio Bentes told me that our brothers among the soldiers had been transformed into machines for carrying out injustices. And who were the guilty parties? By that time we were already two mystics. Our meetings went from feverish love to the feverish pursuit of our ideas. We couldn't even love each other anymore, because we were a single body and had formed a cursed alliance. And so we cast ourselves into the final conspiracy. I return to the same question. Who were the guilty parties? That was the basis on which we and our friends planned to kill the authorities of the Crown one by one . . ."

Translations in notes 4–9 are from Reinaldo Arenas, *The Brightest Star,* pp. 45–106, in *Old Rosa: A Novel in Two Stories,* translated from the Spanish by Ann Tashi Slater and Andrew Hurley (New York: Grove Press, 1989). Note: the Spanish original was published separately; the complete text is translated into English as half of this volume.

4. was that him too? was that the image of him that everyone would carry away? was there no way out? could he not even suffer his digrace, his fall from grace, his misfortune, his fate, with dignity and discretion? could he not be himself even in the moment when he let his terror show? was he forever condemned to live in a world where only frustration made sense and had a place, where the only fitting attitude was burlesque and mockery [. . .]? (69)

5. suddenly he realized that there was no escape, that there was no way out, that all his attempts, all his efforts, had been futile, had been for nothing, and that there were things—aggressive, fixed, unyielding, unbearable, but *real* [. . .]. (83)

6. the eternal tragedy of submission (51).

7. that very night he decided that to save himself he had to start writing, *now* (71).

8. the notebooks Rosa [his sister] had brought him began to fill with, to be awash in, a sea of tiny tiny words, almost scribbled, fast, *fast,* and almost illegible, even to him, *hurry, hurry, keep on, keep on, fast*—of course taking precautions, because there were searches, you couldn't keep diaries, "pansy-ass bullshit," said the lieutenants as official justification for going inexorably, unstoppably, and legally through everyone's correspondence—so taking at least minimal precautions, he scribbled in the notebooks, and on the inside covers, along the spines, in the margins and blank pages of Marxist-Leninist manuals and economics books stolen from the Political Section, he furtively, quickly filled them with his tiny scrawl, and when nobody was looking, under the sheets or standing in the toilet, in line for breakfast sometimes, he even filled the margins of grotesque political posters pasted up on the walls, even announcements *For Internal Camp Circulation* suffered that almost microscopic crablike invasion of virtually indecipherable letters and signs, his labor constantly, incessantly interrupted, yet constant [. . .] *keep on, keep on,* and Arturo went on

scribbling, scrawling over his comrades' letters from home, stolen at midnight, and over the harsh, insulting slogans of the moment [. . . and] one night he found a treasure in the Legal Affairs Office, a whole chestful of the minutes of General Staff meetings, which he unhesitatingly appropriated, and which gave him several weeks' worth of working material [. . .]. (72–73)

9. the first lieutenant orders a search of Arturo's ratty belongings, at which everyone, eyes alight in expectation of cigarettes, money, maybe a can of condensed milk, maybe even jewelry ("You never know about these fags"), begins rummaging: "Letters and photos of more faggots," says one, and strews them on the floor; "Face cream," says another, and smashes it against the wall; and papers, papers, pieces of cardboard, placards, posters, signs, announcements and orders from High Command, papers, papers, and more papers, and all of them written all over, scribbled, marked, scrawled on, out to the very edges: "Those minutes we'd thought were lost," the lieutenant says, "what's that goose doing with the minutes!" and picks up a piece of paper and reads, not without difficulty, then instantly, disgusted, he looks at the corporal and hands him one of the hen-scratched documents—"What'd I tell you," he says, "with these people you've gotta be on your toes every minute, because this guy wasn't satisfied just demoralizing himself, he wanted to demoralize all of us, the whole country, *his* country, *your* country, look at this, look what's he's written here—counterrevolution, open, bald-faced, brass-balled, faggot counterrevolution!"—and so the corporal reads, not without difficulty, and stumbles on words he has never seen or heard before [. . .]. (93–94)

10. But in order to understand this mode of behavior, the outbursts he was unable to contain in moments like these, it is perhaps necessary to remember the episode in his infancy, distant and lost in his memory, but clear and precise whenever he evoked it, of the body in the town plaza which two innocent children stood staring at, one of whom (he, Ernesto) discovered as he gazed on the scene the mystery of love that ends violently. "I was a little boy when by accident I saw the first crime against homosexuals," he told me. "We were wearing our white dust jackets from school with our book bags bumping our shoulders, and my friend and I ran toward the spot where all the people were gathered. He held back, but I pressed forward. Dumbstruck, I saw the dead man lying face down in the dirt under the bitter orange trees [. . .]. It was Fernando, the kid from the sawmill who, according to the adults, had 'bad ways.'"

11. I held back my hand that was about to knock on the glass because, although I was used to Victor's surprises, the scene couldn't help but attract my attention. Just like Ernesto and his encounters, I was used to telling about Victor's comings and goings. I did it in such a way that the facts would seem comical in their disjointed unfolding, since there wasn't any explanation available, just as he used to narrate his adventures, exaggerating the story in order to produce laughter. But retelling was only a way to express the strangeness produced by the inexplicable. Oh, I could understand the reasons, all right, and he would proceed to give them to me, reasons as to why he would now be talking to the doctor on duty right there in the hospital. But I could not understand how this could take place with such naturalness and after scenes like the ones we had just gone through just a few hours ago. Because he would ask me, Which one is

Victor? The one from the police station who tosses money on the ground so that a prisoner who might need it can pick it up? The one in the doorman's apartment who falls down on his knees and transforms the people around him with his prayers? The one who'd been robbed? The one who'd been tricked and who allows himself to be tricked? That one who calls me to go over, because he knows I will, and who's laughing out loud and making the doctors all laugh out loud while he talks? I knocked.

12. Nivaldo drew the curtain with the hope that perhaps he could see Jerônimo out there, perhaps on his way back. Even though he couldn't shout his name, he needed for him to appear so that, by seeing him, he could make him feel how much he loved him. That love was now taking on proportions that were so large he could no longer contain it, and it demanded more room in which to continue growing. Then it would rise up, floating in the air, and from that height it would shout loud and clear so that everybody in the plaza, in the moorage, in the shops, in the bars, in the schools, in the whorehouses could hear his cry filled with passion: "Jerônimo, I love you! Jerônimo, I love you! Jerônimo, I love you! [. . .] But the exaggerated, sudden thrill of freedom often makes people feel momentarily lost. That is what Nivaldo experienced at that moment. The sun flooded into the room and brought with it a vision that was exactly like the one the day before: the set of stairs that was overly pretentious for that place and for the simplicity of the church's façade: the Shell gas station with its shining emblem moving gently in the wind, the police station recently painted in two tones of blue, the business establishments along the other side of the street, and the open space of yellow dirt in front of the church, with a few people walking by here and there up and down the main street. Jerônimo was not among them. He felt himself betrayed by the landscape he wanted to communicate his happiness to but which meanwhile remained drowsily indifferent.

13. It was an overpowering order that left one's voice castrated in his own throat.

14. "So, Nivaldo, you must learn right from the start only to be afraid of dangerous things, those that really exist and that . . ." ("Should I go on lying or not?" he thought in the middle of the sentence, deciding he should) . . . "From now on you will have to face things like malaria, cobras, scorpions, horseflies, injustice, and people—the federal police, Nivaldo!, which you will have to help me fight. And our struggle will be a hard one, you'll see, like the faith in liberty which, for us, includes the right to our love and to the peace that will allow us to continue to live together when all this is over."

15. The novelized self-reports of Félix Chaneton will be a construction of literature if they are an annihilation of given reality.

16. Unhappiness, sordidness, swishiness, and even homosexuality were and are the results of oppression.

17. If with respect to the fairies that, as the reader will have already noticed, are the lowest of classes and the most grotesque within the homosexual community, if with respect to the fairies, I say, we were able to isolate and then reveal in all of their extreme nakedness their very qualities (fear, the desire to overcome their sense of shame, also the inversion of morality, the fog and the turbulent glow, the dream of the worst sort of scorn and condemnation), we would have before us, as something impossible, the absolute universe of the fairies.

This universe radically excludes women, but at the same time it includes them in the very way it denies them by identifying with them or, better, with a certain idea of women. The language spoken here is besieged by pornography triumphant. Its images flourish in the midst of the great filth machos are capable of. Its habits are oriented by the fanaticism of the masturbations that are obliged both to adore and to destroy in their own body the sex that desires itself. Anyone who has savored this lamentable, or better yet, this pitiful and devastating universe where death is no surprise, has prepared his palate for atrophy, mutilation, the agony of starvation, the worst kind of despair. It is without a doubt an aberrant universe, and its inhabitants are sick people, but only because the basis of this pathos lies in madness and horror in an inextricable mixture. As long as there are violent or frightened men, that universe will be *there*. I invite you, reader, to take it into your charge.

18. Anguish chokes me and keeps me from thinking. Carrera is a PIG, but if I separate myself from him, I lose all protection and will turn into a worm. This is the price of my passivity: I am nothing more than a lamentable spectacle that puts me to shame.

19. I have not written these metaphors in order to underscore a progressive plot, but rather to indicate with a phrasing lacking a real basis the gaps that opened up between Carrera and me.

20. *Pablo*'s spectators, if not abominable (which might be too harsh), were obviously scorned individuals, with ideas and actions that were scorned. Carrera's look of control upset them, while at the same time it sank them deeper in their seats. Carrera wrinkled his nose as though smelling a garbage dump or the odor of death. Moreover, he cocked his ear as though listening to the whisperings of someone or something revealing to him the lies and deceits of the pitiful specimens swept by his gaze.

21. Up to this point Carrera and I had been two individuals fascinated by the spectacle of the world. And I told myself once more that I was still young, that I was *only* twenty-five. Later, as time went on, Good would be there waiting for me. Beyond my loneliness, the sordidness of my ignorance, beyond Carrera, my rabid hatred, I would set Good aside for myself: I would study, be something, someone.

22. I don't know if these words ought to have the power to struggle against the flatness of this midday, and beyond that, the flatness of Buenos Aires and Argentina.

Translations in notes 23–30 are from José Donoso, *Hell Has No Limits*, translated by Hallie D. Taylor and Suzanne Jill Levine, pp. 145–229, in *Triple Cross* (New York: E. P. Dutton, 1972).

23. Tell her to come. I want to laugh. It can't be all so damn sad in this town don Alejo's going to tear down and plow under, surrounded by vineyards that are going to swallow it up, and tonight I'll have to go home and sleep with my wife and I don't want to, I want to have fun, that nutty Manuela has to come out and save us, there must be something better than this, she has to come out. (219)

24. Not a hope remained to grieve her, even fear was eliminated. Nothing would ever change, it never had, it would be the same forever.

25. Pancho suddenly becomes quiet watching la Manuela. Watching that thing dancing in the center of the room, all eye sockets, hollows, spasmodic shadows, that thing which is going to die despite its cries, that incredibly repulsive thing that, incredibly, is the party, and dances for him, he knows he aches to touch it and caress it, he doesn't want that writhing thing to be alone there in the center but against his skin, and Pancho lets himself watch and caress from a distance that old queer who is dancing for him and he surrenders to her dance, and now it isn't funny anymore because it's as if he too were gasping for breath. Octavio mustn't know. He can't know. No one must know. (220–221)

26. When Japonesita started talking like that la Manuela felt like screaming, it was as if his daughter were drowning him in words [. . .]. (181)

27. "And la Manuela?"

Japonesita didn't answer.

"And la Manuela, I said?"

"My father has gone to bed." (218)

28. She sensed him shivering near the coals. The poor thing was wet and tired from so much revelry. Feeling that la Manuela was there, Japonesa drew near the corner and touched him. He said nothing. Then she leaned her body against la Manuela's. [. . .]

"They're such bores . . ."

"Like animals."

"It doesn't matter to me. I'm used to it. I don't know why they always do this or something like it to me when I dance, it's as if they were afraid of me. I don't know why if they know I'm just a fag." (195–196)

29. Don't tell me that old whore is sick! Do you think I came to look at your frigid little rabbit's face? No, I came to see la Manuela, that's what I came for. Now, I said, Go call her. I want her to dance for me. (218)

30. She's the only one capable of turning the party into something thrilling, because she's la Manuela. [. . .] They aren't women. She's going to show them what a woman is and how to be a woman. (212).

6. Optical Constructions

1. "Diana, you're drunk!" Das Graças was almost shouting and continued to shake me with so much force that my teeth were rattling.

"Look at that! Look at that!" I pointed to an indistinct figure.

She directed a startled look toward where I indicated. A few persons began to watch us.

"I swear to god if it doesn't look like an old man wearing pants with suspenders, damn it."

"Swear to what?"

"Swear to god. Over there. Wait right here while I go take a look. I'll bet you anything there's a sweet little femme under the table . . ."

"Diana, stop that!"

". . . just full of fun. Wanna bet? I bet to g . . ." The blow I received at that precise moment really brought me up short. But it sure worked. The nausea disappeared, banished by the sense of pain, anger, and shame. I turned stupidly to Das Graças who was standing in front of me, with a concerned look on her dark and long-suffering face, her eyes fixed on me with tenderness and care. She could have been my friend, I still thought. Suddenly, I understood. A suffering that had been repressed up to that point, the suffering of a child, came bursting forth and exploded in loud, violent sobs and my tears flowed free and a large and profound sense of release was now to be able to look upon the good face of Das Graças behind the veil of tears and smoke and to be able to ask the others and everybody and even herself, when she will have forgotten everything and I will be able to ask her forgiveness and to understand things and to be able to accept her invitation to dance and allow her to hold me and comfort herself and forget who I am, me who's a nobody, and accept my arm and forgive me, more than once, for everything.

The translations in notes 2–4 are from Alejandra Pizarnik, *The Bloody Countess,* translated by Alberto Manguel, pp. 70–87 in *Other Fires: Short Fiction by Latin American Women,* edited by Alberto Manguel. New York: Clarkson N. Potter, 1986.

2. Like Sade in his writings, and Gilles de Rais in his crimes, the Countess Bathory reached beyond all limits the uttermost pit of unfettered passions. She is yet another proof that the absolute freedom of the human creature is horrible. (87)

3. The road is covered in snow and, inside the coach, the somber lady wrapped in furs feels bored. Suddenly she calls out the name of one of the girls in her train. The girl is brought to her: the Countess bites her frantically and sticks needles in her flesh. A while later the procession abandons the wounded girl in the snow. The girl tries to run away. She is pursued, captured and pulled back into the coach. A little further along the road they halt: the Countess has ordered cold water. Now the girl is naked, standing in the snow. Night has fallen. A circle of torches surrounds her, held out by impassive footmen. They pour water over the body and the water turns to ice. (The Countess observes this from inside the coach.) The girl attempts one last slight gesture, trying to move closer to the torches—the only source of warmth. More water is poured over her, and there she remains, forever standing, upright, dead. (72–73)

4. She was never afraid, she never trembled. And no compassion, no sympathy or admiration may be felt for her. Only a certain astonishment at the enormity of the horror, a fascination with a white dress that turns red, with the idea of total laceration, with the imagination of a silence starred with cries in which everything reflects an unacceptable beauty. (86–87)

7. Narrations on the Self

1. This photograph of Gastón is the one that appears on the first page of my album. In reality, Jaime's photo should be in first place, but I lost it.

2. I often ask myself, with a slight inner trembling, if maybe I haven't been mistaken in everything. But I want you to understand it's only on rare occasions. Because in general, under the broad firmament of condemnation, but at

the same time with renewed promise, I have lived in accordance with what I want and what I am. Certainly, of course, I have not triumphed in the general sense of the word, nor even in the sense I had proposed to myself before Leonardo showed up. (There he is, the beginning and the end.) But, on the other hand, I have lived without inhibitions. Can you understand that? Not just for some of the time, which is what the majority of you opt for, but forever. I have lived in that fashion, and I feel no bitterness despite the numerous setbacks. Because, after all, that's what's important.

3. In the art of coming up with lines to initiate conversations with boys, I consider myself truly extraordinary. I rarely fail.

4. Right now, even though to a reduced degree, I reexperience how upset I was then, which is unusual after all these years. I would like to record the facts as they occurred. But I hold back because I must submit my story to certain literary constraints, even if that means changing the events in some ways and, especially, if it means losing some spontaneity. But by contrast, it is vital to hush certain things up. Because if I were to reveal them, I am certain that they would scandalize everybody and cause a ruckus.

5. Right now, there is nothing more pleasant to me than to be surrounded by my memories. I see everything in order, day by day, episode by episode. Even though you do not share my opinion, I believe my power to evoke things borders on the marvelous.

6. It has now become a habit for me to find myself bent over my desk writing these notes. The familiarity with pen and paper, the (pleasant) evocations of my days in Guanajuato, the story about my disagreements with Rolando, to references to my economic straits, the calls on the telephone and the knocks at the window—in sum, all the elements that go to make up the story have brought me an unexpected love for this book. My world is taking on a definite outline in these pages. And just as if it were a mirror, here I am contemplating myself as I please.

7. And now I'm writing this, you must understand, only because it burns the hell out of me to keep quiet about it.

8. I wanted to see what would happen if I did something tacky like writing a few tears.

9. It will be discovered, among other things, that the rose lives in time and space, like you and like my love for you. Which is why I'm writing this, so it will last a little while longer.

10. "That's fine, Soledad. We'll get together and have a drink. I'll call you."

By that time I was afraid you'd try to call and get a busy signal. I was ready to promise anything. But she wanted to talk. The guy never reached Julio. The marathon broke up, and the neighbors never found a thing out.

"Are you still in psychoanalysis?"

"No, I stopped going."

"You did the right thing. That's all the more reason I want to talk to you."

"I'll call you on Monday." (Maybe by Monday I'll see Miguel. Even though the weekend is all filled up. And today is already Thursday.)

"You won't call. I know that. But this is the end."

I had already realized that this was a dialogue with you. And I looked at the receiver as though that son-of-a-bitch, fate, were on the other end of the line, playing a dirty trick on me again. And the receiver said:

"Pride doesn't have anything to do with what I'm saying . . ."

It was clear that I was the one talking. And you had turned into me. What I mean is that I was Miguel listening to the complaint impassively, absolutely certain that even though she were to make a decision, feelings cannot be dictated. The best that could be done would not be to call again.

". . . are you there?"

"Yes, I'm here."

"No, because you were so quiet."

"I'm listening."

11. I was really wrong. I've always been wrong. About holes (as my psychoanalyst used to say), about life, about illusions, feelings, presentiments. What I loved was a lie, and what I wanted was a fiction.

The translation in note 12 is from Sylvia Molloy, *Certificate of Absence,* translated by Daniel Balderston with the author (Austin: University of Texas Press, 1989).

12. Today she is writing down what she has done, what she has not done, trying to grasp the fragments of a whole that escapes her. She believes she can recover them, and with them tries to make—or make up—her own private constellation. They are only traces, splinters which make her feel deaf, dumb, without memory. Nonetheless, she tells herself, there was once a vision, a face she can no longer find. Shut up in this room everything seems easier because she can piece things together. By writing, she would like to find out what lies beyond these four walls; or perhaps she would like to find out what lies within them, in this closed space where she has chosen to write. (3)

13. "I can't believe you!"

14. "Because I don't want to stop being furious."

15. Embroidering on writing and cooking.

16. Suddenly, I'm struck by a doubt: Might the needle be something like the thread's wife, concerning itself with the difficult task of piercing the fabric in order then to disappear and leaving its mate outlined in spectacular forms and colors as the only object worthy of admiration and praise? It's a doubt I can't get rid of.

There are threads that turn out to be difficult to pursue. [. . .]

And I say that this business about the thread is very relative, because I've spent hours asking myself, And what can I say about the thread if the best I can do is sew a button on or poorly stitch a hem? if I can barely follow with some sort of coherence this tangled skein that is my life right now?

17. Beneath the sheets, a love that belongs to the Cosmos, two women make love with a secret language, far removed from the world. After all is said and done.

18. Almost all the names have been changed. And almost everything really happened.

19. I imagine us drinking tea, the two of us sitting very close together and telling each other how menstruation often makes our feelings more acute and

leads us from our ovaries to creation. Or, to the contrary, it distances us from creation. How new women take possession of us through their blood, some of them touchingly near to us, while others are alien and terrible. Because our menstrual blood bears the ferocity and the color of life, but also the germ of madness.

8. Utopian Designs

1. Who could give an explanation?

2. The most often banned author in Brazil.

3. Then a strange struggle took place. Fernanda held Paula by the shoulders, while Paula shoved against her in order to free herself, but gently so as not to hurt her. Neither said a thing, but she heard the heavy beating of her heart and felt the other's panting breath on her neck. Fernanda's movements were calculated, malicious, and all her gestures served to open her eyes to things that until then she had never even suspected: that sex, love, desire, or whatever you want to call it was able to provoke that anxiety, was a mystery that could lead to the worst sort of things like that sensation that flooded over her body, making her hesitate and begin to fear that maybe Fernanda would stop what she was trying to do.

4. To be happy, to be what you want to and to have what makes us happy . . . You make me feel good, and I have no desire to hurt you . . . I can't understand why I like you the way I should like a man . . . I can't understand it, I just feel it and that's enough for me . . . I'm not about to ask anybody if that's good or bad. Good? Bad? Why do you like white clothing so much? Why do I like to bring you red roses so much? . . . Why does my father prefer a pipe to a cigarette? Why does my mother enjoy a Manhattan so much?

5. Paula did not avoid Fernanda's gesture, which was to lift the covers and contemplate her with attention.

"I already knew your body was beautiful . . . I had already seen it . . . But not here . . . In my bed . . . Woman-woman . . . Sleep . . . Sleep . . . How am I going to tell what I feel? . . . Everything is a sin . . . Not a sin . . . a crime . . . something dirty . . . *but not here* . . . Here it's all dreams and fantasies . . . a mixture of champagne and clear water . . . Paula, you are water and I'm thirsty . . .

6. Will my brothers write a tender book in which they remember me? Now I know they won't. Either I write that book or they'll toss me in the dump of oblivion.

7. I dreamed about Jesús Lopera the other night. A vivid dream. It's just as vivid as the words I use to recall it are confused. Language is a such a clumsy net, so roughly woven that it lets reality slip through.

8. The last thing I saw was the park, and in the park the statue of the Liberator Bolivar in flames. The marble was burning, the bronze was burning, the horse was burning, the hero was burning. So long, you great son-of-a-bitch!

9. Some members of that crowd that passed through Junín, I want you to know, later caused quite a stir and were reported in cackling tones on the noon, three, six, and nine news reports. They were all mayors, inspectors, attorneys-general, directors, governors, officials, representatives, treasurers, every one of them with his coveted public job and his private wife (the latter really a hag), his

children, their radios and televisions blaring, those high-sounding Antioquia last names [. . .] and the infinite pride of ignorance.

10. Well, just let the world change, because I have no intention of changing.

11. The eternal unanswerable questions of man. Flowing away? That's the word, Heraclites' grand word: *panta rhei,* everything passes. This book, an imitation of life, flows away like a river, potamos, where I bathe myself and where the hippopotamus bathes, and together we pass on like the changing waters.

12. To hell with the government and the novel!

13. I am very given to presuming I discovered the world the first time I opened my eyes.

14. Life is full of conditionals. I've maybe given an account of what the doctor said: a one-percent wretched person. For one reason or another, everything else escapes me. Literature is like that, and life is no different: you don't exist, you don't live, you don't write what you want to, only what you can.

15. Center of the center, heart of the earth.

16. Not seeking the distortion of reality. Why seek that? I have always found reality distorted more than enough.

17. And finally she shouted, come, Salomão, come, because you've got to, and with a stifled groan I threw myself into her, there in the depths where huge barrels of wine filled with tradition fermented, and putting in motion the machines that produce so many mysteries, I deposited my seed, the first in this glorious young land sowed by the hand of man. And as I did this I heard, half in the distance but yet almost nearby, the savage and violent chorus of the animals of Phaeton, their harmony, even when they had to kill in order to eat, obeying, barely, the laws of nature.

18. LET MEN BEWARE.

19. This book speaks to us of commonplaces, trivialities, the false conception of life on the part of those who move with the herd. Characters and behaviors appear here which Torres Molina cuts down mercilessly. She writes by projecting herself in multiple narratives, demystifying the macho's taboos that have become incrusted like splinters in our wracked social body.

20. I meet María.

21. At that moment all my senses are concentrated in my fingers over her clitoral texture, like a delinquent expert trying to pick a lock.

It is necessary to settle for small, subtle, precise movements, while at the same time paying attention to any revealing gesture. Alert to the smallest sign. Without losing the rhythm. Making one attempt after another.

My lips inside yours, and your tongue penetrating me relentlessly.

I feel the grand moment draw near in the demands and the feverishness of our bodies in the increasingly wild and convulsive contact of our caresses and our embraces.

And I am so right about it that she opens up to me as though she were the most marvelous and exotic of wildflowers. And it is then that I spurt the vital liquid into her virginal and awaiting entrails.

22. More than intuiting it, I feel certain that from now on my life will not have a moment's peace.

But that is precisely what I have chosen. Neither to give nor demand a moment's peace.

That's the way we women are!

23. And I'll make the curtains, because María hates sewing.

24. That's impossible. It simply isn't possible, and nevertheless, I've seen the X-rays, and there's not the slightest doubt that a live fetus is growing inside Adrián. The idea that the system won't allow for it no longer makes any sense. This is our way out of humanity. We will be a separate group of strange beings. It's all the same to live the way Adrián wants to or not. In any event, we will no longer be like the others, not even like other homosexuals. And I was the one who never believed we were like other homosexuals, which is why we lived in society, castrated maybe, but in society, hidden and pursued, but in society. There is no doubt that life shows us something new each day, but that child of mine is taking us out of the world.

25. If I used to feel like shit, now I know I really am since Adrián began to say interesting things after he got pregnant and started to talk about life so I began to reread the existentialists in order to understand that when I said something to him or agreed with him, I wasn't assimilating them but rather Adrián's unique vision.

BIBLIOGRAPHY

Primary Sources

Arcidiácono, Carlos. *Ay de mí, Jonathan.* Buenos Aires: Ediciones Corregidor, 1976.

Arenas, Reinaldo. *Arturo, la estrella más brillante.* Barcelona: Montesinos, 1984? English translation (*The Brightest Star*) included in his *Old Rosa: A Novel in Two Stories,* translated by Ann Tashi Slater and Andrew Hurley. New York: Grove Press, 1989.

Arévalo Martínez, Rafael. "El hombre que parecía un caballo." In *El hombre que parecía un caballo,* pp. 9–25. Guatemala City: Editorial Universitaria, 1951.

Barbachano Ponce, Miguel. *El diario de José Toledo.* Mexico City, 1964.

Calva, José Rafael. *Utopia gay.* Mexico City: Editorial Oasis, 1983.

Caminha, Adolfo. *Bom-Crioulo.* Rio de Janeiro: Olivé Editor, 1969. First published in 1895. Translated into English by E. A. Lacey as *Bom-Crioulo: The Black Man and the Cabin Boy.* San Francisco: Gay Sunshine Press, 1982. Spanish translation by Luis Zapata. Mexico City: Editorial Posada, 1987.

Ceballos Maldonado, José. *Después de todo.* 2d ed. Mexico City: Premiá, Red de Jonás, 1986. First published in 1969.

Chocrón, Isaac. *Pájaro de mar por tierra.* Caracas: Editorial Tiempo Nuevo, 1972.

Correas, Carlos. *Los reportajes de Félix Chaneton.* Buenos Aires: Editorial Celtia, 1984.

Denser, Márcia. "Ladies First." In *Diana caçadora,* pp. 73–93. São Paulo: Global Editora, 1986.

D'Halmar, Augusto. *La pasión y muerte del cura Duesto.* 3d ed. Santiago de Chile: Editorial Nascimento, 1969.

Donoso, José. *El lugar sin límites.* Mexico City: Editorial Joaquín Mortiz, 1966. Translated by Hallie D. Taylor and Suzanne Jill Levine as *Hell Has No Limits,* in *Triple Cross.* New York: E. P. Dutton, 1972.

González Castillo, José. *Los invertidos: Obra realista en tres actos.* Buenos Aires: Ediciones del Carro de Tespis, Argentores, 1957.

Hernández Catá, Alfonso. *El ángel de la Sodoma.* Valparaíso: "El Callao," 1929?

Molloy, Sylvia. *En breve cárcel*. Barcelona: Editorial Seix Barral, 1981. Translated by Daniel Balderston with the author as *Certificate of Absence*. Austin: University of Texas Press, 1989.

Penteado, Darcy. *Nivaldo e Jerônimo*. Rio de Janeiro: Codecri, 1981.

Pizarnik, Alejandra. *La condesa sangrienta*. Buenos Aires?: Aquaris, 1971. Translated by Alberto Manguel as *The Bloody Countess*, in *Other Fires: Short Fiction by Latin American Women*, edited by Alberto Manguel. New York: Clarkson N. Potter, 1986.

Rios, Cassandra. *A borboleta branca, romance*. 5th ed. São Paulo: Global Editora e Distribuidora, 1980. First published in 1963.

Roffiel, Rosamaría. *Amora*. Mexico City: Editorial Planeta Mexicana, 1989.

Silva, Aguinaldo. *No país das sombras*. Rio de Janeiro: Civilização Brasileira, 1979.

———. *Primeira carta aos andróginos*. Rio de Janeiro: Pallas, 1975.

Torres Molina, Susana. *Dueña y señora*. 3d ed. Buenos Aires: Ediciones de la Campana, 1984. (Originally published in 1983.)

Vallejo, Fernando. *El fuego secreto*. Bogotá: Planeta Colombiana Editorial, 1986.

Villordo, Oscar Hermes. *La otra mejilla*. Buenos Aires: Editorial Sudamericana, 1986.

Wácquez, Mauricio. *Toda la luz del mediodía*. Santiago de Chile: Editora Zig-Zag, 1964.

Zapata, Luis. *Las aventuras, desventuras y sueños de Adonis García, el vampiro de la Colonia Roma*. Mexico City: Editorial Grijalbo, 1979. Translated by E. A. Lacey as *Adonis García: A Picaresque Novel*. San Francisco: Gay Sunshine Press, 1981.

———. *En jirones*. Mexico City: Editorial Posada, 1985.

Secondary Sources

Acevedo, Ramón L. "Augusto D'Halmar: Novelista." Thesis, Universidad de Puerto Rico, 1976.

Acevedo, Zelmar. *Homosexualidad: Hacia la destrucción de los mitos*. Buenos Aires: Ediciones del Ser, 1985.

Alcoforado, Maria Letícia Guedes. "*Bom-Crioulo* de Adolfo Caminha e a França." *Revista de letras* [Curitiba] 28 (1988): 85–93.

Amat, Nuria. "La erótica del lenguaje en Alejandra Pizarnik y Monique Wittig." *Nueva estafeta* 12 (1979): 47–54.

Argüelles, Lourdes, and B. Ruby Rich. "Homosexuality, Homophobia, and Revolution: Notes toward an Understanding of the Cuban Lesbian and Gay Male Experience." *Signs* 9.4 (1984): 683–699; 11.1 (1985): 120–136.

Armstrong, Nancy, and Leonard Tennenhouse, eds. *The Ideology of Conduct: Essays on Literature and the History of Sexuality*. New York: Methuen, 1987.

Austen, Roger. *Playing the Game: The Homosexual Novel in America*. Indianapolis: Bobbs-Merrill, 1977.

Avellaneda, Andrés. *Censura, autoritarismo y cultura: Argentina, 1960–1983*. Buenos Aires: Centro Editor de América Latina, 1986.

Beaver, Harold. "Homosexual Signs (*In Memory of Roland Barthes*)." *Critical Inquiry* 8 (1981): 99–119.

Bellucci, Mabel. "El anarquismo y su lucha en favor del derecho al placer femenino." *Contribuciones* [Asociación Argentina de Protección Familiar] 10.35 (Julio 1987): 41–45.

Beneyto, Antonio. "Alejandra Pizarnik: Ocultándose en el lenguaje." *Quimera* 34 (Diciembre 1983): 23–27.

Benstock, Shari. "Beyond the Reaches of Feminist Criticism: A Letter from Paris." In *Feminist Issues in Literary Scholarship,* edited by Shari Benstock, pp. 7–29. Bloomington: Indiana University Press, 1987.

Berenguer Carisomo, Arturo. *Las ideas estéticas en el teatro argentino.* Buenos Aires: Comisión Nacional de Cultura, Instituto Nacional de Estudios de Teatro, 1947.

Blanco, José Joaquin. *Función de medianoche.* Mexico City: Era/SEP Cultura, 1986. Originally published in 1981.

———. *La paja en el ojo: Ensayos de crítica.* Puebla, Mex.: ICUAP, Centro de Estudios Contemporáneos, Editorial Universidad Autónoma de Puebla, 1980.

Blau, Herbert. "Disseminating Sodom." *Salmagundi* 58–59 (1982–1983): 221–251.

[*Bom-Crioulo* (review).] *Nova Revista* 2 (1985): no page.

Bronski, Michael. *Culture Clash: The Making of Gay Sensibility.* Boston: South End Press, 1984.

Brookshaw, David. *Race and Color in Brazilian Literature.* Metuchen, N.J.: Scarecrow Press, 1986.

Bruce-Novoa, Juan. "Homosexuality and the Chicano Novel." *Confluencia: Revista Hispánica de Cultura y Literatura* 2.1 (1986): 69–77. Also in *European Perspectives on Hispanic Literature of the United States,* edited by Genvieve Fabre, pp. 98–106. Houston: Arte Público Press, 1988.

Brushwood, John S. *La novela mexicana (1967–1982).* Mexico City: Grijalbo, 1984.

Buil, José. "¿Podría usted quitar sus dientes de mi cuello?" *Revista de la Universidad de México* 34.3 (1979): 53.

Caldas, Waldenyr. "Subliteratura: O fetiche do prazer." *Vozes* 72.3 (1978): 5–12.

Canales, Luis. "O homossexualismo como tema no moderno teatro brasileiro." *Luso-Brazilian Review* 18.1 (1981): 173–181.

Caplan, Pat, ed. *The Cultural Construction of Sexuality.* London: Tavistock Publications, 1987.

Carter, Angela. *The Sadeian Woman and the Ideology of Pornography.* New York: Pantheon Books, 1978.

Castagnino, Raúl H. *Sociología del teatro argentino.* Buenos Aires: Editorial Nova, 1962.

Charney, Maurice. *Sexual Fiction.* London: Methuen, 1981.

Chesebro, James W., ed. *Gayspeak: Gay Male and Lesbian Communication.* New York: Pilgrim Press, 1981.

Chumu, Maya. *Salir a la luz como lesbianas de color.* Seattle: Tsnunami Press, 1980.

Cixous, Hélène. "The Laugh of the Medusa." Translated by Keith and Paula Cohen. In *Critical Theory since 1965*, edited by Hazard Adams and Leroy Searle, pp. 309–320. Tallahassee: University Presses of Florida, 1986.

Cohen, Ed. "Foucauldian Necrologies: 'Gay' 'Politics'? Politically Gay?" *Textual Practices* 2.1 (1988): 87–101.

———. "Writing Gone Wilde: Homoerotic Desire in the Closet of Representation." *PMLA* 102 (1987): 801–813.

Cortázar, Julio. *Nicaragua tan violentamente dulce*. 5th ed. Buenos Aires: Muchnik Editores, 1984.

Daly, Mary. *Gyn/ecology: The Metaethics of Radical Feminism*. Boston: Beacon Books, 1978.

Davis, Murray S. *Smut: Erotic Reality/Obscene Ideology*. Chicago: University of Chicago Press, 1983.

Delpech, François. "La patraña del hombre preñado: Algunas versiones hispánicas." *Nueva Revista de Filología Hispánica* 34.2 (1985–1986): 548–598.

Dowling, William C. *Jameson, Althusser, Marx: An Introduction to the Political Unconscious*. Ithaca, N.Y.: Cornell University Press, 1984.

Duberman, Martin Bauml, Martha Vicinus, and George Chauncey, Jr., eds. *Hidden from History: Reclaiming the Gay and Lesbian Past*. New York: New American Library, 1989.

Dworkin, Andrea. *Intercourse*. New York: Free Press, 1987.

Dynes, Wayne. *Homolexis: A Historical and Cultural Lexicon of Homosexuality*. New York: Gay Academic Union, 1985.

Eagleton, Terry. *Literary Theory: An Introduction*. Minneapolis: University of Minnesota Press, 1983.

Faderman, Lillian. *Surpassing the Love of Men: Romantic Friendship and Love between Women from the Renaissance to the Present*. New York: William Morrow, 1981.

Fiedler, Leslie. *Love and Death in the American Novel*. New York: Criterion Books, 1960.

Foppa, Tito Livio. *Diccionario teatral del Río de la Plata*. Buenos Aires: Argentores, Ediciones del Carro de Tespis, 1961.

Foster, David William. *Alternate Voices in the Contemporary Latin American Narrative*. Columbia: University of Missouri Press, 1985.

———. "Identidades polimórficas y planteo metateatral en *Extraño juguete* de Susana Torres Molina." *Alba de América* 7.12–13 (1989): 75–86.

———. "The Manipulation of the Horizons of Reader Expectation in Two Examples of Argentine Lesbian Writing: Discourse Power and Alternate Sexuality." In *Spanish and Portuguese Distinguished Lecture Series: Selected Texts*, pp. 117–127. Boulder: University of Colorado, Department of Spanish and Portuguese; Society of Spanish and Spanish-American Studies, 1989.

———. "The Monstrous in Two Argentine Novels." *Américas* [English language edition] 24.2 (1972): 33–36.

———. "Narrativa testimonial argentina durante los años del proceso." In *Testimonio y literatura*, edited by René Jara and Hernán Vidal, pp. 138–154. Minneapolis: Institute for the Study of Ideologies and Literature, 1986.

———. "Los parámetros de la narrativa argentina durante el 'Proceso de Reorganización Nacional.'" In *Ficción y política: La narrativa argentina durante el proceso militar,* pp. 96–108. Buenos Aires: Alianza Editorial; Minneapolis: Institute for the Study of Ideologies and Literature, 1987.

———. Review of Luis Zapata, *Adonis García: A Picaresque Novel,* translated by E. A. Lacey, and Winston Leyland, ed., *My Deep Dark Pain Is Love: A Collection of Latin American Gay Fiction. Chasqui* 13.1 (November 1983): 90–92.

Foster, Stephen Wayne. "Latin American Studies." *Cabirion and Gay Books Bulletin* 11 (1984): 2–7, 29.

Foucault, Michel. *The History of Sexuality, Volume I: An Introduction.* Translated from the French by Robert Hurley. New York: Vintage Books/Random House, 1980.

Fry, Peter. "Da hierarquia à igualdade: A construção histórica da homossexualidade." In *Para inglês ver: Identidade e política na cultura brasileira,* pp. 87–115. Rio de Janeiro: Zahar, 1982.

———. "Léonie, Pompinha, Amaro e Aleixo, prostituição, homossexualidade e raça em dois romances naturalistas." In *Caminhos cruzados: Linguagem, antropologia, ciências naturais,* pp. 33–51. São Paulo: Brasiliense, 1982.

García Pinto, Magdalena. "La escritura de la pasión y la pasión de la escritura: *En breve cárcel,* de Sylvia Molloy." *Revista Iberoamericana* 132–133 (1985): 687–696.

———. "Sylvia Molloy." In *Historias íntimas: Conversaciones con diez escritoras latinoamericanas,* pp. 123–147. Hanover, N.H.: Ediciones del Norte, 1988.

Gay Left Collective, eds. *Homosexuality: Power and Politics.* London: Allison and Busby, 1980.

Goldar, Ernesto. *Buenos Aires: Vida cotidiana en la década del 50.* Buenos Aires: Plus Ultra, 1980.

Gómez Ocampo, Gilberto. "La novela del vagabundo." *Boletín Cultural y Bibliográfico* 25.17 (1988): 160–161.

Goodwin, Joseph P. *More Man Than You'll Ever Be; Gay Folklore and Acculturation in Middle America.* Bloomington: Indiana University Press, 1989.

Greenberg, David F. *The Construction of Homosexuality.* Chicago: University of Chicago Press, 1988.

Gregorich, Luis. *Literatura y homosexualidad y otros ensayos.* Buenos Aires: Editorial Legasa, 1985.

Hoffman, William M. "Introduction." In *Gay Plays: The First Collection,* pp. vii–xxxix. New York: Avon Books, 1979.

Hohldfeldt, Antônio. "A condição feminina reivindicada." *Suplemento Literário de Minas Gerais* 992 (5-X-1985): 10.

Hokenson, Jan. "The Pronouns of Gomorrha: A Lesbian Prose Tradition." *Frontiers* 10.1 (1988): 62–69.

"Homosexuality: Sacrilege, Vision, Politics." *Salmagundi* 58–59 (1982–1983): entire issue.

"Homosexuality in Cuba: A Threat to Public Morality?" *Connexions: An International Women's Quarterly* 2 (1981): 18–19.

Howes, Robert. "Adolfo Caminha's Bom-Crioulo." In Adolfo Caminha, *Bom-*

Crioulo: The Black Man and the Cabin Boy, translated by E. A. Lacey, pp. 11–21. San Francisco: Gay Sunshine Press, 1982.

———. "The Literature of Outsiders: The Literature of the Gay Community in Latin America." In *Latin American Masses and Minorities: Their Images and Realities,* edited by Dan C. Hazen, 1:288–304, 580–591. Madison: SALALM Secretariat, Memorial Library, University of Wisconsin, 1985. SALALM no. 30.

Jaén, Didier T. "La neo-picaresca en México: Elena Poniatowska y Luis Zapata." *Tinta* 1.5 (1987): 23–29.

Jameson, Fredric. "Architecture and the Critique of Ideology." In *The Ideologies of Theory: Essays, 1971–1986, Volume 2, Syntax of History.* Minneapolis: University of Minnesota Press, 1988.

———. "Metacommentary." *PMLA* 86 (1971): 9–18. Also in his *The Ideologies of Theory: Essays, 1971–1986,* 1:3–16. Minneapolis: University of Minnesota Press, 1988.

———. *The Political Unconscious: Narrative as a Socially Symbolic Act.* Ithaca, N.Y.: Cornell University Press, 1981.

———. *The Prison-House of Language: A Critical Account of Structuralism and Russian Formalism.* Princeton: Princeton University Press, 1972.

Jáuregui, Carlos Luis. *La homosexualidad en la Argentina.* Buenos Aires: Ediciones Tarso, 1978.

Jockl, Alejandro. *Ahora, los gay.* Buenos Aires: Ediciones de la Pluma, 1984.

Jones, Willis Knapp. *Behind Spanish American Footlights.* Austin: University of Texas Press, 1966.

Kaminsky, Amy. "Lesbian Cartographers: Body, Text, Geography." In *Cultural and Historical Grounding for Hispanic and Luso-Brazilian Feminist Criticism,* edited by Hernán Vidal, pp. 223–256. Minneapolis: Institute for Study of Ideologies and Literature, 1989.

Kappeler, Susanne. *The Pornography of Representation.* Cambridge: Polity Press, 1986.

Karlinsky, Simon. "La literatura gay en la Rusia bolchevique." *Quimera* 24 (1982): 8–11.

Kellogg, Stuart. "Introduction: The Uses of Homosexuality in Literature." *Journal of Homosexuality* 8.3–4 (1983): 1–12.

———, ed. *Literary Visions of Homosexuality.* New York: Haworth Press, 1983; Harrington Park Press, 1985.

Kerr, Lucille. *Suspended Fictions: Reading Novels by Manuel Puig.* Urbana: University of Illinois Press, 1987.

Lagmanovich, David. "La poesía de Alejandra Pizarnik." In *Instituto Internacional de Literatura Iberoamericana, XVII Congreso,* pp. 885–895. Madrid: Cultura Hispánica del Centro Iberoamericano de Cooperación, 1978.

Lasarte V., Francisco. "Más allá del surrealismo: La poesía de Alejandra Pizarnik." *Revista Iberoamericana* 125 (1983): 867–877.

Lau Jaiven, Ana. *La nueva ola del feminismo en México: Conciencia y acción de lucha de las mujeres.* Mexico City: Grupo Editorial Planeta, 1987.

Leland, Christopher Towne. *The Last Happy Men: The Generation of 1922, Fiction, and the Argentine Reality.* Syracuse: Syracuse University Press, 1986.

Levin, James. *The Gay Novel.* New York: Irvington Publishers, 1983.
Leyland, Winston, ed. *My Deep Dark Pain Is Love: A Collection of Latin American Gay Fiction.* Translated from Spanish and Portuguese by E. A. Lacey. San Francisco: Gay Sunshine Press, 1983.
———. *Now the Volcano: An Anthology of Latin American Gay Literature.* Translated by Erskine Lane, Franklin D. Blanton, and Simon Karlinsky. San Francisco: Gay Sunshine Press, 1979.
Lima, Délcio Monteiro de. *Os homoeróticos.* Rio de Janeiro: Francisco Alves, 1983.
Loos, Dorothy Scott. *The Naturalistic Novel of Brazil.* New York: Hispanic Institute in the United States, 1963.
Lopes Júnior, Francisco Caetano. "Uma subjetividade outra." Ms.
MacRae, Edward. "Os respetáveis militantes e as bichas loucas." In *Caminhos cruzados: Linguagem, antropologia, ciências naturais,* pp. 99–124. São Paulo: Brasiliense, 1982.
Malinow, Inés. [Juicio crítico]. In *Poesía argentina contemporánea* I/6.2833–2840. Buenos Aires: Fundación Argentina para la Poesía, 1978–.
Marañón, Gregorio. "Prólogo." In Alfonso Hernández Catá, *El ángel de la Sodoma,* pp. 9–41. Valparaíso: "El Callao," 1929?
Martin, Robert K. *The Homosexual Tradition in American Poetry.* Austin: University of Texas Press, 1979.
Martínez, Fabio. "Fernando Vallejo: El ángel del Apocalipsis." *Boletín Cultural y Bibliográfico* [Bogotá] 25.14 (1988): 35–41.
Masiello, Francine R. "*En breve cárcel:* La producción del sujeto." *Hispamérica* 41 (1985): 103–112.
Meyers, Jeffrey. *Homosexuality and Literature, 1890–1930.* Montreal: McGill-Queen's University Press, 1977.
Míccolis, Leila, and Herbert Daniel. *Jacarés e lobisomens: Dois ensaios sobre a homossexualidade.* Rio de Janeiro: Achiamé, 1983.
Mielli, Mario. *Homosexuality and Liberation: Elements of a Gay Critique.* Translated by David Fernbach. London: Gay Men's Press, 1980.
Miller, Nancy K. "Emphasis Added: Plots and Plausibilities in Women's Fiction." *PMLA* 96.1 (1981): 36–48.
Montaner, Carlos Alberto. "Sexo malo." In *Informe secreto sobre la revolución cubana,* pp. 173–177. Madrid: Ediciones Sedmay, 1976.
Montero, Oscar. "'En breve cárcel': La Diana, la violencia y la mujer que escribe." In *La sartén por el mango: Encuentro de escritoras latinoamericanas,* edited by Patricia Elena González and Eliana Ortega, pp. 111–118. Río Piedras: Ediciones Huracán, 1984.
Montes Huidobro, Matías. *Exilio.* Honolulu: Editorial Persona, 1988.
Moody, Raymond Albert. "The Life and Prose Style of Rafael Arévalo Martínez." Ph.D. dissertation, University of California at Los Angeles, 1967.
Moraes, Maria Quartim de. "A 'nova' moral sexual das revistas femininas." In *Sexo e poder,* edited by Guido Montega, pp. 67–83. São Paulo: Editora Brasiliense, 1979.
Mott, Luiz. *Escravidão, homossexualidade e demonologia.* São Paulo: Icone, 1988.

———. *O lesbianismo no Brasil.* Porto Alegre: Mercado Aberto, 1987.
Muñoz, Elías Miguel. "El discurso utópico de la sexualidad en *El beso de la mujer araña* de Manuel Puig." *Revista Iberoamericana* 135–136 (1986): 361–378.
———. *El discurso utópico de la sexualidad en Manuel Puig.* Madrid: Editorial Pliegos, 1987.
Murray, Stephen O., ed. *Male Homosexuality in Central and South America.* San Francisco: Instituto Obregón; New York: GAU-NY, 1987.
Norton, Rictor. *The Homosexual Literary Tradition: An Interpretation.* New York: Revisionist Press, 1974.
Ordaz, Luis. "José González Castillo: Sainetero popular y dramaturgo." *Revista de Estudios de Teatro* 2.6 (1963): 32–35.
Oved, Jaacov. *El anarquismo y el movimiento obrero en Argentina.* Mexico City: Siglo XXI Editores, 1978.
Pellón, Gustavo. "The Loss of Reason and the Sin *Contra Natura* in Lezama's *Paradiso.*" *Revista de Estudios Hispánicos* 19.2 (1985): 21–35.
Penrose, Valentine. *Erzsébet Báthory, la comtesse sanglante.* Paris: Marcure de France, 1962. Translated by Alexander Trocchi as *The Bloody Countess.* London: Calder and Boyars, 1970.
Peri Rossi, Cristina. "Alejandra Pizarnik o la tentación de la muerte." *Cuadernos Hispanoamericanos* 273 (1973): 584–588.
Perlongher, Néstor Osvaldo. *O negócio do michê: Prostituição viril em São Paulo.* São Paulo: Editora Brasiliense, 1987.
Phillips, Eileen, ed. *The Left and the Erotic.* London: Lawrence and Wishart, 1983.
Piña, Cristina. "Alejandra Pizarnik o el yo transformado en lenguaje." *Revista Nacional de Cultura* [Caracas] 251 (1983): 69–78.
Pratt, Mary Louise. *Toward a Speech Act Theory of Literary Discourse.* Bloomington: Indiana University Press, 1977.
Puig, Manuel. "Losing Readers in Argentina." *Index on Censorship* 14.5 (1985): 55–57.
Ramos, Juanita, ed. *Compañeras: Antología lesbiana latina.* New York: Latin Lesbian History Project, 1984.
Rechy, John. *The Sexual Outlaw: A Documentary.* Rev. ed. New York: Grove Press, 1985. Originally published in 1977.
Reedy, Daniel R. "La dualidad del 'yo' en 'El hombre que parecía un caballo'." In Instituto Internacional de Literatura Iberoamericana, *El ensayo y la crítica literaria en Iberoamérica,* pp. 167–174. Toronto: University of Toronto, 1970.
Reinhardt, Karl J. "The Image of Gays in Chicano Prose Fiction." *Explorations in Ethnic Studies* 4.2 (1981): 41–55.
Reis, Roberto. *A permanência do círculo: Hierarquia no romance brasileiro.* Niterói: Universidade Federal Fluminense, Editora Universitária, 1987.
Ribeiro, João Felipe de. *Roteiro de Adolfo Caminha.* Rio de Janeiro: Livraria São José, 1957.
Ross, Judith Wilson. "Ethics and the Language of AIDS." *Federation Review: The Journal of the State Humanities Councils* 9.3 (May/June 1986): 15–19.

Rozencvaig, Perla. "Entrevista: Reinaldo Arenas." *Hispamérica* 28 (1981): 41–48.

Running, Thorpe. "The Poetry of Alejandra Pizarnik." *Chasqui* 14.2–3 (1985): 45–55.

Russ, Joanna. *Magic Mommas, Trembling Sisters, Puritans and Perverts: Feminist Essays*. Trumansburg, N.Y.: Crossing Press, 1985.

Salgado, María A. *Rafael Arévalo Martínez*. Boston: Twayne, 1979.

Sarotte, G. M. *Comme un frère, comme un amant: L'homosexualité masculine dans le roman et le théâtre américains de Herman Melville à James Baldwin*. Paris: Flammarion, 1976. Translated as *Like a Brother, like a Lover*. New York: Anchor/Doubleday, 1978.

Scarry, Elaine. *The Body in Pain: The Making and Unmaking of the World*. New York: Oxford University Press, 1985.

Schaefer-Rodríguez, Claudia. "The Power of Subversive Imagination: Homosexual Utopian Discourse in Contemporary Mexican Literature." *Latin American Literary Review* 33 (1989): 29–41.

Schneider, Luis Mario. "El tema homosexual en la nueva narrativa mexicana." *Casa del tiempo* [Mexico] 49–50 (1985): 82–86.

Scholes, Robert E. *Structuralist Fabulation: An Essay on Fiction of the Future*. Notre Dame: University of Notre Dame Press, 1975.

Schwartz, Kessel. "Homosexuality as a Theme in Representative Contemporary Spanish American Novels." *Kentucky Romance Quarterly* 22 (1975): 247–257.

Schwartz, Perla. "Alejandra Pizarnik: Los límites del exilio interior." In *El quebranto del silencio: Mujeres poetas suicidas del siglo XX*, pp. 95–101. Mexico City: Editorial Diana, 1989.

Shaw, Donald A. "Notes on the Presentation of Sexuality in the Modern Spanish-American Novel." *Bulletin of Hispanic Studies* 59 (1982): 275–282.

Soble, Alan, ed. *The Philosophy of Sex: Contemporary Readings*. Totowa, N.J.: Rowman and Littlefield, 1981.

Stambolian, George, and Richard Howard, eds. *Homosexualities and French Literature: Cultural Contexts/Critical Texts*. Ithaca: Cornell University Press, 1979.

Steuernagal, Trudy. "Contemporary Homosexual Fiction and Gay Rights Movement." *Journal of Popular Culture* 20.3 (1986): 125–134.

Stevenson, John Allen. "A Vampire in the Mirror: The Sexuality of *Dracula*." *PMLA* 103 (1988): 139–149.

Süssekind, Flora. *Tal Brasil, qual romance? Uma ideologia estética e sua história: O naturalismo*. Rio de Janeiro: Achiamé, 1984.

Todd, Janet. *Feminist Literary History; A Defense*. Cambridge: Polity Press, 1988.

Trevisan, João S. *Perverts in Paradise*. Translated by Martin Foreman. London: GMP Publications, 1986. Originally published as *Devassos no paraíso* (1986).

Vela, Rubén. "Alejandra Pizarnik: Una poesía existencial." *Repertorio latinoamericano* 55 (1983): 4–7.

Vestrini, Miyó. *Isaac Chocrón frente al espejo*. Caracas: Editorial Ateneo de Caracas, 1980.
Vidal, Gore. *The City and the Pillar*. New York: E. P. Dutton, 1948.
Vidal, Hernán. *Poética de la población marginal: Fundamentos materialistas para una historiografía estética*. Minneapolis: Prisma Institute, 1987.
Villanueva, Alfredo. "Machismo vs. Gayness: Latin American Fiction." *Gay Sunshine* 29–30 (1976): 22.
Viñas, David. *Anarquistas en América latina*. Mexico City: Editorial Katún, 1983.
WAUDIG (University of Washington Discourse Analysis Group). "Resisting the Public Discourse of AIDS." *Textual Practice* 3.3 (1989): 388–396.
Weeks, Jeffrey. *Sexuality*. Chichester: Ellis Horwood; London/New York: Tavistock, 1986.
———. *Sexuality and Its Discontents: Meanings, Myths and Modern Sexualities*. London: Routledge and Kegan Paul, 1985.
Weinrich, James D. *Sexual Landscapes: Why We Are What We Are; Why We Love Whom We Love*. New York: Charles Scribners, 1987.
Whitam, Frederick L., and Robin M. Mathy. *Male Homosexuality in Four Societies: Brazil, Guatemala, the Philippines, and the United States*. New York: Praeger, 1985.
White, Edmund. *States of Desire: Travels in Gay America*. New York: E. P. Dutton, 1983. Originally published in 1980.
White, Hayden V. "The Noble Savage Theme as Fetish." In *Tropics of Discourse: Essays in Cultural Criticism*, pp. 188–197. Baltimore: Johns Hopkins University Press, 1978.
Wittig, Monique. *The Lesbian Body*. Translated by David Le Vay. New York: William Morrow, 1975.
Young, Allen. *Gays under the Cuban Revolution*. San Francisco: Grey Fox Press, 1981.
Young, Ian. *The Male Homosexual in Literature: A Bibliography*. Metuchen, N.J.: Scarecrow Press, 1975.
Zapata, Luis. "Prólogo." In Adolfo Caminha, *Bom-Crioulo*, pp. 9–22. Mexico City: Editorial Posada, 1987.

INDEX